METHODS OF INQUIRY FOR INTELLIGENCE ANALYSIS

Security and Professional Intelligence Education Series (SPIES)

Series Editor: Dr. Jan Goldman

In this post–September 11, 2001, era there has been rapid growth in the number of professional intelligence training and educational programs across the United States and abroad. Colleges and universities, as well as high schools, are developing programs and courses in homeland security, intelligence analysis, and law enforcement, in support of national security.

The Security and Professional Intelligence Education Series (SPIES) was first designed for individuals studying for careers in intelligence and to help improve the skills of those already in the profession; however, it was also developed to educate the public on how intelligence work is conducted and should be conducted in this important and vital profession.

1. *Communicating with Intelligence: Writing and Briefing in the Intelligence and National Security Communities*, by James S. Major, 2008.
2. *A Spy's Résumé: Confessions of a Maverick Intelligence Professional and Misadventure Capitalist*, by Marc Anthony Viola, 2008.
3. *An Introduction to Intelligence Research and Analysis*, by Jerome Clauser, revised and edited by Jan Goldman, 2008.
4. *Writing Classified and Unclassified Papers for National Security*, by James S. Major, 2009.
5. *Strategic Intelligence: A Handbook for Practitioners, Managers, and Users*, revised edition by Don McDowell, 2009.
6. *Partly Cloudy: Ethics in War, Espionage, Covert Action, and Interrogation*, by David L. Perry, 2009.
7. *Tokyo Rose / An American Patriot: A Dual Biography*, by Frederick P. Close, 2010.
8. *Ethics of Spying: A Reader for the Intelligence Professional*, edited by Jan Goldman, 2006.
9. *Ethics of Spying: A Reader for the Intelligence Professional*, Volume 2, edited by Jan Goldman, 2010.
10. *A Woman's War: The Professional and Personal Journey of the Navy's First African American Female Intelligence Officer*, by Gail Harris, 2010.
11. *Handbook of Scientific Methods of Inquiry for Intelligence Analysis*, by Hank Prunckun, 2010.
12. *Handbook of Warning Intelligence: Assessing the Threat to National Security*, by Cynthia Grabo, 2010.
13. *Keeping U.S. Intelligence Effective: The Need for a Revolution in Intelligence Affairs*, by William J. Lahneman, 2011.
14. *Words of Intelligence: An Intelligence Professional's Lexicon for Domestic and Foreign Threats, Second Edition*, by Jan Goldman, 2011.
15. *Counterintelligence Theory and Practice*, by Hank Prunckun, 2012.
16. *Balancing Liberty and Security: An Ethical Study of U.S. Foreign Intelligence Surveillance, 2001–2009*, by Michelle Louise Atkin, 2013.
17. *The Art of Intelligence: Simulations, Exercises, and Games*, edited by William J. Lahneman and Rubén Arcos, 2014.
18. *Communicating with Intelligence: Writing and Briefing in National Security*, by James S. Major, 2014.
19. *Quantitative Intelligence Analysis: Applied Analytic Models, Simulations and Games*, by Edward Waltz, 2014.
20. *Scientific Methods of Inquiry for Intelligence Analysis, Second Edition*, by Hank Prunckun, 2015.
21. *The Handbook of Warning Intelligence: Assessing the Threat to National Security–The Complete Declassified Edition*, by Cynthia Grabo, 2015.
22. *Intelligence and Information Policy for National Security: Key Terms and Concepts*, by Jan Goldman and Susan Maret, 2016.
23. *Handbook of European Intelligence Cultures*, edited by Bob de Graaff and James M. Nyce, with Chelsea Locke, 2016.
24. *Partly Cloudy: Ethics in War, Espionage, Covert Action, and Interrogation, Second Edition*, by David L. Perry, 2016.
25. *Humanitarian Intelligence: A Practitioner's Guide to Crisis Analysis and Project Design*, by Andrej Zwitter, 2016.
26. *Shattered Illusions: KGB Cold War Espionage in Canada*, by Donald G. Mahar, 2017.
27. *Intelligence Engineering: Operating Beyond the Conventional*, by Adam D. M. Svendsen, 2017.
28. *Reasoning for Intelligence Analysts: A Multidimensional Approach of Traits, Techniques, and Targets*, by Noel Hendrickson, 2018.
29. *Counterintelligence Theory and Practice, Second Edition*, by Hank Prunckun, 2019.
30. *Methods of Inquiry for Intelligence Analysis, Third Edition*, by Hank Prunckun, 2019.
31. *The Art of Intelligence: More Simulations, Exercises, and Games*, edited by Rubén Arcos and William J. Lahneman.

To view the books on our website, please visit https://rowman.com/Action/SERIES/RL/SPIES or scan the QR code below.

METHODS OF INQUIRY FOR INTELLIGENCE ANALYSIS

THIRD EDITION

HANK PRUNCKUN

Charles Sturt University

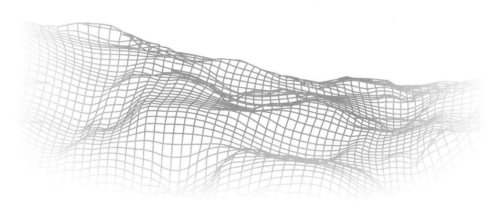

ROWMAN & LITTLEFIELD
Lanham • Boulder • New York • London

Executive Editor: Traci Crowell
Assistant Editor: Deni Remsberg
Senior Marketing Manager: Amy Whitaker
Interior Designer: Ilze Lemesis

Credits and acknowledgments for material borrowed from other sources, and reproduced with permission, appear on the appropriate page within the text.

Published by Rowman & Littlefield
An imprint of The Rowman & Littlefield Publishing Group, Inc.
4501 Forbes Boulevard, Suite 200, Lanham, Maryland 20706
www.rowman.com

6 Tinworth Street, London SE11 5AL, United Kingdom

British Library Cataloguing in Publication Information Available

Library of Congress Cataloging-in-Publication Data

Names: Prunckun, Hank, 1954– author.
Title: Methods of inquiry for intelligence analysis / Hank Prunckun.
Other titles: Handbook of scientific methods of inquiry for intelligence analysis
Description: Third edition. | Lanham : Rowman & Littlefield, [2019] | Series: Security and professional intelligence education series (SPIES) ; 30 | Includes bibliographical references and index.
Identifiers: LCCN 2018059664 (print) | LCCN 2019000905 (ebook) | ISBN 9781538125885 (electronic) | ISBN 9781538125861 (cloth : alk. paper) | ISBN 9781538125878 (pbk. : alk. paper)
Subjects: LCSH: Intelligence service—Methodology—Handbooks, manuals, etc. | Science—Methodology—Handbooks, manuals, etc. | Social sciences—Methodology—Handbooks, manuals, etc. | Behavioral assessment—Methodology—Handbooks, manuals, etc.
Classification: LCC JF1525.I6 (ebook) | LCC JF1525.I6 P78 2019 (print) | DDC 327.12072—dc23
LC record available at https://lccn.loc.gov/2018059664

The secret nature of intelligence work prevents the cadres of scholar-spies from being recognized for their contribution to society's safety. However, I acknowledge their research by dedicating this book to all analysts who work anonymously.

Contents

4 Clandestine and Covert Sources of Information   53

5 Open Sources of Information   71

Foreword

This third edition of Hank Prunckun's *Methods of Inquiry for Intelligence Analysis* has been revised and updated to help teach the world's future intelligence analysts. Designed for analytical courses, it does not attempt to cover the extremely broad and complex fields of intelligence collection, with its many literal and nonliteral sources, or the related topics, such as the intelligence-policy relationship, or issues, such as oversight or politicization of intelligence judgments. Prunckun wisely leaves those topics to other volumes.

In revising this book, Prunckun notes the tremendous change in the intelligence field since the terror attacks of September 11, 2001. With the greatly increased focus on counterterrorism, intelligence efforts have increasingly focused on small, non-nation-state groups and individuals. It is interesting to observe that national security intelligence efforts have often merged with more traditional law enforcement investigations and assessments. He also points out the impact of the Internet and social media, which have led to the age of "big data" requiring sophisticated and automated collation and analysis techniques.

Intelligence is a critical element in any power equation allowing decision advantage to leaders in various communities that employ intelligence—national security, military, law enforcement, security, business, and other private sector endeavors.

I am particularly impressed with the various chapters that address sources of information, methods of analysis, and the types of reports used in intelligence work because these chapters will help aspiring intelligence analysts understand the practical aspects of working in this fantastic field of endeavor. These chapters are relevant to strategic, operational, and tactical intelligence analyses that span a range of purposes and users—from governmental to the private sector.

There are several chapters that address sources of information that are critical for intelligence analysis. Chapters 4 and 5 on clandestine and open sources discuss the value and shortfalls of such sources, including social media and the challenges of data mining. An important element in these chapters is the discussion of techniques for vetting information of many types and origins and of the problems that analysts can face in processing these data.

Chapters 6 and 7 focus on qualitative and quantitative analysis types and methods of analysis. These are followed by short, focused chapters on key report types—target profiles, operational assessments, vehicle route security (i.e., protective intelligence), threat assessments, vulnerability assessments, risk assessments, and national security policy assessments. Prunckun provides examples of each kind of report. This is a unique feature of the book that will be very useful for students.

Chapter 8 addresses geointelligence, the long-standing use of maps, and the modern application of technology that has made this an important intelligence province. This information is provided in simple terms that anyone can understand.

The value of this new edition of *Methods of Inquiry for Intelligence Analysis* derives from several factors. It is focused on its principal topic—analysis, which is the heart of the intelligence profession—without the extraneous excursions common to many books about intelligence. It illustrates the uses and importance of intelligence analysis to various communities that use intelligence, not just the military or national security fields. Its focus on methods of analysis is comprehensive and invaluable. The examples of types of reports—their expected contents and contexts—provide practical guidance to students of the craft. Warnings of problems with sources—misinformation, attempts at deception, and so on—and shortcomings in analytical approaches are important to help develop analysts' critical thinking. Also, the incorporation of discussion questions in each chapter is useful for instructors.

Methods of Inquiry for Intelligence Analysis is a well-focused text for intelligence analysis, but it is also valuable to other intelligence-related courses as supplementary reading.

Peter C. Oleson, BA, MA
Former Assistant Director for Plans and Policy,
U.S. Defence Intelligence Agency
Former Director for Intelligence and Space
Policy, U.S. Secretary of Defence
Board of Directors, Association of Former Intelligence Officers
Senior Editor, *Intelligencer: Journal of U.S. Intelligence Studies*

Preface

In the first two editions to this book, I argued that no other profession has experienced change to the same extent as that of intelligence since the terrorist attacks of September 11, 2001. Now, in its third edition, I have not wavered from this view. Over the years, the role of intelligence has continued to grow, and its mission remains complex.

Growth and complexity have been evidenced by government and private sector security agencies that are recruiting intelligence analysts to process what has become a voluminous amount of raw information that flows into these agencies' data collection systems. There is even interest being expressed by nongovernment organizations (NGOs) to incorporate intelligence into their operations. This is an interesting step for a sector that has traditionally shied away from any association with *intelligence*, demonstrating the value intelligence provides for planners.

The demand for intelligence analysts has been met by colleges and universities that offer intelligence study programs so that candidates for analytical positions can begin their duties without protracted on-the-job instruction. This third edition is not just a summary of existing knowledge; it provides instruction into the essential analytic skills that are critical for undertaking intelligence work. In this regard, this edition provides the theoretical foundations as well as practical insights into the craft of producing intelligence. Therefore, it is equally useful for academic researchers and "scholar-spies."

This edition has been reorganized and improved to address the subject of intelligence analysis with a grounding in what I argue are the origins of intelligence research—the scientific method of inquiry at the core of such academic disciplines as sociology, anthropology, criminology, psychology, political science, history, economics, education, and library science. Although there are many intelligence texts covering certain aspects of topics discussed in this book, in my view this third edition is more comprehensive because it covers the topic in a holistic way—more than a textbook on analytic techniques—and is a serious piece of research on the theory and practice of intelligence analysis.

While the literature on intelligence abounds with works on spy gadgetry and covert surveillance, one must look wider for material on intelligence research and analysis. Although there are several texts on analytic techniques, this book goes further—it not only presents the reader with a range of analytical methods used in secret research, but also provides instruction on how to write such reports and gives examples. In this way, students can get a feel for what will be expected of them once they are employed as analysts. By doing so, it shows how secret intelligence fits into the larger research framework.

This third edition not only discusses the essentials of applied intelligence research but also analyzes the function, structure, and operational methods involved in intelligence work. It explores how an analyst will be required to obtain data via covert methods and discusses some of the ethical issues of working with this classified information. It also examines how intelligence data are validated by an analyst, in marked contrast to how the same task is performed by a social science researcher. The reader is left with little doubt about the theoretical foundations of intelligence, how intelligence is developed, and how it is processed in an environment that has security and secrecy at its core.

The need for such a book was borne out of my personal experience as a researcher and analyst. In many of the positions I held during my operational career, I relied on texts in other academic disciplines since none in my discipline addressed the craft of intelligence. Occasionally, I found texts in the field of criminal justice and police science that were of value, but, again, they addressed issues faced by analysts obliquely. There are several excellent texts for industry-specific applications—for instance, national security intelligence, military intelligence, or law enforcement intelligence—but these texts were narrow in focus (e.g., foreign policy–centric or police-centric) and did not apply the principles of intelligence across the spectrum of industries that ply this craft.

The third edition of *Methods of Inquiry for Intelligence Analysis* examines how these concepts apply in the world almost two decades after the 9/11 attacks—an environment that has fewer boundaries between what may have been military intelligence and, say, business intelligence, and so forth. This reorganized edition examines how applied research methods are used by intelligence practitioners to conduct the secret work they do. It is a systematic exploration of the theoretical concepts within the intelligence discipline, thereby providing scholars and practitioners with the knowledge of how to be effective researchers in a variety of intelligence settings: military, national security, law enforcement, business, and the private sector.

The book comprises fifteen chapters that fit quarter- and semester-length college courses. Each chapter presents important concepts that progressively build students' understanding of intelligence research and analysis. This edition includes new material that was not available for the first two editions. This discussion addresses topics such as some ethical dilemmas of using covertly obtained information and an example of vehicle route security report, as well as examples of what threat, vulnerability, and risk assessments look like. There is also a new chapter on writing national security assessments, and case studies added throughout. Moreover, all chapters have undergone revision to ensure that their content reflects new developments and thinking relevant to the craft of intelligence analysis.

Finally, I appreciated and benefited from the comments of the many reviewers of this edition—Mark Feulner, Florida State University; Garth den Heyer, Arizona State University; Kurt F. Jensen, Carleton University; Ken Stiles, Virginia Tech; and Damien Van Puyvelde, University of Glasgow.

Chapter 1

Intelligence Theory

Intelligence Research—A Hard Row to Hoe

It could only be described as a typical winter's day in late January 1993. Like on most work days, a line of traffic came to a halt at a set of traffic lights on the eastbound lane of Virginia Route 123. It was located just outside the entrance to the Central Intelligence Agency (CIA) headquarters in Fairfax County, Virginia. In the line of cars waiting to enter the CIA compound were staffers and various contactors. It was a routine day for them as well as the many intelligence analysts who were already at work.

On such a day, one wouldn't expect analysts to face anything more dangerous than the hazard posed by some careless driver. But intelligence work—no matter how remote analysts are from the James Bond–like scenarios of intelligence gathering—is a profession fraught with danger.

On January 23, 1993, a Pakistani assassin[1] stopped at that traffic signal, got out of his car, and walked calmly from vehicle to vehicle shooting the male occupants with his AK-47 assault rifle. He only stopped firing, as he later confessed, because he ran out of targets. Among those dead and wounded were intelligence analysts.

Although this book is a critical discussion of intelligence research—a seemingly urbane profession—make no mistake, intelligence work carries with it dangers. The CIA Memorial Wall (and Book of Honor) displays stars that represent those who gave their lives for their country in the service of intelligence.[2] And yes, among these people were analysts who conducted the genteel craft of intelligence research. It is a "hard row to hoe," both mentally and physically. As the former CIA director Robert Gates once stated: "The nation is at peace because we in intelligence are constantly at war."[3]

Why Intelligence?

Why is there so much concern with intelligence? It is because intelligence enables one to exercise control over a given situation. In this sense, control equates to power. Ira Cohen, in his classic treatment of the study of power, wrote:

> Power is sought because without power the security and even the ability of [one] to continue to exist is generally decreased. Without power, [one] has no ability to deter another . . . from actions whose consequences threaten the vital interests of the former. Without power [one] cannot cause another . . . to do that which the former desires but which the latter desires not to do. Power is sought because the more power that [one] has, the greater is the number of [his or her] available options. The more options available to [one], the greater [his or her] security. The greater [his or her] security, the better off [he or she is]. [He or she is] more secure in [his or her] life and in the enjoyment of [his or her] private property.[4]

Intelligence is, therefore, not a form of clairvoyance used to predict the future, but an exact science based on sound quantitative and qualitative research methods. Lowenthal astutely pointed out: "Intelligence is not about truth. If something were known to be true, states would not need intelligence agencies to collect the information or analyze it. . . . [So,] we should think of intelligence as a proximate reality. . . . [Intelligence agencies] can rarely be assured that even their best and most considered analysis is true. Their goals are intelligence products that are reliable, unbiased, and honest (that is, free from politicization)."[5] In this regard, intelligence enables the analyst to present options to decision makers that provide them with an advantage over the opposition but are, at the same time, based on defensible conclusions.

> Intelligence has given nations understanding of an adversary's intentions and covertly advanced policy implementation. For companies, intelligence has assisted strategic planning, risk assessments, market decisions, R&D, and investments. For criminals, intelligence has provided forewarning of law enforcement actions, aided unlawful enterprises—including the subversion of police and politicians—and allowed intimidation of witnesses. Of course, there are many other uses.[6]

At this juncture, it should be noted that such conclusions are not absolute, and there will always be some level of probability or uncertainty involved with presenting intelligence findings (i.e., proximate reality). Nevertheless, uncertainty can be reduced and conclusion limits further defined so that decision makers understand the boundaries. This must be contrasted with making decisions based on "a hunch," "instinct," "luck," "gut feel," "belief," "faith," "trust," "hope," or "experience."

Having said that, the word *intelligence*, to some people, conjures up assorted notions of spying and espionage, secrets, and a world of exotic gadgetry. Yet, to others, the word is closely associated with the Orwellian concept of "big brother"—a world of hardball politics and an uncompromising quest for influence.

To some degree, intelligence work is associated with these concepts, but, here, the study of intelligence is approached from the focus of the analytic methods that turn information into intelligence. This process is based on methods used in applied research rather than on the James Bond–like devices used by cinema heroes or by some of the world's brutal police states in exercising authoritarian oppression.

In the post–September 11, 2001, world, colleges and universities across the globe have responded to the need to develop intelligence courses for the new cadre of analysts needed to support national security. Much of what is taught in these courses will also be applicable to other types of intelligence: law enforcement, military, business, and private sector intelligence. The growth of these educational programs means that training aids are also needed to instruct new analysts in the scientific methods of inquiry for intelligence research.

Information versus Intelligence

Trying to define *information* is difficult but not impossible. Information is like gravity and electricity, as it cannot be defined by tangible examples. Nevertheless, its properties can be observed and described, thus enabling improvement in the analytic methods that produce intelligence. The problem hard sciences face in trying to define gravity and electricity has never prevented engineers from designing and building applications that involve these phenomena. Therefore, a lack of a physical variable does not prevent analysts from producing intelligence from what we call *information*.

· ·

Information is the unrefined raw material used to produce finished, focused intelligence. Without information, intelligence could not exist.

· ·

It is quite safe to say that every facet of our lives, whether central or incidental, is in some way related to information. We rely on an alarm clock to wake us in the morning, the newspaper to tell us what is happening in the world beyond the end of our street, the radio to alert us if rain is expected, an array of indicator lights and meters on our car's dashboard to tell us about the car's performance as we drive to work, traffic lights and signs to alert us to road conditions, and on we could go until the clock tells us it's time to lay our work aside and to go off to sleep.

Individuals, organizations, and, indeed, whole societies owe their survival to information. The concept of community is only possible because of our ability to collect, store, retrieve, and transfer information from one person or body corporate to another. The more complex our society, the more it necessitates the conversion of information into intelligence.

Intelligence Defined

There are many definitions of *intelligence* and this appears to have given rise to some scholars asserting that there is no agreed position on what the term means. This is simply not the case. Although there may be as many definitions as there are intelligence scholars, the differences amount to mere wordsmithing. This is because the various definitions in circulation have commonalities that can be narrowed to four meanings.

Dictionaries use what is referred to as an "order of definitions" in cases where there are multiple definitions. They order the definitions by synchronic semantic analysis to clarify the different meanings. Taking this approach, the many uses of the term *intelligence* that appear in the subject literature can be deduced to mean:

1. Actions or processes used to produce knowledge;
2. The body of knowledge thereby produced;[7]
3. Organizations that deal in knowledge (e.g., an intelligence agency); and
4. The reports and briefings produced for decision makers in the process or by such organizations.[8]

However, it is axiomatic that these four meanings take place in the context of secrecy. Otherwise, these definitions could apply to other forms of research. Moreover, in this book, intelligence as a process (i.e., definition 1 above) is categorized by the different functions it performs. *Knowledge* in the context of intelligence equates to *insight* or, viewed another way, the ability to *reduce uncertainty*. Insight (in other words, *advantage*), and therefore, certainty, offers mankind the ability to make decisions that enable civilizations to take better control over the "unknown." But, it should be noted that insights are not produced through mystic rituals; insights are produced through processes based on sound quantitative and qualitative research methods that culminate in *defensible conclusions*. In this sense, insights relate to *probability* and/or *prediction*. Expressed as an equation, intelligence could be shown as:

(secrecy (information + analysis = intelligence ∴ insight ⇒ reduces uncertainty))

The elements of this equation will be discussed in more detail at the end of this chapter when we examine the intelligence theory.

Intelligence as Knowledge

As a body of knowledge, intelligence deals with an adversary, a potential adversary, or a possible area of operation that is useful to managers in planning and carrying out their organization's mandate. Terms like *target, subject, person of interest, subject of interest* are some of the ways intelligence manifests itself as knowledge. To demonstrate, consider the following notional examples:

National Security Context. Intelligence from agents in the Caribbean alerts us to the imminent passage of legislation in Cuba that will legalize a multi-party, democratic political system.

Military Context. We have recently received intelligence indicating the Russian government has authorized the deployment of its newly developed UXB anti-aircraft missile system on the Crimean border with the Ukraine. This intelligence indicates the system will be operational during the week beginning April 1.

Law Enforcement Context. We have intelligence indicating the Orinsky Gang is planning to break into the automatic teller machine located at the Springfield shopping center this Friday night.

Business Context. Intelligence suggests Nero Entertainment is about to begin an advertising campaign in the northeast this autumn, attempting to capture customers between the age range twenty-one and forty-one.

Private Sector Context.[9] Two Japanese whaling boats were observed yesterday leaving port and heading for the northwestern Pacific. Intelligence passed on by a crew member was that the vessels were aiming to catch 200 whales for "scientific research."

Intelligence as a Process

The intelligence process is a series of procedures or steps which form what has been traditionally termed the *intelligence cycle*. In recent years, the term *intelligence process* has gained popularity over *intelligence cycle* because it has been recognized that it is not really a cycle per se but a process. Nonetheless, this cycle, or process, is initiated by a decision maker who poses a question or requests advice. This is termed an *intelligence requirement* (in some intelligence agencies, such as the military, this is referred to as *essential elements of intelligence*—EEI). The intelligence requirements are forwarded to an intelligence agency and the process begins.

The intelligence process consists of seven steps (see figure 1.1), with the first five focusing on converting raw data[10] into finished, focused intelligence:

1. Direction setting (i.e., problem formulation and planning);
2. Information collection;
3. Data collation;
4. Data manipulation and processing; and
5. Data analysis.

FIGURE 1.1 The intelligence process.

This resulting intelligence is then treated with two further steps:

6. Report writing; and
7. Dissemination (which would include provision for feedback).

Depending upon the initial intelligence requirements (e.g., the research objective), a single "loop" maybe enough to complete the intelligence research project and provide the decision maker with the insight sought. However, in practice, further data may need to be collected and the cycle may begin again, or the process may have two or more tasks being performed at once and may double back before advancing again. For instance, once the research question has been formulated and the data collection plan devised, an outline of the report may begin and, as the more readily available pieces of information flow in, a database or spreadsheet may be constructed and the data collated.

Moreover, even before all the data are received, some preliminary analysis may be carried out and, depending upon the results (e.g., at the collation stage, which some analysts view as low-grade analysis), further information may be requested (e.g., if, by chance, these results show the data would be inadequate to answer the research question or a serious limitation is noted). This would mean that the data collection plan is revised and field operatives called on to gather more or different data, and so on.

While a specific intelligence operation is underway, the analytic process will be continuous—forming the so-called *cycle*. As new information is being collected and collated, other data will be manipulated and analyzed. The resulting outcomes will be disseminated either for immediate use and/or to set new collection goals.

The dissemination of the intelligence product can take a variety of forms. For instance, in the case of business intelligence, it could be the background history of a company or one of its executives, the diagram of a company's office layout, identification of new projects being researched by the company, prediction of the intended release of a new product, data on staff salaries, the classification and number of personnel on a company's payroll, and the like.

The intelligence process is not unique to intelligence research but has parallels with research processes in other academic disciplines.[11] For example, the research process that is used in applied social research shares the same cyclical pattern:

- Establish a plan for information collection and carry out initial field work;
- Observe, discuss, and collect data;
- Analyze the data and write the report; and
- Distribute the report and gather feedback that can be used to formulate further disseminate strategies.

Data versus Information

Some intelligence scholars make a distinction between the terms *data* and *information*. According to *The American Heritage Dictionary for the English Language* the word *data* means: "Information, especially information organized for analysis or used for the basis for a decision."[12] In the context of intelligence research, the terms can generally be used interchangeably as analysts rely on *data* for analysis and decision-making purposes. From this perspective, *data*[13] is therefore *information*. Trying to create a distinction between these two terms, in contrast to common usage, could be said to be an exercise in abstractness that adds nothing to our understanding, but does add to our confusion.

Intelligence Theory

Having looked at intelligence and contrasted it with concepts such as information and data, as well as examined the difference between intelligence and investigation and discussed intelligence as knowledge and as a process, it is incumbent to now examine the theory that underscores intelligence.

Why should we know about the theory of intelligence if we can define it and, once defined, recognize intelligence in any of its four meanings? Because theory offers both scholars and practitioners the ability to understand how and why intelligence is what it is and does what it does. Without a theory, it is difficult to posit a view about an intelligence-related phenomenon and then test that hypothesis through empirical observations to see if the results support the hypothesis or reject it.

· ·

Conducting intelligence research is like shining a light in a dark place.

· ·

Although scholars have called for a theory of intelligence for decades, unfortunately until 2009 the literature was largely devoid of such theorizing. Gill, Marrin, and Phythian published an anthology of papers that year that attempted to address the "missing" intelligence theory issue.[14] Among these essays were treatments by key opinion leaders such as professors David Kahn, Michael Warner, and Jennifer Sims. Although there are other scholars who have discussed the issue elsewhere in the subject literature, these researchers were, arguably, at the time of writing of this book, in the forefront of the debate. However, surveying the theories they advanced, it is evident that there was little consensus between the models. Nonetheless, these scholars are to be commended for advancing the debate by contributing to the discourse.

To take their work further, this chapter proposes another theory—one that is not military- or national security–centric—because the world of intelligence is no longer able to operate within such neatly defined parameters. The post–9/11 world is vastly different from the one following Cold War operations. The reasons why these old demarcations have blurred will become more evident when our discussion turns to intelligence taxonomy, anatomy, and typology in chapter 2.

Grounded Theory of Intelligence

A grounded theory approach, which was used to develop a complementary theory of counterintelligence, was applied to observations made by surveying the subject literature, which was then distilled to formulate an intelligence theory.[15] This theory has its roots in the definition that was put forward earlier in this chapter. Although there have been many definitions of intelligence, with some scholars disagreeing on the semantic construction of "this or that" definition, it was possible to extract the core meaning, which resulted in the four unencumbered definitions presented earlier. These definitions, therefore, become the first four of five principles on which the theory rests. To reiterate, these principles are:

1. Actions or processes used to produce knowledge;
2. The body of knowledge thereby produced;
3. Organizations that deal in knowledge;
4. The reports and briefings produced for decision makers in the process or by such organizations; and
5. The fifth principle is that, for intelligence to transcend the bounds of mere research, it needs to be potted in some form of secrecy.

If the fifth principle is not present, *intelligence* is just *research*. This is because either enterprise—intelligence or research—results in knowledge. It could be argued that knowledge leads to insight, and insight results in reducing uncertainty in decision making, but unless secrecy is involved, it remains mere research. Having said that, secrecy will be context driven—what is secret for one agency may not be for another, or it may not be in a certain situation. The equation expressed earlier in this chapter presents a logical model for the theory of intelligence:

(secrecy (information + analysis = intelligence ∴ insight ⇒ reduces uncertainty))

Expressed in narrative form, intelligence theory might go something like this: Under the veil of secrecy, analysts obtain information and analyze it. This process results in intelligence (knowledge) and therefore provides insight to decision makers (reports and/or briefings), which in turn reduces uncertainty. This takes place within an organization (or unit within an organization, etc.) whose role is to engage in intelligence (secret research).

The following example demonstrates a case when the principle of secrecy is removed from the model. Take the case of pharmaceutical research being conducted by a notional university laboratory for a drug to treat the effects of some common form of arthritis. Using the intelligence model, it can be seen that all the principles apply—analysts (researchers) obtain information and analyze it. This results in knowledge and, therefore, provides insights to decision makers (in this case, the development of a suitable drug), which in turn reduces uncertainly (that is, it gives certainty to manufacturing or other processes involved in the drug's effectiveness and/or production). What is different is the lack of secrecy. This makes such research open—outsiders could, potentially, access this information (e.g., from journal articles, conference papers, personal communication with the researchers via e-mail or lab visits).

If secrecy is applied, the studies being conducted by our notional university becomes intelligence—*business intelligence* to place it in the correct typological classification (see chapter 2). But not all aspects need to be secret; only one component needs to be secret.

Compare the supposed case of university drug research to military analysts who might be researching a question about the development of a new weapons system by an unfriendly nation. During their inquiries, military analysts may access open-source information—say, the curricula vitae of certain academics in that nation who are known to be experts in the particular technology needed to develop such a weapons system. Clearly, these data are freely available on the websites of universities that employ them; but the fact that the research project is secret, the methods of analysis are classified, and other aspects of the endeavor are undisclosed makes this *intelligence*.

Axioms

There are four supporting axioms that underpin the four principles. These can be considered to be generally accepted truths, or conditions, that allow the theory to stand. Stated, these axioms are that intelligence can be either defensive or offensive, and that intelligence needs to be timely, as well as it needs to be defensible.

Defensive Intelligence

Defensive intelligence is concerned with providing decision makers with insights into how to deal with threats, vulnerabilities, and risks. Defensive intelligence is applicable to all five typological classifications discussed in chapter 2—national security, military, law enforcement, business, and private sector intelligence. Defensive intelligence can be concerned with several related aspects of defense—for example, prevention, preparation, mitigation, damage control/response, and recovery (and perhaps other areas).

Offensive Intelligence

Intelligence can be used to assist decision makers plan offensive missions. A simple example is that of targeting in the military. Targeting analysts use intelligence to task military assets so they can damage or destroy enemy capabilities, provide advice for immediate fire or maneuver, or support deep offensive operations. Examples of the application of offensive intelligence to other intelligence typological classifications are conceivable (see chapter 2). Offensive intelligence might include estimative or strategic intelligence because these categories of research projects concern themselves with outmaneuvering imminent threats.

Timely Availability

For intelligence to be useful, it must be provided in a timely fashion. If an intelligence report or briefing is not provided to decision makers on time, it is prima facie that the insights cannot be used. *Timely* may also include the notion of *continuous*—which is applicable in cases where an event is unfolding and updated intelligence is needed on a regular basic.

Defensibility

Defensibility considers several related notions. These include the need for the analytic process that produces intelligence to be transparent and replicable. The analytic process should be transparent to those who are within the defined circle of trust, but not to anyone outside that circle.

The reason for transparency is to allow those reading the reports, or receiving the briefing, to, if desired, reproduce the results. But to do so would be most unusual; nevertheless, what is likely is that a process of review will be carried out in the same vein an academic research report is peer reviewed for methodological soundness. This underscores the fact that intelligence is based on the same research principles as other types of applied research—they use scientific methods of inquiry that are based on sound quantitative and qualitative research methods (though it is acknowledged that access to reliable information can be more difficult).

Some scholars refer to this as *auditable*. Regardless of whatever term is used, replication means that, say, the reader of an intelligence report can understand the collection methods, collation and analysis techniques used (and can understand why these were selected), and be able to derive similar conclusions as the analyst did from the study's findings. It is not to say that the next time the intelligence cycle is repeated the same findings will be produced—it means that if the same data and methods used to arrive at the position articulated in the report are employed, it would be reasonable to expect similar results.

The fact that the environment in which intelligence operates is dynamic does not stand in the way of the concept of replication. Applied social research is analogously the same—rarely does an issue under investigation remain static. There are numerous independent variables in any research question that can be added, removed, or changed. This applies to intelligence research too.

If transparency and the ability to replicate an intelligence study are present, then the findings can be "defended." Tied to this notion are the concepts of relevance and accuracy—concepts which are often discussed in relation to intelligence research reports. The argument here is that, if the axiom of defensibility is maintained, then, by default, these aspects are catered for, as are the concepts of validity and reliability.

Discussion

Why does it matter that we have an intelligence theory? Because theory allows us to test propositions—questions about, say, the efficacy of certain intelligence approaches, operational methods, or procedural practices, as well as other issues facing the profession. For instance, it allows us to test the effectiveness of intelligence concerns in terms of outcomes, outputs, and processes. As Walsh put it, it allows for the development of the discipline of intelligence.[16]

So, what would intelligence scholars and practitioners test with such a theory? Well, prominent among the list of possible responses is the so-called phenomena of *intelligence failures*. For example, research questions that explore the issue of how the organization of intelligence agencies (principle 3) impacts on the analytic processes (principle 1) and the resulting dynamics might result in an "intelligence failure."

Using this theory, other research questions can be formulated and tested. Take, for instance, the following indicative examples: *Does the level of secrecy affect the operational efficiency? Is operational effectiveness contingent upon the organizational structure of the intelligence agency?* Since this is a universal theory of intelligence, it allows for the context to be varied while still being tested by the same theory. For instance, *a purely defensive approach to national security issues (which would be specified) is less effective than one that incorporates offensive measures, but in a business intelligence context, incorporating an offensive role will be counterproductive.* Using such hypotheses, scholars can then define variables and operationalize them. Take the hypothesis above as an example: *offensive measures* could be operationalized into, say, agents, wiretaps, surveillance drones, walk-ins, or any number of other manifestations of the concept of offensive information gathering.

As with all theories, this theory can then be tested empirically. Findings of empirical studies—ones based on valid and reliable data—can then guide good practice. In sum, this intelligence theory could not be described as conceptually dense, but, nevertheless, it is one that articulates the five axioms that explain why intelligence practice is performed as it is, or as it should be.

It is hoped that this intelligence theory will be refined so that the theoretical base that underpins the craft is better understood. "All being well, one would anticipate that, in the fullness of time, this and other yet to be articulated [intelligence] theories will spawn better policy options. These policy options will therefore be based on defensible conclusions that are grounded in empirical research."[17]

Key Words and Phrases

The key words and phrases associated with this chapter are listed below. Demonstrate your understanding of each by writing either a short definition or a one- or two-sentence explanation.

intelligence cycle   target
intelligence requirement

Study Questions

1. By way of example, define the term *intelligence*.

2. Explain the difference between *intelligence* and *information*.

3. Explain the difference between *intelligence* and *investigation*.

4. List the five principles and four axioms that comprise Prunckun's intelligence theory.

Learning Activity

From the intelligence cycle that is displayed in figure 1.1, we see that one of the key stages is *collation*. Some may argue that this stage is not only a stage but also a preliminary part of the analysis stage. Using a spreadsheet, construct a table that will allow you to collate the following data items: date, event, country of occurrence, type of military force, and impact. Now, obtain at least six newspaper articles that discuss a military event that has occurred somewhere in the world. Collate the information relating to that newspaper article into the spreadsheet, extracting a summary of the details (i.e., a simple qualitative description) and inserting it into the corresponding table. Having completed this activity, reflect on what you have produced and on the logic that was required to produce it. Based on this reflection, discuss why the two views of collation hold sway. That is, discuss why the collation stage is both a separate stage and a part of the analytical process.

Notes

1. George Tenet with Bill Harlow, *At the Center of the Storm: My Years at the CIA* (New York: HarperCollins, 2007), 41–42.
2. Ted Gup, *The Book of Honor: Covert Lives and Classified Deaths at the CIA* (New York: Doubleday, 2000).
3. Charles Lathrop, *The Literary Spy: The Ultimate Source for Quotations on Espionage and Intelligence* (New Haven, CT: Yale University Press, 2004), 205.
4. Ira S. Cohen, *Realpolitik: Theory and Practice* (Encino, California: Dickenson Publishing, 1975), 41–42.
5. Mark M. Lowenthal, *Intelligence: From Secrets to Policy*, fourth edition (Washington, DC: CQ Press, 2009), 6.
6. John MacGaffin and Peter Oleson, "Decision Advantage, Decision Confidence: The Why of Intelligence," *Intelligencer: Journal of U.S. Intelligence Studies*, 21, no. 3 (2015): 41.
7. Terry L. Schroeder, *Intelligence Specialist 3 & 2, vol. 1* (Washington, DC: Naval Education and Training Program Development Center, 1983), 2-1.
8. Christopher Andrew, Richard Aldrich, and Wesley Wark, *Secret Intelligence: A Reader* (London: Routledge, 2009), 1.
9. Private sector intelligence is a wide category that includes nongovernment agencies.
10. *Raw information* is sometimes referred to as *unassessed intelligence*.
11. Henry Prunckun, "The Intelligence Analyst as Social Scientist: A Comparison of Research Methods," *Police Studies* 19, no. 3 (1996): 70–72.
12. William Morris, ed., *The American Heritage Dictionary for the English Language* (Boston: American Heritage Publishing Co. and Houghton Mifflin Company, 1971), 336.
13. Note that the term *data* is both singular and plural.
14. Peter Gill, Stephen Marrin, and Mark Phythian, eds., *Intelligence Theory: Key Questions and Debates* (New York: Routledge, 2009).

15   In 2011–12, I advanced a theory of counterintelligence. I saw it as a way to fill the void in the subject literature that had existed for decades. My paper on this issue, along with the method I used, was published in the *American Intelligence Journal* (Volume 29, Number 2, December 2011, pp. 6–15), and then later published as Hank Prunckun, *Counterintelligence Theory and Practice* (Lanham, MD: Rowman & Littlefield, 2012).

16   Patrick F. Walsh, *Intelligence and Intelligence Analysis* (London: Routledge, 2011), 295–97.

17   Prunckun, *Counterintelligence Theory and Practice*, 48.

Chapter 2

Intelligence Organizational Structures

Taxonomy of Intelligence Research

Intelligence can be classified into four categories: basic, tactical, operational, and strategic. However, the term *basic intelligence* is a bit of a misnomer. The term infers that somehow it is elementary or simple, but it is neither of these things. Basic intelligence is concerned with analyzing historical topics. The purpose is to provide information that can be used for a variety of research projects, as well as for operational reasons. An example of the latter is where an operative or agent is developing a "cover" or "legend" and needs facts about what a place looked like at a particular time.

Some scholars have asserted that research needs to be predictive to be considered intelligence. However, when regarding basic intelligence, one can conclude that this is not the case. As pointed out in chapter 1, the aspect that differentiates research from intelligence is not prediction, but *secrecy*.[1]

· ·

Analysts are estimators, not clairvoyants. In the best of circumstances, a well-trained analyst cannot read an opponent's mind. Analysts can explain a trend or understand a motive, but they will not know everything. Policymakers will need to accept the limitations of intelligence efforts.[2]

· ·

The central tenet of basic intelligence is that it must be easily accessible. So, in this sense, a better description for basic intelligence might be *historical*, *universal*, or *collective* intelligence.[3]

Tactical intelligence provides support for an operation that is either under way or about to begin. Allied to the concept of tactical intelligence is what could be considered the category of *current intelligence*. Current intelligence includes reports and briefings that keep intelligence consumers apprised of developments regarding the various issues under consideration. Facts and figures produced in providing current intelligence reports could find their way into an agency's basic intelligence holdings.

Depending on the jurisdiction and/or agency, tactical intelligence is sometimes called *field intelligence* or *line intelligence* in a law enforcement context and *combat intelligence* in a military setting. These are processes and reports that fit within a defined location or the specific issue under investigation. Tactical intelligence produces such products as crime charts and maintains a "watching brief" regarding crime trends or security issues. Target profile is a form of tactical intelligence report that will be discussed in chapter 9.

Operational intelligence is information that contributes directly to the achievement of a wider goal, whereas strategic intelligence relates to long-term forecasts or broader conclusions on larger objectives. An operational assessment is a type of strategic intelligence report that will be discussed in chapter 10. This report investigates what is happening beyond the tactical level (e.g., apprehension, interdiction), but it is not predictive like strategic intelligence (i.e., long-term implications) and is, therefore, considered operational. Nevertheless, a popular convention has been to use the term *tactical* for these assessments. In previous editions of this book, the term *tactical assessment* was used.[4] But in hindsight, this anomaly may have caused confusion when developing such an assessment—it would be easy to mistake the scope of the report based on this inconsistent use of the term.

In British Commonwealth countries, strategic intelligence reports are termed *assessments* and in the United States they are called *estimates* (hence, the term *estimative intelligence* is sometimes used synonymously with *strategic intelligence*).

It should also be noted that a special category of strategic intelligence is called *warning intelligence*. Warning intelligence has a narrower focus because it is usually concerned with providing cautionary advice about an event or situation that is likely to occur soon or at a specified point in time.[5] These time frames are forward looking, but usually short term. Depending on the issue and the context, this time frame could be hours, days, or weeks. Perhaps months, but, intuitively, if an estimate is focused on a time frame of many months it is likely to be strategic intelligence. Although there is no hard-and-fast rule to what is or is not warning intelligence, judgment needs to be exercised as to what category applies. Certainly, if the issue under study is defined in terms of a year or more, it is unlikely to be warning intelligence.

The scope of these taxonomical categories is described below in point form as well as shown diagrammatically in figure 2.1. Note the narrower focus and shorter predictive time frame of warning intelligence as compared to strategic intelligence. However, for most purposes discussed in this book, tactical, operational, and strategic intelligence will be the focus.

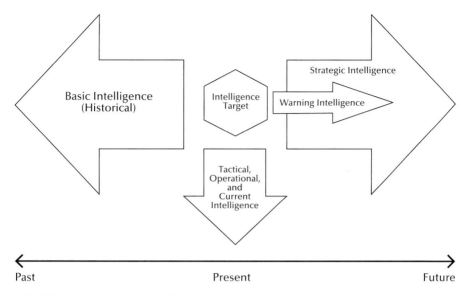

FIGURE 2.1 Graphical view of the taxonomical categories of intelligence.

Basic Intelligence

- Provides an encyclopedia-like compilation of facts and figures;
- Covers a variety of topics, issues, events, situations, places, and people spanning many decades or even centuries;
- Can be used by research analysts as well as operational personnel; and
- Can be easily accessed for quick reference.

Tactical Intelligence

- Provides immediate insight that supports a specific operation;
- Oriented toward an individual target or an activity over the short term; and
- Provides day-to-day updates on unfolding events or developing situations (i.e., *current intelligence*).

Operational Intelligence

- Is short-range or time limited but usually covers a slightly longer time frame than tactical intelligence; and
- Consists of patterns or operational mode activities that provide a wider perspective than does tactical intelligence.

Strategic Intelligence

- Considered to be a higher form of intelligence because of the involvedness of the research;
- Provides a comprehensive view of a target and/or associated activity;
- Comments on future possibilities or identifies potential issues;
- Provides advice on threats, risks, and vulnerabilities;

- Provides warning about the likelihood of certain events or situations (see the previous discussion about warning intelligence);
- Provides options for planning and policy development;
- Assists in allocating resources; and
- Requires subject area knowledge of the target, area of activity, or phenomena.

Although there appears to be an obvious separation between these classes of intelligence, in certain situations a given piece of information may be relevant to more than one—say, to meet a tactical objective as well as a strategic goal.

In military intelligence, there are other categories of tactical, operational, and strategic intelligence specific to a branch of an armed service, such as combat intelligence to the army:

- Provides military commanders with advice on the threat posed by an enemy through a process known as *intelligence preparation of the battlefield* (IPB);
- Provides knowledge of an enemy's *order of battle*—that is, a list of military units, the type of equipment it carries, and the capabilities of that equipment, as well as the location of the units and other information specific to the battlefield environment;
- Provides analysis of the weather and geographical features likely to be encountered by a commander when conducting combat operations; and
- Assists commanders in executing existing plans that are based on sound decisions—decisions that consider the enemy's intentions, capabilities, vulnerabilities, and, therefore, the likely courses of action.

Naval intelligence has categories that are specific to its mission, such as intelligence for amphibious operations, intelligence for antisubmarine warfare, and intelligence for air operations. The air force has categories within this taxonomy of tactical, operational, and strategic intelligence that are applicable to its areas of concern and operations in air and space, as well as to information warfare in cyberspace—for instance, indications and warning intelligence, and target intelligence (i.e., target development and battle damage assessment).

Anatomy of Intelligence

Just as the human anatomy is comprised of different components, so too is the anatomy of intelligence: applied intelligence research, counterintelligence, espionage, counterespionage, and covert operations.

Applied Intelligence Research

Basic research, or theoretical research as it is sometimes known in other academic disciplines, is concerned with research for its own sake—that is, when undertaken, it has no practical application in mind. It is knowledge for knowledge's sake. The findings of such research are sometimes used later in an applied setting, but at the time of conducting the research, this is not the aim.

By contrast, applied research has a practical purpose—to offer a basis for decision making (i.e., to provide insight or reduce uncertainty). Intelligence is, in this sense, applied research: it is the outcome of processing raw information that has been collected from a variety of sources—open, semi-open, official, clandestine, or covert.[6]

. . . .

Information gathered by intelligence services or compiled by the analyst is of little use unless it is got into the hands of the "consumers," the policymakers.[7]

. . . .

Once the information is in the hands of an intelligence analyst, it is evaluated and any irrelevant information discarded. The pieces of information pertinent to the matter under investigation are then analyzed, interpreted, and formed into a finished *product*. This product can take the form of an oral briefing, a written briefing, a target profile, a tactical assessment, a strategic estimate, or any number of other forms of reports. These products are then disseminated to the end user (known as the *customer* or *consumer*). The intelligence process can be summarized as analysis that leads to the production of deep, thorough, or meaningful understanding about a matter. An overview of some of the key intelligence topics and their potential taxonomical uses is given in table 2.1.

Counterintelligence

Counterintelligence is concerned with deterrence and detection. It is a security-focused function, but it is not security. However, security is used defensively within counterintelligence. That is, the thrust of counterintelligence is to protect an agency (or its client) from infiltration by an adversary, to protect against inadvertent leakage of confidential information, to make secure its installations and material against espionage, subversion, sabotage, terrorism, and other forms of politically motivated violence, and to facilitate secure transfer of key technologies and/or equipment. It is an active model that calls on defensive as well as offensive methods of security and uses research and analysis.

Even though there is a clear distinction between intelligence and counterintelligence, the demarcation line can be thin. That is, information concerning an adversary's attempts to penetrate one's own or a partner agency, discovered via the counterintelligence function, can feed the intelligence side, revealing an opponent's information voids as well as highlighting their capabilities and

TABLE 2.1 Selected Intelligence Topics and their Potential Uses

Topic	Potential Taxonomical Uses
Adversarial Attacks (in various manifestations)	Warning (Operational and Strategic)
Agriculture	Strategic
Aquaculture	Strategic
Arts, Culture, and Literature	Basic
Biographic	Basic
Building/Construction Industry	Strategic
Civic Organizations	Basic, Tactical, Operational, and Strategic
Civil Infrastructure	Operational and Strategic
Crime and Justice (including civil justice)	Operational and Strategic
Diplomatic	Tactical, Operational, and Strategic
Economic/Financial	Operational and Strategic
Educational	Operational and Strategic
Energy	Strategic
Environmental	Tactical, Operational, and Strategic
Foreign Trade	Strategic
Genealogical	Basic, Tactical, and Operational
Geological	Basic
Government	Strategic
Health	Strategic
Historic	Basic
Law Enforcement (including regulatory and compliance enforcement)	Tactical, Operational, and Strategic
Legal/Legislative	Strategic
Manufacturing/Industry	Strategic
Media	Tactical and Operational
Military/Defense	Tactical, Operational, and Strategic
Mining/Minerals	Strategic
Political (includes many subtopics)	Basic, Tactical, Operational, and Strategic
Religious	Basic, Tactical, Operational, and Strategic
Science	Strategic
Social (includes many subtopics)	Basic, Tactical, Operational, and Strategic
Space	Operational and Strategic
Sport	Basic Intelligence
Technological	Tactical, Operational, and Strategic
Telecommunications	Tactical, Operational, and Strategic
Transportation—Passenger and Cargo	Tactical, Operational, and Strategic
Vital Statistics	Basic

possible intentions. So, counterintelligence can be both an activity that is carried out and a product that is produced to inform decision makers.[8]

Espionage

This is the classic form of information gathering dating back centuries, and it forms part of the second step of the intelligence cycle. Espionage, or colloquially, spying, traditionally utilizes undercover agents. Having said that, a distinction must be made that an *agent* is someone who acts on behalf of another person or organization (e.g., a private investigator is an agent for a client who hires them to make inquiries), whereas an *officer* (or an *operative*) is someone who is charged with an authority that requires them to discharge a statutory responsibility (e.g., a Boston police officer). So, an agent is someone whom an intelligence officer recruits to obtain secrets on behalf of the operative's agency.[9] In such situations, the recruiting officer was traditionally known as a *case officer* but is now termed an *operations officer*.[10]

These agents (undercover) are placed in, or recruited while in, positions that allow them to view, overhear, or otherwise obtain information that could not be gained in any other way. Generally speaking, agents betray their country for ideological or monetary reasons, or for revenge, lust for power, or for the thrill involved, or it could be for the risk or mystique involved in the activity, or to fulfill some fantasy.[11] However, with technological improvements, more technical means of espionage (i.e., technical surveillance and unobtrusive methods) are favored over the classic use of espionage agents. It could be said that this worked reasonably well during the Cold War when intelligence agencies faced actors that were states.

· ·

Espionage is not a James Bond–like game. Rather, it is a serious business that can have deadly consequences. The Wall of Honor at CIA headquarters holds testimony to this fact. In 2002, it was reported to hold seventy-nine stars, each representing an officer of the agency who gave his or her life in the service of country. Forty-eight of those officers have their names listed in the Book of Honor,[12] but the remaining (at that time) were anonymous, as their services to the nation were still classified.[13]

· ·

On the one hand, an agent can provide an agency with a stream of intelligence for years. On the other, a defector (a specific type of spy) can only provide the agency with intelligence which is current at the time of his or her defection, though much can be learned about past operations and methods from debriefing them. Both types of spies are needed in the "great game,"[14] but each has its strengths and limitations. Although spies are often only viewed as being active in the world of national security intelligence, spies and defectors can perform these same roles in other types of intelligence work, including business intelligence and law enforcement intelligence.[15]

But since the al-Qaeda attacks of September 11, 2001, intelligence agencies recognized the importance of having agents in place to gather data.[16] One reason for the shift to technically gathered data was the comparatively high cost of running field agents and improving the reliability of the data collected (e.g., aerial and satellite photographs are not susceptible to exaggerating the truth as an agent might be. These data simply show what is there and what is not).

The events of September 11 and the subsequent terrorist attacks in Bali, Madrid, and London show that the advantages of technically gathered data were of little value against terrorist cells operating in a vastly different fashion from that of, say, a foreign government's military. This type of confrontation, and other nontraditional challenges to a state-centric paradigm, no longer applies. Nations now face threats from weak and corrupt governments, rogue states, sub-state and trans-state actors, as well as international, organized criminal groups, radical ethnic and religious groups, and right-wing political groups. All these threats pose special data collection problems that defy a purely technical approach.

When it comes to describing *cover*—a plausible story about all facets of the operative's life—there are essentially two types: official cover and nonofficial cover (NOC, pronounced *knock*).[17] NOC is also referred to as commercial cover, when the operative works for a phantom company created and maintained by an intelligence agency. The former are personnel posing as government employees of some description, and the latter are those who on the surface have no connection with the government.

The NOC operatives have been described as the truest practitioners of espionage, as they always operate on their own, with no protection from their government. In the case of foreign espionage, if they are caught abroad, they may be tortured during interrogation and perhaps executed. If this happens, no media conference will be held, and no one will hear about the event. The NOC operatives operate alone and die alone.

Nonetheless, espionage still employs audio surveillance devices, radio frequency devices, and special photographic equipment, including space-based reconnaissance satellites. The use of such devices can provide the intelligence analyst with an exponential gain in both the quantity and, under the right circumstances, the quality of the information gathered. However, it is at the peril of the intelligence agency that it neglects data collection by human sources. Because the espionage function features so heavily in intelligence work, chapter 4 explores various forms of covert and clandestine sources of information gathering.

Counterespionage

Counterespionage is concerned with detection, deception,[18] and neutralizing the effectiveness of an adversary's intelligence activities. On the surface, counterespionage presents as a form of spying—collecting classified information through a network of agents—which it is, except that it is the acquisition of data not from another nation's government or military but from the opposition's intelligence service. It is in some ways related to counterintelligence but differs in others. Counterintelligence could be viewed as the defensive side of the craft, whereas counterespionage is the offensive side. An agency cannot have the latter without the former, so the two work in tandem.

· ·

Counterespionage is often touted as the aristocratic sector of secret operations. In the romantic image the counterespionage man is pitted against his fellow professionals on the other side who are trying to get his nation's secrets. His job is to foil them. It is a true adversary relationship unlike the espionage situation, in which two men work together to purloin secrets. Most spy stories are not about spying but about counterspying.[19]

· ·

Counterespionage is a precise function and is, arguably, the most subtle and sophisticated of all intelligence functions. It calls for the engineering of complex strategies that deliberately puts one's agent(s) in contact with an opposition's intelligence personnel. This is done so that information can be obtained, or the adversary can be fed disinformation which will hopefully lead to confusion, thus disrupting the adversary's operations and allowing the perpetrator to "prosper"—and prosper can be interpreted in many ways. False information can also be planted; so, like a "barium meal," the route that this information travels within the opposition's intelligence apparatus can be traced to confirm penetration by a mole or expose other security leaks or discover information hitherto unknown. It could be argued that counterespionage could not carry out its mission without the support of the methods and practices of counterintelligence.[20]

Covert Operations

Although scholars sometimes argue that covert operations fall into a somewhat gray area of intelligence work—being neither intelligence work nor military operations—it's posited here that covert ops are, in fact, one of the prime policy options for which intelligence is produced. Intelligence work and covert operations go hand in glove. Intelligence professionals who view covert action as a repulsive cousin of intelligence work are misguided in their thinking. If they believe that they are only information gatherers or analysts of data and that the outcome is simply to produce reports, assessments, and estimates, then they are naïve. They need to recall that the outcome of their activities is not related to some polite discussion about the academic merits of how the principal adversary or opposition might be influenced. It should be clear to anyone working in intelligence that the end state is to defeat the opposition and/or prevent the opposition from defeating you.

On a policy scale that ranges from doing nothing up to engaging in all-out military engagement, covert action lies somewhere in the middle. So, how could intelligence professionals not see that their work might affect policy outcomes that could maintain the status quo at one extreme, but could escalate to inflicting death on large numbers of people or destroying entire cities at the other? How could they not see covert action as just another policy option, albeit a *secret policy option*, within this policy continuum? Choosing one option over another is, after all, based on the results of their intelligence work.

Sometimes referred to as *covert action*,[21] *special activities*,[22] or *special ops*,[23] it uses various methods of information gathering including that of research and analysis, but incorporates advice and counsel, financial and material support, as well as technical assistance to individuals, groups, or businesses which are opposed to, or working in competition with, a target or adversary.

Covert operations, or *black ops* as it is sometimes referred to, is a function by which the perpetrator analyzes the information collected through espionage and observation to strengthen his allies and to weaken, destabilize, or destroy his opponents.[24] A few of the tactics used in covert operations include political agitation, propaganda, election rigging, bribing high officials, blackmailing key political figures, demolishing key facilities, targeted killings, promoting rebellions and insurrections, as well as a wide variety of "monkey-wrenching" tactics[25] in the physical world and in cyberspace. Listing these tactics in such a blunt way should not be interpreted as condemnation or admonishment—in the world of realpolitik their use is a valid policy option. But the effectiveness of covert operations is contingent upon the perpetrator's involvement remaining hidden or, at least, deniable, and this relies on intelligence work (specially, counterintelligence).

On the one hand, if a "plausible denial"[26] can be maintained, then the rewards of such ventures can be enormous. On the other hand, if the perpetrator's involvement is discovered, the consequences of this activity can be catastrophic. For example, in 1985 the French government was concerned about protests by Greenpeace regarding nuclear testing on the Pacific atoll of Mururoa. So, on July 10, 1985, French intelligence operatives from the Direction Générale de la Sécurité Extérieure (in English, the Directorate General for External Security) mined Greenpeace's *Rainbow Warrior* in Auckland Harbour, New Zealand, with an explosive charge. The vessel sank, drowning one person aboard.

. . . .

If intelligence is about trying to understand or predict an event using secret methods of inquiry, then covert action is about making an impact on an event using secret tactics.

. . . .

New Zealand police mounted an investigation into the incident and two French operatives were arrested, tried, and found guilty. They were then sent to prison. The other French operatives managed to evade capture and escaped. The incident was not only an embarrassment to the French government but carried political ramifications that affected the French government for many years. Had the operation been carried out successfully—that is, had the operatives managed to escape undetected—then the results of the op would have been much different.

Although it could be thought that agents who perform covert operations do this exclusively, it should be kept in mind that any agent who is recruited as a spy can be diverted to perform covert operations. Yes, there may be agents who specialize in covert operations, but it does not necessarily follow that they are the only ones who perform this function, especially when the situation calls for speed of execution, in which case, improvisation by using an agent in place may be the approach selected.

Summary

One way to summarize the relationship between the different anatomical parts of intelligence is to show it in a modified Johari Window.[27] Table 2.2 displays the four "panes" in the so-called window metaphor. Across the top is displayed the agency's perspective on information and along the left side is the opposition's perspective. So, the intersection of each perspective shows the intelligence function that is needed by the agency in relation to each information type.

TABLE 2.2 **The Relationship between Information and the Various Anatomical Parts of Intelligence Viewed from an Agency's Standpoint**

		Agency	
		Known	**Unknown**
Opposition	**Known**	Applied Intelligence Research	Espionage
	Unknown	Counterintelligence	Counterespionage and Covert Ops

Starting at the upper left quadrant, we see that, where information is known to both an intelligence agency and its opposition, the information is (likely) common knowledge (e.g., open-source information) and not subject to any specialized intelligence function; though it is the livelihood of the applied intelligence research function. Having said that, it is important to note that analysts performing the applied intelligence research function will use information from all four quadrants. For simplicity, this function is shown at the upper left quadrant only.

In the upper right quadrant, these data are unknown to the agency but known to the opposition; so, for the agency to obtain this information, the espionage function needs to be employed. In the lower left quadrant, we have data that are known to the agency but unknown to the opposition. In these cases, the counterintelligence function needs to be exercised. Finally, the lower right quadrant shows that neither the agency nor the opposition knows about this information, but both seek to acquire it. This is where counterespionage and covert operations come into play.

Typology of Intelligence

Intelligence is structured according to type (or class), and the typology is based on the environment in which the organization operates. There are five major classes of intelligence: national security (which includes foreign policy and international politics), military, law enforcement, business, and private. A sixth type, emergency services (e.g., firefighters and search-and-rescue teams), also has intelligence cells but, although it is given the name *intelligence*, does not perform the same function or the same level of analysis as the other five types.[28] Because of these limitations, this type of intelligence is not considered within the pages of this book.

It is important to note these environments can overlap—for example, an investigation into the capability of a terrorist cell may be of interest to local law enforcement agencies as well as to agencies involved in national security, the military, and some private security firms. Moreover, regarding military intelligence, it is, in some cases, intimately aligned with national security because it informs about the intent and capabilities of an adversary not only to military commanders but also to political leaders who are responsible for authorizing the use of military force and directing strategic military policy.

In addition to the overlap or close working partnership, the same methods of operation, tactics, devices, information storage systems, and methods of analysis are used by each intelligence type. This is because information holds no bounds as to its usefulness, and a piece of data could conceivably be the target for more than one type of intelligence user. In other words, the difference between the various types of intelligence lies in the end use or general thrust of the intelligence operation.

National Security Intelligence

National security intelligence is conducted by the various branches of a nation's armed forces, foreign diplomatic service, and, depending on the country, its atomic energy authority. It is sometimes referred to as *foreign policy* intelligence, depending on the context. Nations with advanced economies generally tend to have a central agency that acts to coordinate subsidiary intelligence agencies and the collection and processing of information from all sources. Other nations, in contrast, have a unified system with one supreme agency taking on all three roles—coordination, collection, and analysis.

The types of information sought by national security intelligence analysts can be the current political issues facing a foreign government; the health, education, and social structures of the country; its social problems; or its legal institutions. They may include issues concerning food production and distribution, world resources (e.g., oil and potable water), international trade relationships, world migration patterns and changes in the ethnic composition of nations, as well as the state of the global monetary order. Without a doubt, they seek also information on foreign technological developments, nuclear matters, and almost anything to do with foreign weapons production, defense industries, defense installations, and military capabilities.

However, in the post–9/11 security environment, there is a nexus between national security intelligence and law enforcement intelligence. This is due to the threat international terrorists pose to civil society. Prior to the 9/11 attacks, national security analysts and law enforcement analysts did not "fully understand the fundamental roles and limitations of their counterparts. This led to communications errors and frustrations, ultimately leading to decreased effectiveness."[29] Although this situation has changed in the intervening years, it underscores the point that there is an overlap in these security environments.[30]

Military Intelligence

Military decisions carry a heavy burden of responsibility. As such, these decisions impact not only the lives of the fighting forces but also a nation's liberty. Military intelligence concerns itself with matters key to fighting a war—"enemy strength, capabilities, and vulnerabilities as well as information on weather and terrain."[31] In addition to dealing with these fundamental concerns, intelligence produced by the military "has to be timely, accurate, adequate, and usable."[32]

Military intelligence is decision making by commanders about both the operational environment and the forces (whether they are hostile, friendly, or neutral) and the civilian population in the operational (or potential) area. A nation's military will carry out intelligence activities regardless of whether it is at war or at peace (i.e., to prevent a surprise attack or to transition to a war footing at short notice) and at three levels—tactical, operational, and strategic.

It would be most unusual for any army, navy, or air force not to have some form of military intelligence capability. It may take the form of a specialist unit, or it may be part of another government service. Staff can be from the military or civilians assigned to the intelligence agency because of their technical or analytical abilities. Military personnel who do not have such skills are often trained at special colleges, which are set up specifically for this purpose.

Law Enforcement Intelligence

Law enforcement intelligence aims to increase the accuracy of decisions made by commanders. Intelligence provides senior officers with advice needed to make sound decisions and, in this regard, provides a focus on those criminal activities that would generally go undetected until they evolve into a community problem. These agencies are much wider than just police and include compliance and regulatory agencies that perform law enforcement functions (which can be quite numerous), such as immigration, customs services, and prison intelligence units.

Law enforcement intelligence also encompasses agencies engaged in combating the threat posed by foreign and internal subversion, espionage, sabotage, and terrorism. Other law enforcement agencies protect national security and foreign policy interests by enforcing export regulations relating to prohibited dual-use items, such as certain hardware technology, software, chemicals, and nuclear material (e.g., U.S. Department of Commerce's Office of Export Enforcement).

Depending on the agency and its mission, the analysts who staff these units may be referred to by different names, such as project officers, collators, intelligence analysts, crime analysts, criminal intelligence analysts, and so forth.[33] The reason for these different names could be historical or based on industrial agreements. The titles may also reflect some level of discrimination between the levels of critical thinking that are required to perform the tasks. For instance, a collator may perform simple analytic tasks using a few rudimental research methods, whereas an analyst may be required to show high levels of analytic thinking as well as an understanding of advanced research methodologies (and/or subject expertise).

Business Intelligence

Business intelligence is concerned with the acquisition of trade-related secrets and commercial information that is held confidential from competing firms. Business intelligence is also referred as *competitor intelligence* (or *competitive intelligence*) and *corporate intelligence*.[34] Although the media has exposed much about the unethical behavior of some intelligence practitioners, it is safe to say that a good deal of information is gathered through open and semi-open sources. The focus of this activity can be on several levels—local, regional, national, or even international. Business intelligence is not limited to the realms of companies and corporations themselves but can also include private investigation firms that specialize in this type of inquiry (i.e., spies-for-hire), as well as intelligence agencies of foreign nations. In the latter group are foreign military and national security agencies that target trade, economic, and technological information. "A former FBI counterintelligence officer described as a 'reasonable estimate' the claim that China has in place up to 25,000 intelligence officers and had recruited 15,000 informants already in the United States. . . . Those with valuable technological and scientific information will be asked to pass it on."[35]

Sometimes other terms are used by businesses to "soften" what might be aggressive practices associated with the term *intelligence*. *Market intelligence* (or simply, *market research*), *product intelligence* (or *product research*), or *customer/client intelligence* are all terms that can be heard in business circles, but, when used, they usually mean *business intelligence*.

Private Sector Intelligence

To describe what constitutes private sector intelligence is not straightforward—this is because it is a diverse type of intelligence. In this book, it will be viewed as firms and private agents who offer their services in secret research for fee or reward to the public. A simple definition might be: private sector intelligence is secret research conducted by nongovernment entities.[36]

Although the term *private* implies an individual, there is some overlap in what constitutes private sector intelligence and what may be business intelligence or even national security intelligence. The ultimate determiner is who is contracting the spy-for-hire.

Private sector intelligence practitioners offer a range of specialist services that go beyond the bounds of the average private investigator or private detective. Often the private intelligence practitioner comes from a background in law enforcement, military, or national security intelligence work. Their specialties may be in background investigations or surveillance. They may have extensive training in the use of state-of-the-art optical or electronic audio surveillance equipment, and they would be familiar with the techniques of intelligence analysis. They may offer advice on business counterintelligence and electronic audio countermeasures (debugging). They may also specialize in providing close personal protection for important public figures, crisis and risk management, cyber security, and business continuity planning.

Private sector intelligence agencies could (arguably) include commercial organizations that maintain databases for specialized inquiry work, for example, credit reporting. Likewise, private sector intelligence agencies might even encompass what are called policy institutes (or think tanks) where research agencies engage in scholarly investigation for fee-paying clients. Private sector intelligence practitioners are being viewed by some of their government counterparts as a viable supplementary alternative deemed necessary in cases where resources are constrained.

Although private investigators might dominate this field, many, and perhaps most, are not because intelligence is about structured thinking—devising research questions, formulating data collection plans, collecting and collating data, and analyzing the data. Many of those who practice in private sector intelligence are other than private investigators. Some, for instance, come from backgrounds in policy; some are subject area experts; some might be methodologists; some are data analysts; and so on.

But, this is not to say that all these private sector intelligence practitioners have policy, analytical, or research backgrounds; it is likely that a large percentage comprises private investigators. In fact, subject area experts are now discussing how private investigators can adapt sophisticated intelligence methods to conduct inquiries in the post–9/11 security environment.[37] By way of example, in August 2013, a symposium on the *Privatization of Intelligence* was held in Canberra—Australia's national capital—where leading academic and intelligence practitioners gathered to discuss the latest developments and their implications for the future of the profession.[38]

Key Words and Phrases

The key words and phrases associated with this chapter are listed below. Demonstrate your understanding of each by writing either a short definition or a one- or two-sentence explanation.

applied intelligence research
business intelligence
counterespionage
counterintelligence
cover

espionage
essential elements of intelligence
military intelligence
national security intelligence
private sector intelligence

Study Questions

1. Provide an overview of the five major classes of intelligence as well as the functions each performs within this typological framework.
2. Describe what is different between the four major categories of intelligence—basic, tactical, operational, and strategic.
3. Identify two intelligence consumers in a military setting and describe how they might use intelligence products.
4. What type of intelligence would it be if an analyst was tasked to assist field operatives to locate the individuals responsible for a terrorist attack on an iconic landmark? Explain why.

Learning Activity

Research the businesses in one of the following nations that engage in private sector intelligence—Australia, Canada, New Zealand, the United Kingdom, or the United

States. List the types of services these businesses provide and compare them to the types of tasks in which you know government intelligence agencies are engaged. Examining the list of private sector activities, are you able to suggest whether any of these could be contracted to a private firm by a government agency? Speculate as to what the advantages and disadvantages might be, and then conclude with your consideration as to when and why one or more might be contracted out.

Notes

1. If, to some scholars, "prediction" is "knowing in advance" and all intelligence needs to be able to do this, then it does not fit with analyses that are not able to predict but merely weigh the probability that an event might take place, or a person/group may do something, and so on. Prediction implies that a future can be known, when, in fact, intelligence is not able to do this—intelligence research may only be able to test the likelihood of a hypothesis (i.e., reduce uncertainty). This has been highlighted by former U.S. Director of National Intelligence, James R. Clapper, who pointed out that, intelligence reduces "uncertainty for decision makers as much as possible, whether they're in the Oval Office, at the negotiating table, or on the battlefield (p. 49)." And "intelligence work [is] about acquiring and assessing foreign secrets, not predicting events or reading minds (p. 159)." James. R. Clapper with Trey Brown, *Facts and Fears: Hard Truths from a Life in Intelligence* (New York: Viking, 2018), 49.

2. Frank J. Cilluffo, Ronald A. Marks and George C. Salmoiraghi (2002), "The Use and Limits of U.S. Intelligence," *Washington Quarterly*, 25:1, 72.

3. In this regard, researchers with library science degrees can be most helpful in developing basic intelligence systems (Dr. Edna Reid, Federal Bureau of Investigation, Washington, DC, personal communication, June 7, 2011).

4. See, for instance, the United Kingdom's *National Intelligence Model* (London: National Criminal Intelligence Service, 2000), which uses the term *tactical assessment* instead of *operation assessment*.

5. Cynthia M. Grabo, *Anticipating Surprise: Analysis for Strategic Warning* (Lanham, MD: University Press of America, 2004).

6. Roy Godson, *Dirty Tricks or Trump Cards: U.S. Covert Action and Counterintelligence* (Washington, DC: Brassey's, 1995), 303.

7. Allen W. Dulles, *The Craft of Intelligence* (New Delhi: Manas Publications, 2007), 149.

8. See Hank Prunckun, *Counterintelligence Theory and Practice, Second Edition* (Lanham, MD: Rowman & Littlefield, 2019) for a more in-depth discussion of the counterintelligence function. See also, Hank Prunckun, "A Grounded Theory of Counterintelligence," *American Intelligence Journal* 29, no. 2 (December 2011): 6–15.

9. Ellis M. Zacharias, *Secret Missions: The Story of an Intelligence Officer* (New York: G.P. Putnam's Sons, 1946).

10. Robert Baer, *See No Evil: The True Story of a Ground Soldier in the CIA's War on Terrorism* (New York: Crown Publishers, 2002), 273; Melissa Boyle Mahle, *Denial and Deception: An Insider's View of the CIA from Iran-Contra to 9/11* (New York: Nation Books, 2004), 37, 54, and 370.

11. Fredrick P. Hitz, *The Great Game: The Myth and Reality of Espionage* (New York: Alfred A. Knopf, 2004).

12. Gup, *The Book of Honor*.

13. T.J. Waters, *Class 11: Inside the CIA's First Post-9/11 Spy Class* (New York: Dutton, 2006), 4.

14. Hitz, *The Great Game*, 3.

15. For a detailed discussion on the case-managing agents, see Jefferson Mack, *Running a Ring of Spies: Spycraft and Black Operations in the Real World of Espionage* (Boulder, CO: Paladin Press, 1996).

16. Baer, *See No Evil*; Mahle, *Denial and Deception*; and Waters, *Class 11*.

17. Mahle, *Denial and Deception*, 141, 149–50, 233, 370.

18. For a discussion about how pervasive deception is in this area of intelligence work, see the personal story of a family member who lived with his father who was a spy, by Scott C. Johnson, *The Wolf and the Watchman: A CIA Childhood* (New York: W.W. Norton and Company, 2013).

19 Harry Rositzke, *CIA's Secret Operations: Espionage, Counterespionage, and Covert Action* (New York: Reader's Digest Press, 1977), 119.

20 Prunckun, *Counterintelligence Theory and Practice, Second Edition.*

21 Godson, *Dirty Tricks or Trump Cards,* 2–3, 304.

22 William J. Daugherty, *Executive Secrets: Covert Action and the Presidency* (University of Kentucky Press, 2004), 13–15, and note 7 at 228.

23 Hitz, *The Great Game,* 5.

24 See, for instance, Dennis Fiery, *Out of Business: Force a Company, Business or Store to Close Its Doors ... For Good* (Port Townsend, WA: Loompanics Unlimited, 1999).

25 As an example, recall the case of Donald H. Segretti, who, during the 1972 U.S. presidential election campaign, conducted "opposition research" to assist Richard Nixon's reelection. "His goal was to create as much bitterness and disunity within the Democratic Party as he could." Segretti was "recruited by [H.R.] Halderman's appointments secretary, Dwight Chapin, for the political game of 'dirty tricks.'" Quotes from Tony Ulasewicz with Stuart A. McKeever, *The President's Private Eye: The Journey of Detective Tony U. from NYPD to the Nixon White House* (Westport, CT: MACSAM Publishing Co., 1990), 240. Also, during the era of the Watergate Affair, there were other *monkey-wrenching* campaigns planned or conducted. For details see G. Gordon Liddy, *Will: The Autobiography of G. Gordon Liddy* (London: Severn House, 1981). Finally, there is a sizable body of literature outlining how to conduct such campaigns. By way of example, these are a few indicative titles: George Hayduke, *Get Even: The Complete Book of Dirty Tricks* (Boulder, CO: Paladin Press, 1980); George Hayduke, *Byte Me: Hayduke's Guide to Computer-Generated Revenge* (Boulder, CO: Paladin Press, 2000); John Jackson, *The Black Book of Revenge: The Complete Manual of Hardcore Dirty Tricks and Schemes* (El Dorado, AR: Desert Publications, 1991); and Victor Santoro, *Political Trashing* (Port Townsend, WA: Loompanics Unlimited, 1987).

26 Peter Grabosky and Michael Stohl, *Crime and Terrorism* (London: Sage Publications, 2010), 53 and 64. See also, Richard A. Best, Jr., and Andrew Feicket, *CRS Report for Congress: Special Operations Forces (SOF) and CIA Paramilitary Operations: Issues for Congress* (Washington, DC: Congressional Research Service, Library of Congress, December 6, 2006), 5.

27 The framework shown in table 2.2 was adapted from the concept developed by Joseph Luft and Henry (Harry) Ingham for understanding interactions: "The Johari Window: A Graphic Model of Interpersonal Awareness," in *Proceedings of the Western Training Laboratory in Group Development* (Los Angeles: University of California, Los Angeles, Extension Office, 1955).

28 Emergency Management Australia, *Operations Centre Management,* second edition (Canberra, Australia: Emergency Management Australia, 2001), 5–10; and Emergency Management Australia, *Land Search Operations,* second edition (Canberra, Australia: Emergency Management Australia, 1997).

29 David L. Carter, "Law Enforcement Intelligence and National Security Intelligence: Exploring the Differences," *International Association of Law Enforcement Intelligence Analysts Journal* 21, no. 1 (November 2012): 1.

30 Walsh, *Intelligence and Intelligence Analysis.*

31 Joseph A. McChristian, *The Role of Military Intelligence: 1965–1967* (Washington, DC: GPO, 1974), 3.

32 McChristian, *The Role of Military Intelligence,* 3.

33 Walsh, *Intelligence and Intelligence Analysis,* 245.

34 Leonard M. Fuld, *Competitor Intelligence: How to Get It—How to Use It* (New York: John Wiley and Sons, 1985); and Richard Eells and Peter Nehemkis, *Corporate Intelligence and Espionage: A Blueprint of Corporate Decision Making* (New York: Macmillan Publishing Company, 1984), 78.

35 Clive Hamilton, *Silent Invasion: China's Influence in Australia* (Melbourne: Hardie Grant Books, 2018), 153.

36 Eells and Nehemkis, *Corporate Intelligence and Espionage,* 185.

37 See Hank Prunckun, ed., *Intelligence and Private Investigation: Developing Sophisticated Methods for Conducting Inquiries* (Springfield, IL: Charles C Thomas, 2013).

38 A selection of the unclassified papers that were presented at this symposium was later published in a special issue of *Salus Journal* (see vol. 1, no. 2, November 2013).

Chapter 3

The Intelligence Research Process

Problem Formulation

Problem formulation is the center of intelligence research. Aristotle is attributed as saying "Well begun is half done," and this proverb resonates with the intelligence research process. So, how do decision makers formulate their questions, and how do analysts arrive at the hypotheses that form the basis of their research projects? Because intelligence research is applied, the questions under investigation will have real-world origins. Whether the origin is geopolitical (national security intelligence), financial markets (business intelligence), criminal activity (law enforcement intelligence), or issues involving an adversary's order of battle (military intelligence), the questions decision makers pose are concerned with how to address the problem. Intelligence provides insight to guide possible options based on defensible conclusions derived from evidence-centered study. In practice, this means writing reports based on empirical research.

. . . .

Intelligence has to "educate its customers [but] this is a formidable task. . . . They have to be convinced of what it can and what it cannot achieve" by asking the right questions, at the right time and without flooding the system.[1]

. . . .

Having said that, there are times when analysts are asked to provide decision makers with possible scenarios of what the future holds for an environment. In such cases, analysts are free to establish their own theories and create their own research questions.

While analysts can provide intelligence, the competing demands of tactical field commanders (e.g., executive directors in a business setting) and strategic decision makers can flood the intelligence system, thereby rendering it ineffective. Therefore, what is asked of an intelligence unit should be minimal and specific.

For instance, a single but nonspecific intelligence request can be quite counterproductive. Take the tactical intelligence example of a field commander who asks to "see all the aerial photos relating to the terrain north of the Orrenabad Desert." This may result in gigabytes of assorted classified imagery being delivered to the commander's computer hours or days after the time it is needed, rendering the information useless if he or she had intended to use it to plan an attack. Therefore, specific requests assist intelligence analysts and reciprocate by yielding answers more useful to the decision makers when choosing the most appropriate operational options. Requests need to be specific by using questions such as:

- How many troops does the enemy have positioned north of the Orrenabad Desert?
- What is the enemy's order of battle?
- Will the weather be favorable to launch a frontal assault on these positions over the next twenty-four hours?
- If an attack is launched, can resupply of friendly forces be assured?
- Can air support provide both suppressing fire in the advance and evacuation of the wounded?

"How we ask a question, when and where we ask, whom we ask and what we ask about will all influence the kind of response that we get."[2] "There is no specific formula of 'one-size-fits-all' approach to asking good questions,"[3] but there are three characteristics, or foundational requirements, that comprise a good question: understanding what specific information is needed; understanding that the wording of the question is important to get the correct information; and then putting forward that question to those able to supply the answer.

Literature Review

To start the writing process, the first step is to conduct a literature review. The purpose of the literature review is to seek research related to the issue under investigation, to establish the problem's conceptual as well as a theoretical context. But literature review can be an abbreviated form of review, especially when it is applied to tactical projects. Although it may be not referred to as a literature review in the tactical setting, it might be called "background," "context," or "situation." This section of the report may only be a paragraph or two as opposed to the much longer length in a strategic intelligence report. Regardless, the literature review places the analyst's project in the context of the wider issue. "No man is an island unto himself," wrote the poet John Donne, and his message, though intended for a different audience, applies to intelligence problems.[4] No research question exists in isolation from other issues. The literature review allows analysts to develop and ground their arguments or, simply, to "tell their stories." For analysts undertaking a new research project, a literature review is one of the first steps. Analysts need to discuss the theoretical base they intend to use to test their hypothesis. For law enforcement analysts, this might include deterrence theory, target hardening, rationale choice theory, differential association, social disorganization, or any number of other criminological theories.

• •

In the social and behavioral sciences, the term *hypothesis* is used to pose a question. In intelligence research, the term *explanation* is sometimes substituted for hypothesis. In this book, the term hypothesis will be used.

• •

For national security intelligence, analysts might consider the use of sociological (e.g., Edwin Sutherland's theory on white-collar crime[5]), anthropological, psychological, political science, historical, economic (especially as they relate to illicit drug importation), business (in relation to organized crime and antiterrorism), or even military theories (e.g., counterterrorism and counterinsurgency) and apply them to the issue under investigation.

The theory component of the literature review should have its own subheading (or some such literary device) so the reader does not have to "hunt" for this information. Obviously, in a tactical intelligence report, theory may not feature at all, as the purpose of the report is to address a specific, short-term issue.

The literature review should talk about why the issue is being studied and how the theory (i.e., the presumed relationship between the variables), if applied to the problem, could help, improve, solve, make more efficient, and so on. Effectively, it states what benefit the study's findings might have for decision makers or how the research results of the study might "push back the frontiers of knowledge."

Analysts need to demonstrate that they understand what research has already been conducted and how their research will either add to it, address an area that has not yet been explored, or, if a different theory is being used, why changes might be expected that are yet to be realized. The key concepts and terms need to be discussed so they can be "operationalized" in the methodology.

It is unlikely the analysts will find research that is the same as the inquiries they are making (unless they are conducting a reexamination of previously conducted research). From this perspective, there will be no issue so unique the analyst cannot locate some piece of related research to inform the current scholarly investigation.

As with other forms of empirical research, intelligence research seeks to push back the boundaries of knowledge by adding to what is known. Therefore, the literature review allows the analyst to introduce the problem under investigation expressed as a research question[6] or hypothesis, so the reader of the report can understand how it fits within the wider context, how exploration of the problem will provide understanding, and how to provide critical insight into solving it.

On a practical point, reviewing the literature allows the analyst to gain an appreciation of some of the problems encountered in previous studies and, therefore, avoid repeating the same mistakes. These problems are often in methodological issues including inappropriate sample size or selection method, invalid measurement instruments, data reliability issues, or inappropriate statistical analysis (e.g., autocorrelation of time-series data is a commonly experienced problem).

The ancillary benefit of a literature review is the discovery of secondary data sources that could be used in the study. For instance, an analyst may come across quotations from field notes or interviews and these can be used as sources of data. Even though the literature review sets the scene and appears in the forefront of the research report, the analyst can always refer to the literature in the results section of the report as a means of validating certain aspects of the findings.

Methodology

In empirical research, this is the most important aspect of the investigation process, especially regarding strategic intelligence. However, like the literature review, the method section is mainly applicable to strategic intelligence projects. A tactical intelligence report may state the method it used, but it would be abbreviated and may only be a paragraph that summarizes the study's overall approach.

If the analyst has crafted the research question well and placed it in its historical (and if applicable, theoretical) framework, it will guide the rest of the research process. As the methodology deals with the tangible aspects of the study, the analyst will need to define the concepts being studied so they can be measured (i.e., operationalized).

Some intelligence scholars suggest that there are four categories of analytic methods—expert judgment, structure analysis, quantitative methods using expert-generated data, and quantitative methods using empirical data.[7] These methods can be categorized according to this argument, but this book takes another view of how such a taxonomy is constructed.

It is argued that there are only two methodological categories—quantitative and qualitative. Within the quantitative category fall quantitative methods using expert-generated data and quantitative methods using empirical data. Under the taxonomical category of qualitative methods are expert judgments and structure analyses, as well as other methods. Put simply, data that are gathered in numeric form lend themselves to a range of quantitative analytic tests; whereas, data that are unstructured, when collected, can be analyzed by various qualitative methods. By way of example, the text of a political speech is unstructured data—it is simply words that represent a person's thoughts. Therefore, the speech can be analyzed using qualitative methods, say, expert judgment (which is a form of pros-vs-con/force field analysis in narrative form), or the content of the speech can be given numeric structure and analyzed using, for instance, the Flesch Reading Ease or the Flesch-Kincaid Grade Level tests, or other methods (see chapter 6 for more details).

In chapter 7, we discuss the four levels of how quantitative data are "measured": nominal data, ordinal data, interval data, and ratio data. Each level of measurement represents an increase in the type of statistical tests that are permissible. The type of data that is collected determines which statistical test can be conducted. High-level data can be converted to low-level measures, but the opposite is not possible—if ordinal data are collected, for example, they cannot be converted to ratio data.

So, in this regard, what some intelligence scholars have asserted about there being four categories of data has painted an incomplete picture. Unstructured (qualitative) data can be analyzed as is or given structure to be analyzed using quantitative tests. Numeric data (quantitative) can be analyzed using a method commensurate with its level of measurement; or it can be converted to a lower level of measurement (e.g., ordinal or categorical) and analyzed using a qualitative technique (e.g., thematic analysis, competing hypotheses, or others).

The most popular research designs include evaluations (to plan intervention programs/operations), case studies (what is going on?), longitudinal studies (has there been any change over time?), comparisons (are A and B different?), cross-sectional studies (are A and B different at this point in time?), longitudinal comparisons (are A and B different over time?), and experiments or quasi-experimental studies (what effect does A have on B?).

The methodology requires analysts to identify the type of data they need to collect (whether these data are from primary and secondary sources or in qualitative or quantitative forms, or both) and how these data will be collated and analyzed (e.g., statistically or content analysis) to test their hypothesis.

Analysts also need to consider related issues, including sample size and control for confounding variables (i.e., the potential that what they are observing is due to something else that they are not measuring). These extraneous influences may pose limitations for their research (e.g., possible alternative explanations for the relationship between A and B) or there could be limits inherent in the data.

Intelligence Collection Plan

Analysts use the information collection plan as a method to design and manage their data acquisition. The plan is a simple device structuring the analyst's thinking to develop a picture of the data and what is required, where it exists, and how it can be gathered. It outlines time frames for collection of each piece of information for the research project, and allows checking when data have been collected, as well as assessing whether there are outstanding items. Therefore, the intelligence collection plan can be either a simple collection blueprint or a combined collection and management strategy. These can take the form of idea maps, fishbone diagrams, and data collection tables.

Because the objectives of individual intelligence agencies are so diverse, there are no set formats for collection plans. Nonetheless, a good collection plan should be couched in precise terms reflecting the following:

- The decision makers' *intelligence requirements* (IR) or *intelligence collection requirements* (ICR);
- The resources needed to collect data;
- What priority each data item has in relation to other data and within the whole data collection scheme;
- Who is responsible for collecting each data item; and
- The progress tracking of each data item.

The plan should be flexible to allow adjustment as changes in intelligence requirements emerge or if the objective of the research project alters.

In some agencies, there are two additional methods of acquiring information—the *statement of intelligence interest* and *essential elements of information* (EEI was discussed in chapter 1). The former is a standing request to receive finished intelligence publications when released for dissemination. Usually, analysts register their interests in topics under investigation, and the reports are forwarded to them for consideration when they become available. The standing request can be viewed as an order that remains in force until canceled; as new material is lodged, it is sent to the analyst. Essential elements of information are time-urgent requests for information (e.g., ground forces engaged in combat operations require EEI).

Idea Mapping

A mind map is type of idea map. It is a diagram representing a set of related thoughts. Mind maps can take a variety of forms, but the two most popular are hierarchical lists and spider diagrams. A hierarchical list is an aggregate of many items into a structure that ranks each in some order—for example, low to high, urgent to less important, and so on. Spider diagrams resemble a spider web. At the center is the issue being explored and lines are draw from it to link to related concepts. As the diagram develops, it creates a visual representation (e.g., figure 3.1). Which is better? In practice, it comes down to personal preference—some researchers think in terms of lists, while others are visual.

Concept maps are very similar to mind maps but differ in this regard: where the subthemes are shown in a mind map, concept maps show connections between various idea nodes using descriptive words. In this sense, concept maps show the relationship between multiple ideas and, hence, are useful for depicting concepts diagrammatically. They can be useful in mapping sources of information as shown in figure 3.1.[8]

Concept maps offer the analyst a way of taking large numbers of related but hitherto unstructured sources of data and collating them so that their relationships become clear. Figure 3.1 shows the beginning of a concept map relating to an intelligence research project on illicit drug importation. The distinguishing descriptive feature—the use of labels for each linking line—helps explain the relationships between the ideas in the nodes. Although only one idea is represented in this figure, many more can be included, as can be related ideas.

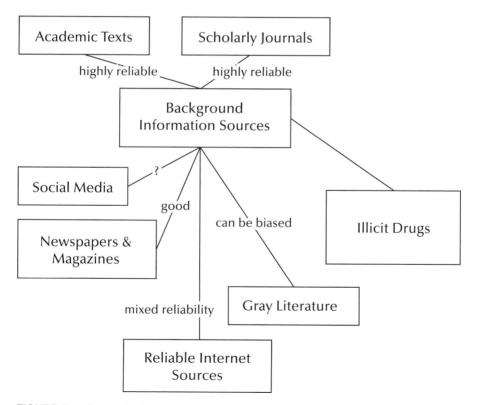

FIGURE 3.1 Data collection plan using a concept map.

If a software package is used, it can make linking quicker and it also makes rearranging ideas easier.

Fishbone Diagram

A fishbone diagram can also be used to coordinate an information collection plan.[9] A fishbone analysis is usually conducted to identify and explore cause-and-effect issues but can be adapted by analysts to help manage the collection process.

The research question or intelligence target is posted at the right-hand side of the diagram (the fish's "head" in figure 3.2). The major bones of the fish are constructed by listing the different agencies or sources of information, and the minor bones subtend from the major bones, listing the data items required. As each piece of data is received, it can be crossed off the diagram with the effect of producing a visual aid as to overall progress. The pictorial information can be converted into a progress report in narrative form or into a statistical summary.

Data Collection Table

A data collection table can also be used to organize an analyst's data requirements (see table 3.1). Across the top of the table, the analyst lists the key issues

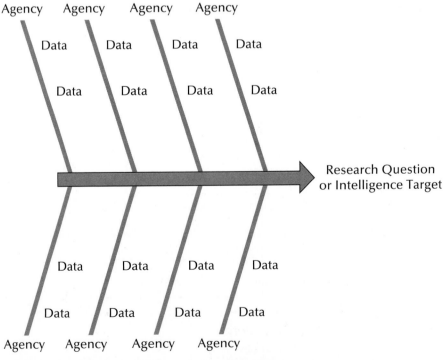

FIGURE 3.2   Data collection plan using a fishbone diagram.

TABLE 3.1 **Data Collection Plan in Table Form**

Type of Data	Source	Risk	Expense	Priority
Statistical	*Aerospace Facts and Figures*	Nil	Cost of purchasing annual volume or online subscription	High
	Handbook of Airline Statistics	Nil	Cost of purchase	Medium
Manufacturers	*World Aviation Directory*	Nil	Cost of purchase	High
	Interavia ABC: World Directory of Aviation and Astronautics	Nil	Cost of purchase	Medium
Associations	*Aerospace Industries Association of America*	Nil	Cost of purchase	Low

for consideration. There are five shown, but other issues could be included in this row depending upon the target and the ramifications associated with the research project. Other issues could include legal constraints, administration, communication, timing, and data security.

Starting with "type of data," the analyst states the type of questions they need answered, placing each category in the row below. The analyst could substitute type of data with specific questions that need to be answered. This is followed by completing each cell by moving from left to right across the rows. Table 3.1 is an example for the aerospace industry compiled by a notional private sector intelligence firm.

Data Collection

Information can be gathered from a variety of sources. The diversity of these sources is exemplified by category in the following lists. Many of the information sources are the same for the five different types of intelligence practitioners—national security, military, law enforcement, business, and private sector intelligence. As such, it is conceivable that a single piece of information could have application to each functional intelligence group (e.g., information relating to a terrorist cell could be of interest to law enforcement intelligence officers that have a responsibility to prevent and deter such attacks on the homeland). Likewise, the same information could be of interest to:

- National security and military intelligence: whether the cell is based overseas or operates internationally;

- Business intelligence: whether the target of the terrorists is their industry or their facilities; or
- Groups employing private sector intelligence, such as the antinuclear lobby: to highlight the vulnerable nature of a nuclear facility in relation to terrorism.

To highlight the various sources of information, as well as the diversity available, consider these lists. But, in doing so, also compare that there are some sources that can be used in the five types of intelligence work that were discussed in chapter 2.

National Security Intelligence

- Open-source information (particularly the Internet);
- Clandestine operatives (official cover);
- Covert operatives (nonofficial cover);
- Recruited agents;
- Diplomatic missions and embassies;
- Surveillance aircraft;
- Surveillance satellites;
- Electronic intercepts;
- Defectors;
- University and independent research bodies; and
- Other government departments.

Military Intelligence

- Open-source information (particularly the Internet);
- Surveillance planes;
- Surveillance satellites;
- Electronic intercepts;
- Reconnaissance teams;
- Field operatives;
- Diplomatic missions and embassies;
- Defectors;
- Prisoners;
- Civilian inhabitants;
- University and independent research bodies; and
- Other government departments.

Law Enforcement Intelligence

- The public;
- Crime investigators (detectives);
- Patrol officers;
- Police records;
- The media;

- Businesses;
- Open-source information (particularly the Internet);
- Government departments and agencies;
- Informants;
- Citizens;
- Covert surveillance (physical and electronic);
- Undercover operatives; and
- Other law enforcement agencies and government departments.

Business Intelligence

- Open-source information (particularly the Internet);
- A business's own internal records;
- Information supplied by other businesses;
- The media, trade, and other open-source publications;
- Sales personnel;
- Customers;
- Distributors;
- Raw material and component suppliers;
- Government departments and agencies;
- A business's research and development section(s);
- University and independent research bodies;
- Market research surveys;
- Reverse engineering; and
- Covert physical surveillance (e.g., a hired private investigator).

Private Sector Intelligence

- An organization's own internal records;
- Open-source information (particularly the Internet);
- Information supplied by other organizations;
- The media, trade, and other open-source publications;
- Staff;
- The public;
- Government departments and agencies;
- An organization's research section;
- University and independent research bodies;
- Surveys; and
- Covert physical surveillance (e.g., a hired private investigator).

Data Evaluation

Evaluating information is an integral step within the analytic process and usually takes place as information is gathered. The data are evaluated according to the reliability of the source and the validity of the actual information. When evaluating information, the analyst asks many questions, including:

- How reliable is the information source?
- Has the source provided information before?
- How accurate is the information?
- How recent is the information?

With some types of intelligence, particularly national security intelligence and military intelligence, deception is a concern. In such cases, analysts need to evaluate data to distinguish between objective information and that tainted by bias.

Secondary sources such as government press offices, commercial news organizations, (nongovernment organization) spokespersons, and other information providers can intentionally or unintentionally add, delete, modify, or otherwise filter the information they make available to the public. These sources may also convey one message in English for U.S. or international consumption and a different non-English message for local or regional consumption. It is important to know the background of open sources and the purpose of the public information to distinguish objective facts from information that lacks merit, contains bias, or is part of an effort to deceive the reader.[10]

The evaluation process firstly assesses the source's reliability and, secondly, the information's accuracy. In theory, this process is performed on each piece of information collected. However, in agencies collecting large volumes of data, this may be an automated process where a generic rating is assigned if the data are merely stored, but if it is retrieved and used in an intelligence research project, the data items are then reevaluated. Each piece of data is assigned an alphanumeric rating indicating the degree of confidence the analyst has in that piece of information. This system is known by various names by the American, British, Canadian, Australian and New Zealand militaries,[11] including "source

TABLE 3.2 Source Reliability Codes

	Admiralty Ratings	
Code	Descriptors	Estimated Truth Based on Past Reporting (%)
A	Completely Reliable	100
B	Usually Reliable	80
C	Fairly Reliable	60
D	Not Usually Reliable	40
E	Unreliable	20
F	Cannot be Judged	50
G	Unintentionally Misleading	0
H	Deliberately Deception	0

TABLE 3.3 Information Accuracy Estimates

		Admiralty Ratings
Code	**Descriptors**	**Estimated Probability of Truth (%)**
1	Confirmed	100
2	Probably True	80
3	Possibility True	60
4	Doubtful	40
5	Improbable	20
6	Cannot be Judged	50
7	Misinformation	0
8	Disinformation	0

and reliability matrix,"[12] NATO System, Admiralty Code, but are based on the British World War II so-called *Admiralty Grading System*. A system grounded on this approach, but enhanced by the author, is shown in tables 3.2 and 3.3.[13] It is important to point out that in table 3.3 there is a difference between *misinformation* (which is unintentional) and *disinformation* (which is outright deception, that is, intentional).[14]

As an example, imagine a field operative obtains a piece of information from an agent in place, but this agent is a new source that has never been exploited before. The reliability for this piece of information would therefore have to be F—the reliability cannot be judged. If the information obtained came from a database that has been the source of previous information (i.e., from another agent) and has proven to be truthful in almost every instance, then an accuracy code of 2 would be assigned. The combined code would be printed on the document to show its overall rating. Customarily, accuracy rating precedes the reliability code—for instance, F-2. Having said that, it needs to be pointed out that the ratings must be logical; assigning a rating of, say, E-2 (unreliable source but probably true) or H-3 (deliberately deceptive but possibly true) would raise questions in the consumer's mind about whether the evaluation process was rational.

Regarding the accuracy code 6 of table 3.3—misinformation—the analyst should be cognizant that they may obtain data that are *unintentionally* incorrect, illogical, or contradicted by other sources. In these cases, a code of 7 is appropriate. As for disinformation (code 8), these are data that are shown by other sources to be *deliberately* false or misleading (i.e., provided for the purposes of deception, perhaps as part of an opposition's counterintelligence operation).

Although the admiralty ratings represent an objective position, they are derived through a subjective process because judgment plays the key role. When assigning a rating, the analyst must consider such things as the accuracy of previous information provided by the source and the source's field capabilities (i.e., does the source have access and the ability to obtain what has been delivered?). Evaluation is a difficult process but an important one, as personal or agency bias can adversely affect the results of an intelligence research project. A good evaluation is the result of the source's reliability being evaluated independently of the credibility of the information. Information discovered to be irrelevant to the issue under investigation should be disposed of according to the analyst's agency document destruction policy (e.g., shredding).[15]

Data Collation

Collation takes place after the data have been evaluated, whereby the analyst brings together the disparate pieces of information so that the data can be subject to some form of analysis. The collation process also acts to remove irrelevant, incorrect, or worthless information, which may be collected due to error, misdirection, or compulsiveness. Such data should be destroyed immediately after being identified; otherwise, it will not only cause congestion in the intelligence database but also may place the analyst and the agency in legal jeopardy if a judicial officer tasked with overseeing the agency's operations deems holding such data to be contrary to law.

The remaining data are then stored to be retrieved easily by the analyst. If the data are in an unstructured form, this can be done by:

- Registering the information (i.e., officially acknowledging receipt of the data);
- Indexing;
- Cross-referencing; and
- Key wording.

These data can then be filed so that an electronic database can be interrogated by the analyst using one or more analytic methods. Typically, unstructured data are stored on the agency's enterprise server that is accessed by the analyst's computer workstation, which in turn is likely to be networked with other workstations and servers within the agency.

Data Analysis

Information is analyzed to draw conclusions about an activity, a person(s), a group(s), or an organization(s) at the center of inquiry to provide insight for the decision maker (i.e., *information* is analyzed to produce *intelligence*). The analytical process can be described in several steps that comprise:

- Examining the collected data;
- Sorting facts from opinions (i.e., evaluation of the information);
- Developing inferences (by means of statistical or logical deductions);
- Discussing the strengths and limitations of the various inferences (e.g., based on probabilities); and
- Drawing conclusions from these results and making recommendations in accordance with the decision maker's intelligence requirements.

Despite the complexity of data analysis, the process of analyzing data is generally straightforward. Intelligence research projects mostly perform analyses following a three-step process:

1. Preparing the data by "cleaning" errors and anomalies that may have crept in during the collection phase;
2. Organizing the data so it can be described statistically if quantitative and in other ways if qualitative; and
3. Testing the research hypothesis (or model) using either statistical tests or specialized analytic techniques (depending on the type of data).

The first step—preparing the data—starts with some form of logging that allows the analyst to check what has been collected against the information collection plan. Once assured all data items are present, the analyst checks the data for accuracy, which involves entering the data into a software program. Depending on the type of data being processed, it may mean "double entering" the data to ensure there are no mistakes in data entry or checking that the data item is within a specified range or in a certain format. Software programs designed for data analysis will usually have "error trapping" sub-routes that highlight such errors or allow the analyst to set parameters depending upon the data being manipulated.

The purpose of using a software package is to provide some form of organization to the data so that descriptive analysis can be performed. Most analytic software has this function and will produce a range of descriptive statistics forming the basis for testing the research hypothesis. Descriptive statistics are not only part of both quantitative research and qualitative projects, but also important as they describe what is going on. Such descriptions include graphical representations (e.g., pie diagrams, bar charts, or line graphs) coupled with a narrative discussing the various quanta.

Inference Development and Drawing Conclusions

The final phase of the intelligence research process is testing the research hypothesis. This can be done using statistics or another technique if the data are qualitative. The overall purpose is to draw conclusions allowing the analyst to extrapolate meaning from the data to some level beyond the immediate. Based on the sample data, an analyst may form some inference that could be applied to the general population from which the sample was derived. Alternatively, an analyst may use inferential statistics to form a judgment about the probability that the observations regarding two groups are the result of some variable acting on one of the groups, and the difference would not have occurred if chance was the only factor.

An *inference* is a statement (or proposition or judgment) drawn from data that have been subject to some form of analysis. In this way, the statement follows logically (either deductively or inductively) from the data. Inferences may be based on as little as one or two premises, or they can feature many premises in a cascading fashion depending on the data and the original research question. A simple example of an inference based on a deductive process consisting of two premises is:

- People are criminals because they have been found guilty of breaking the law.
- Jack Knife has been found guilty of breaking the law.
- Therefore, Jack Knife is a criminal.

You will note, in the deductive reasoning process, the analyst moves from specific data items to a general position. In inductive reasoning, the opposite takes place—the analyst starts with a generalized position and moves to the specific, as seen in this example:

- Country Q is like Country X.
- Country Q provides a haven for terrorists.
- Therefore, Country X provides a haven for terrorists.

In the first example, both premises are true; therefore, the inference is valid. Although the premises in the inductive reasoning example are not false, there are many other particulars (i.e., variables) that need to be considered before the analyst can draw the inference that has been presented about Country X's providing a safe haven for terrorists.

The striking feature of the two approaches is that inferences developed by using deductive reasoning do not suffer the same degree of uncertainty as those developed by inductive reasoning. Nevertheless, inductive data analysis is useful in certain situations, such as exploratory qualitative case studies.

· ·

A general (logical) truth of a matter cannot be established by examining only one, or a few, of the variables, as there are potentially a very large number (some might argue, infinite) of variables that need to be weighed in an inductive argument.

· ·

Contrast this with a deductive argument where the premises and their conclusion are so integrally related that, if the premises are true, then the conclusion must also be true. For inductive reasoning to be valid, it requires all the initial premises to be true; as this is not possible, an inductive argument can only establish a degree of likelihood or probability.

Deductive reasoning produces either a valid argument or an invalid argument. Inductive reasoning can only produce a cogent, or sound (i.e., probable), argument.

Interpreting information is a cognitive process based on general knowledge, life experience, common sense, and data collected in relation to the issues under investigation. This process involves identifying new issues and postulating the significance of these issues, which might include being viewed from the perspective of the target.[16] The "so what?" questions can be answered in the interpretative process: what does this information mean in relation to the issue under study? The answers provide a useful starting point to formulate future courses of action and make recommendations.

It is equally important to discover evidence of disagreement in the data as it is to find evidence that supports the research hypothesis. Differences add density to the conclusions drawn. Therefore, analysts should look for outliers and rival explanations in the data.

Report Dissemination

Dissemination is the term commonly used for the last phase of the intelligence process where the report or briefing (termed the *product*) is delivered to the decision maker. Because intelligence reports vary in size from one-page briefings (e.g., tactical or operational reports) to book-length studies (e.g., strategic assessments), it is hard to categorically state who the end user will be within an agency or even at what level of political leadership it may ultimately end up (recall also that some intelligence reports are only disseminated to other analysts).

In the case of business intelligence, an intelligence report may be received by a board of directors (i.e., nonexecutive level), or it might be considered by the corporate executives who make day-to-day decisions about the business. Then, again, it may only be read by a division-level manager who simply needs the insights to plan production schedules.

In the case of national security intelligence, strategic reports, unless in the form of a national estimate (essentially a synopsis of a much larger document), will not be read by a decision maker. Likely, strategic reports will only be read in their entirety by one of the decision maker's staff or advisers. These personnel will extract what they consider the key findings (and these may not be the key findings of the study) and brief the decision maker themselves. A strategic intelligence study may even be destined for a subject specialist, who may be a fellow intelligence analyst within another agency.

Key Words and Phrases

The key words and phrases associated with this chapter are listed below. Demonstrate your understanding of each by writing either a short definition or a one- or two-sentence explanation.

admiralty rating
concept maps
deductive logic
disinformation
inductive logic

inferences
information accuracy
intelligence collection plan
intelligence collection requirements
misinformation

Study Questions

1. Identify two reasons for conducting a literature review and explain their importance to the overall intelligence research process.

2. What are some of the benefits of data collation? List two issues and describe the positive impact of each.

3. Why formulate an information collection plan? Discuss what could go wrong if a plan is not incorporated into an intelligence research project.

4. Explain the purpose of using a software package for collating data.

Learning Activity

Review the difference between inductive and deductive reasoning. Construct two simple inductive arguments and two simple deductive arguments. Provide a short explanation as to why each is so.

Notes

1 Walter Laqueur, "Spying and Democracy: The Future of Intelligence," *Current* 2, no. 86 (March/April 1986): 25–34.
2 Charles Vandepeer, *Asking Good Questions: A Practical Guide* (Golden Grove Village, South Australia: Freshwater Publishing and Training, 2017), 67.
3 Charles Vandepeer, *Asking Good Questions*, 78.
4 John Donne, "Meditation XVII," in John Donne, *Devotions upon Emergent Occasions*, ed. Anthony Raspa (Oxford: Oxford University Press, 1987), 87.
5 Edwin H. Sutherland, *White Collar Crime: The Uncut Version* (New Haven, CT: Yale University Press, 1983).
6 In qualitative studies, the research question is sometimes referenced to as a "statement of guiding purpose."
7 Richards J. Heuer, Jr., and Randolph H. Pherson, *Structured Analytic Techniques for Intelligence Analysis* (Washington, DC: CQ Press, 2011), 21–24.
8 Joseph D. Novak, *Learning, Creating, and Using Knowledge: Concept Maps as Facilitative Tools in Schools and Corporations*, second edition (New York: Routledge, 2010).
9 A fishbone diagram is also known as the "Ishikawa" diagram by the Japanese academic Kaoru Ishikawa to promote quality management process. Although this type of chart is generally used for cause-and-effect analysis in industry and commerce, it can, nevertheless, be adapted for other purposes, including, as shown here, information collection plans for intelligence analysts.
10 U.S. Department of the Army, *FMI 2-22.9: Open Source Intelligence* (Washington, DC: Department of the Army, 2006), 2–10.
11 Chiefs of Staff, *Understanding and Intelligence Support to Joint Operations (JDP 2-00), 3rd edition* (London: Ministry of Defence, 2011), 3–21.
12 U.S. Department of the Army, *Human Intelligence Collection Operations, Field Manual 2-22.3 (FM 34-52)* (Washington, DC: U.S. Army, 2006), B1–B2.
13 To explain the difference, we need to revisit the history of the scale. It was developed for tactical military purposes during World War II. Its purpose is to assign some level of certainly to information that would be the basis for combat operations (i.e., immediately or within a short time). In this context, the Admiralty grading system is fine. However, once an analyst starts to consider issues beyond operational matters, such as warning intelligence and strategic intelligence issues, then this scale presents inadequacies. This is because the scale is unable to consider unintentional misleading (misinformation) and intentionally deceptive information (disinformation) that are hallmarks of an opposition's counterintelligence operations. The "enhanced" scale presented here incorporates these two additional classes of information sources.
14 Robert M. Clark and William L. Mitchell, *Deception: Counterdeception and Counterintelligence* (Los Angeles: Sage, 2019), 9.
15 International Association of Chiefs of Police, *Law Enforcement Policy on the Use of Criminal Intelligence: A Manual for Police Executives* (Gaithersburg, MD: IACP, 1985); Jack Morris, *The Criminal Intelligence File: A Handbook to Guide the Storage and Use of Confidential Law Enforcement Materials* (Loomis, CA: Palmer Press, 1992); and Prunckun, *Counterintelligence Theory and Practice*.
16 Anonymous (Michael F. Scheuer), *Through Our Enemies' Eyes: Osama bin Laden, Radical Islam, and the Future of America* (Washington, DC: Brassey's, 2002).

Chapter 4

Clandestine and Covert Sources of Information

Clandestine or Covert?

The source of information can be viewed as a spectrum, ranging from open and semi-open sources to clandestine and covert. While open-source information will be discussed in chapter 5, this chapter discusses sources at the other end of the information spectrum that are available to the intelligence analyst—those considered to be surreptitious in some way. Because of the intrinsically safe nature of open-source information, the same high level of consideration and planning is required to obtain these data when compared to organizing data collection by clandestine and covert means.

Clandestine data collection, although akin to covert collection, is different in that clandestine collection operates in the open—visible to the target but disguised so that it does not appear to be what it seems. *Covert* operations are carried out in secret. They are hidden; not visible to the target even in a disguised form. They are, to some degree, intrusive, but because they are invisible, the target has no knowledge that the collection operation is being conducted.

These two approaches are discussed here. Included in this discussion are the essential methods that comprise: (1) undercover operatives; (2) informants/agents; (3) physical surveillance; (4) electronic surveillance; (5) informants; (6) mail covers; and (7) waste collection. Analysts may want to consider these methods in their collection plans because an attempt to obtain information via open methods might be fruitless—for instance, secretive methods being used by the target to conceal information. In such cases, the only way to obtain the data is to penetrate the security measures via one of these surreptitious approaches.

Undercover Operatives

Undercover operatives can get close to individuals or inside organizations to make firsthand observations. The use of operatives is risky for the operatives themselves as well as for the organization by which they are employed. These risks are both physical and psychological. The decision to use an undercover operative, hence, comes with ethical considerations for its authorization.

. . . .

The objective of the undercover [operative] is to infiltrate "as deep as possible and [gather information] on the opposition or enemy."[1]

. . . .

The operative risks physical harm in the form of bodily injury and death as well as a range of psychological injuries spanning from mild anxiety to psychiatric disorders. The physical risks are more apparent, as one can easily visualize the ramifications of having to penetrate an illegal enterprise. The psychological injuries arise from the stresses associated with working in isolation, working in a dangerous environment, and, perhaps, engaging in an activity that is illegal (including consuming illicit drugs and alcohol in binge quantities) and, to the operative, personally immoral.

Nevertheless, the data that can be obtained from an undercover operative can be very valuable because it is an opportunity to get a glimpse of the target's intentions, thereby providing an insight into the target's thinking, rationale, and behaviors that could not be obtained by other means. However, given the risks and the monetary costs of "running" a field operative, it is a method that is not often used in the first instance. It is usually reserved as a means of last resort or for targets that pose an imminent danger to community or national security.

Because the operative will be in direct contact with the target, several issues must be kept in mind. The most important thing is that the operative's identity must be guarded with utmost secrecy. If knowledge of the operative leaks to the target, not only will the operative's cover be "blown," but also the operative is likely to suffer injury or death.

Part of the operative's brief is to obtain evidence of wrongdoing in a law enforcement context, or classified intelligence in the case of national security. Evidence may be in the form of admissions, but intelligence data may be in the form of indicators of intent. To capture these data, the operative can either commit the details to memory and then record them later for transmission back to the analyst's agency or use some electronic device that transmits the data live for recording and transcription. The latter is the most reliable and the best solution, as it doesn't rely on the operative's ability to remember the details, which, from an intelligence point of view, can be critical. Data can be qualitative (e.g., discussions with the target) and quantitative (e.g., numbers of items, times, routes, colors, preferences, and so on).

Informants and Agents

Using informants, or agents, to gather information places a safe distance between the agency's operations and the target. An informant is someone who has indicated willingness to assist the agency in achieving its goals and is like an agent who acts on the agency's behalf (a proxy)—whether that is to arrest a drug trafficker, close a trademark infringement ring, or sell state secrets to the agency or its government. Informants and agents do these things for a variety of reasons. As T.J. Waters discussed in his memoir *Class 11: Inside the CIA's First Post-9/11 Spy Class*:

> Values + beliefs = behavior. This is what you need to keep in mind. Know your target's motivations in the context of their values and beliefs. Values govern behavior as motivation for our actions. Beliefs are how we express our values to ourselves and others. . . . We must understand the agent's history, the background fundamentals of how they became who they are to understand their motivations.[2]

TEXTBOX 4.1 | **Case Study**

The processes for handling informants or agents vary from agency to agency and from informant to informant, or agent to agent, but, in general, the process of employing these people starts with some form of "registration." This serves several purposes, the main being accountability of funds (or other gratuities) that will be paid to them for service.

Corruption is a temptation when running informants because the system relies on the honesty of the agent handlers to pass over the full amount of funds without "skimming" any for themselves. Also, there is the temptation to run fictitious agents to collect payment; this ruse was made legendary by Graham Greene in his book *Our Man in Havana*, whose main character, Jim Wormold, ran an entire spy network that did not exist but regularly passed on intelligence reports, which were, of course, fictitious.[1]

Although the *Our Man in Havana* situation may sound like the plot from the pages of a spy thriller, it has a basis in real espionage operations; these ethical issues have been confirmed by an ex-case officer: "Most seasoned operations officers[2] have had that unsettling experience of going to a 'cold meeting,' only to find out the 'agent' did not know he had been recruited, or simply did not exist."[3] It is also reaffirmed by a former legislative counsel to the director of central intelligence and deputy chief of operations for Europe who stated, "A CIA spy runner in Western Europe in the 1980s apparently duped his colleagues for five years with lengthy fictitious reports from imaginary European agents on local attitudes toward NATO and skepticism about U.S. commitment to come to the defense of its European allies in the event of a Soviet attack."[4]

As such, informants are photographed, fingerprinted, and their vital statistics recorded on an official register. This register is maintained by the agency, and the data it contains are classified so only those that have a need-to-know can access it. This helps to protect the agent's identity and, therefore, safety.

[1] Graham Greene, *Our Man in Havana* (London: Heinemann, 1958).
[2] *Operations officer* is the current term used for the traditional title of *case officer*.
[3] Mahle, *Denial and Deception*, 231.
[4] Hitz, *The Great Game*, 124.

The data that informants can provide will vary greatly—from accurate and reliable down to inaccurate and unreliable (see discussion of the Admiralty scale in chapter 3). If the agents are not trained in observation skills or memory-retention techniques, the data they will provide may be sketchy. If, however, they are trained—as in the case of a foreign intelligence operative who has "swapped sides"—the data may be very sound. But having said that, experience shows that trying to establish the veracity and value of an agent's reports is difficult. It may also be difficult to establish their bona fides.[3]

To overcome training shortcomings, a listening device may be employed (such as a body transmitter), but this option may be reserved for when the informant is only used once or twice because the risk of discovery and personal harm is great—with each use, the chance of detection increases. Also, there must be an agency listening post nearby to receive the transmitter's signals and record the audio. Having a van or other vehicle containing the listening post equipment parked near the target's location may raise unduly suspicion.

If an apartment is rented close by to set up a more permanent listening post, this will incur added financial costs and open another possible source of leaks—for instance, the realtor or landlord may "talk" if the agency has rented the property openly without using a cover. If the agency has rented the premises under a cover, the foot traffic in and out of the building may expose the operation. As with undercover operatives, the use of an informant or agent to gather data must be weighed against the risks: exposure of the operation; harm to the informant; the likelihood of obtaining the information sought; and the likelihood of obtaining that information accurately.

Regarding the last point, it will always be the case that the analyst needs to try to verify the accuracy and reliability of the agent's data. There may be many ways of doing this, but one example is to compare the data against similar information provided by the same source. Whatever way it is done, it should be borne in mind that there is some degree of uncertainty inherent in running informants. Their motivation can be greed, revenge, or exchange for some favor (e.g., reduced jail sentence), anything *but* the pursuit of truth.

Physical Surveillance

Physical surveillance is the act of making observations of people, vehicles, or the activities occurring at specific locations. Many research methodologies use observation as the key means of collecting data. This can take the form of a researcher standing on a street corner and counting pedestrians as they pass by or enter a building, or it could be a data collector who records the number of vehicles that pass an intersection or travel along a suburban street. Surveillance used in intelligence operations is usually covert and takes the form of either moving surveillance or fixed surveillance.

· ·

Operatives "assigned to a surveillance operation should possess a reasonable amount of resourcefulness and adaptability so that [they] can effectively blend with the environment, both in appearance and conduct."[4]

· ·

Physical surveillance may take place either at a fixed location, which is known as a *stakeout*, or in a continually moving situation, referred to as a *tail*. Physical surveillance is often used to supplement information which has been obtained from open sources. It can also be used early in an operation to accelerate the generation of leads, corroborate existing information, or obtain details that would not be available through other avenues of inquiry.

Fixed surveillance is a tedious and time-consuming activity, but its value should never be underestimated. Its strength lies with the field operative, who is tasked with a single mission—to obtain details about the target. The results can be pivotal to any intelligence research project. Unlike social research where a data collector stands in the open with a clipboard and makes observations, the covert surveillance officer, termed an *operative*, may sit for hours in the darkened interior of a van or in the back seat of a car, electronically recording the comings and goings of the target and associates.

Moving surveillance is when the operative follows the target. The objectives of the moving surveillance are the same as a fixed surveillance but, in addition, the target is tailed wherever they go. The most common form of moving surveillance is via car, as this is the usual mode of transportation people use. Surveillance on public transport—aircraft, ferry, bus, train, and tram—is also possible, but the level of risk of detection increases, as following a target in such proximity makes the operative's task more difficult.

A benefit of covert surveillance is to validate the information coming from undercover operatives and informants/agents. For instance, a surveillance operative should be able to independently verify that, say, an informant did meet with the target on the day and time provided by an informant. Although it is unlikely that the operative will be able to verify what was said between the parties, validating the meeting may go a long way in establishing an informant's creditability, especially if the pattern is repeated. However, there may be other ways of validating the details of a meeting if a surveillance operative is able to videotape the meeting.

For instance, the length of the meeting may be able to suggest whether the details the informant has purported during the conversation are accurate—a two-minute conversation on a street corner outside a coffee shop is not consistent with details of a long planning meeting over a lengthy meal at a restaurant. Surveillance would be able to shed light on this. Likewise, the body language of the two as they talk may indicate how well the meeting went—was there aggravation, frustration, disbelief, threats, or did it conclude with mutual admiration, gratitude, and a relaxed atmosphere? Such independent observations could prove valuable in supplementing or validating other covertly obtained data. The important point is that surveillance is actual observation, not self-reported information; the latter can be subject to any number of biases.

Vehicles in the Open

A target's motor vehicle is another source of potentially valuable information. Walk down a street in the business district of any city or town, or among cars parked in a parking lot, and view the interior of the cars as you pass. Chances are that you will see many personal and, perhaps, confidential items left in plain view. Back seats, front seats, and dashboards can be littered with objects and papers that could provide rich information or act as leads in finding other sources of information. Permits affixed to windows have numerous facts that are potentially of interest, as do bumper stickers with political messages.

This is a form of physical surveillance not often thought about or incorporated into an information collection plan—perhaps because it is so obvious that analysts overlook it as a source of data. Unless the target practices counterintelligence, there are usually a few pieces of information that could be helpful to an intelligence research project. If the vehicle is devoid of objects or papers, this could mean that the target is fastidiously tidy (which might be valuable in itself) or that he is practicing sound operational security. Having said that, if the target is suspected of being one who is cunning (e.g., a foreign intelligence service's operative or a terrorist), and investigators obtain information from a vehicle "in the open," then be aware that it could have been planted as a means of deception (see deliberately deceptive information in chapter 3 in the section "Data Evaluation").

Optically Aided Surveillance

Because operatives rely on their eyesight in conducting physical surveillance, various devices are used to assist them in extending their vision. Using technology also assists operatives in positioning themselves much further away from the target than could normally be achieved with unaided sight, thus reducing the possibility of discovery.

The principal and traditional device used in physical surveillance is a pair of binoculars.[5] Binoculars are an optical device consisting of two prism-operated telescopes fixed in parallel. This configuration enables an operative (sometimes termed the *surveillant*) to view a magnified image of the subject using both eyes. Binoculars have been designed to provide both magnifying power and light-gathering capabilities. The latter is essential for surveillance work at dusk and at night. Binoculars that have a built-in digital camera are also available commercially.

Viewing a subject at distances that exceed the effective range of binoculars is accomplished by using a telescope. The magnifying power of the telescope ranges from twenty to several hundred times that of normal vision. Binoculars, in comparison, have magnifying power ranging from about six to twenty times that of normal vision.

A periscope is a viewing device, usually present in submarines, but at sometimes used in land-based information gathering. Small, portable, high-quality devices are used to peer into high, inaccessible windows, over walls, and around corners. Periscopes are also used in applications such as surveillance vans (e.g., mounted on the roof). With the availability of so-called "action cameras," a form of periscope can be constructed by placing the camera on the end of a pole (which can be telescopic for concealment in transport). The camera can then be lifted over the obstructing wall, fence, and so forth, or lifted to view through a window that would be too high to see into otherwise and the target area recorded for analysis.

Continued developments in optical technology have now made low-light (night) viewers available at affordable prices. These units are designated as either "active" or "passive" night vision devices. The first group, the active devices, comprises devices that operate by using an infrared light beam. The surveillant projects the invisible beam of energy so that it illuminates the subject. The image is then viewed with special equipment, which converts the infrared radiation into the visible light spectrum. The second range of devices operates by amplifying the existing background light—moon, stars, streetlights, and so on—by several thousand times, thus literally turning night into day through the sights of the surveillant's night scope.

Covert Photography

In the context of intelligence work, covert photography refers to what is generally termed *surveillance photography*.[6] In conducting covert photography, by far the most commonly used camera is a digital single lens reflex (SLR) (which replaced the 35-millimeter-film-based camera). However, in some unique situations, such as surreptitious copying of documents, a subminiature camera may be used. The value of subminiature cameras lies in their concealable size or concealable form (e.g., mobile/cell phones with built-in cameras). Nevertheless, the advantage of digital SLRs is their fast (light-sensitive) lenses. The ability to download images, edit them using commercial software, and send them over the Internet (including live streaming) applies to all digital photography.

As with binoculars and telescopes in physical observation, telephoto lenses play an important role in covert photography. A reflective mirror lens (catadioptric) not only enables a surveillant to greatly reduce the physical size of his equipment, making concealment easier, it acts to extend the operational distances. Basically, catadioptric lenses use a system of mirrors to compress the light's optical path. Magnification (measured in the focal length of the lens) varies from about 100 to 2,000 millimeters.

Digital video cameras are also popular for surveillance work. These cameras are no larger than SLRs—and, in a growing number of models, smaller—so they are often used with a telephoto lens, thus allowing surveillants to record their observations from safe distances. As digital technologies continue to develop, it is likely we will see cameras with higher-definition resolutions, and they will be more affordable. The application of these devices for covert surveillance will also increase the span of applications.

Mobile/cellular telephones have video recording capabilities as part of their functioning and therefore make ideal covert cameras (though there is a degrading of image quality when compared to a dedicated video camera). Eyeglass-style digital recording devices are being developed that can take photographs and video, as well as access the Internet. Information and images taken by these devices can be uploaded to and downloaded from the Internet via the wearer's voice commands.

In the case of a fixed position surveillance (a stakeout), a time-lapse option can be used to provide extended coverage from a single digital memory device. To achieve this, time-lapse photography operates in a frame-by-frame mode that greatly reduces the demand for electronic memory storage (twenty-five frames per second is considered real-time recording). Many state-of-the-art video cameras can be built into such items as briefcases, books, wall clocks, smoke alarms, writing pens, paintings, and plants.

A growing number of devices marketed as "action cameras" that can be attached to parts of vehicles—for example, windows—as well as personal equipment such as helmets, utility belts, and so on. Take, for example, the case where a surveillance operative needs to watch a fixed location for long periods of time, he or she would normally be required to sit in their vehicle and use various screening devices, like window shades, so they remain hidden inside. But they also need to be able to immediately take photographs of people or events. However, with an action camera mounted on, say, the dashboard of a car, the vehicle could be parked overlooking the target area and the camera angled to record the desired field of view (see figure 4.1). Many hours, or perhaps days, worth of digital images could be obtained while the car is parked unoccupied. Once the digital images are retrieved, they can be fast-forwarded to the event(s) of interest. Variations of this technique are possible, such as live streaming the images, thus reducing suspicion and hence the chance the operative is discovered, exposing the operation.

FIGURE 4.1 Traditional covert photography. Here an operative is observing the target from a car. Her stakeout could be replaced by an "action camera" mounted on the dashboard of an unattended vehicle. *Source*: Photograph by the author and provided by courtesy of CC Thomas Publisher, Ltd.

Aerial Photography

Aerial photography from both rotary- and fixed-wing aircraft is another effective method of information gathering. The history of aerial surveillance dates to the mid-nineteenth century when the first photograph was taken from a French military (hot air) balloon.

Since that time, many developments have occurred in photoreconnaissance. The technology currently available ranges from reconnaissance satellites and ultra-sophisticated spy planes down to the light plane-for-hire with conventional handheld photographic equipment. The former, of course, are used by intelligence agencies of various nations, while the latter would probably be used on a rental basis by smaller agencies on an ad hoc basis.

At one time, remote-control model aircraft were the province of model enthusiasts. However, many commercially available remote-controlled aircraft of varying sizes are equipped with digital cameras for carrying out surveillance work. There are both rotary-wing and fixed-wing versions, and both varieties function in the same way as military unmanned aerial vehicles (UAVs), or, as they are commonly referred to, *drones*. These drones can carry multiple cameras, individually controlled so that several ground targets can be tracked simultaneously. Software, then, can be used so that each camera maintains focus on a target of interest, or it can be programmed to have a camera, or cameras, scan for targets that meet a preset set of conditions. Once these visual data are obtained, other software can be used to generate, for instance, social network charts of the people observed.

Internet-based mapping facilities give analysts an easy and cost-effective option for obtaining aerial photographs. Websites provide satellite images of the earth and cover almost all locations on the globe. Intelligence analysts can select several different types of views: satellite imagery, maps, and terrain, or combinations. Street-level views are also available. Although these sources would not be practical for an analyst who is monitoring an arms control agreement (for the most part, these are static images refreshed only occasionally), they may be all that is needed to brief a local police or private investigation surveillance team as to, say, reconnoiter the terrain surrounding the target's place of business. Some of these are of very high quality, so much so that the news media reported that Norway's National Security Authority blocked the U.S. company Apple Inc. from flying over Oslo—the nation's capital—to take three-dimensional photographs for use in its mapping application. It was reported that the intelligence agency feared these high-quality maps could be used to undermine national security.[7]

Electronic Surveillance

As a general principle, where the opposition has established a high degree of operational security (i.e., defensive counterintelligence measures), the

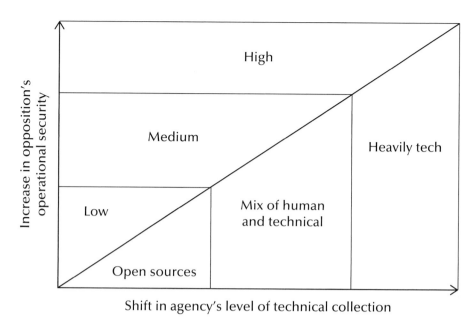

FIGURE 4.2 Relationship between operational security and technical data collection methods.

penetration of human operatives and agents will be prevented. This may also be a result of other factors, such as cultural, ethnic, religious, language, or other natural barriers. In these situations, data collection methods often shift to more technical means. This shift should not be at the total expense of attempting to have human sources in place who can provide reports based on direct observations. The relationship between operational security and a shift in technical collection methods is shown in figure 4.2.

Electronic surveillance is most likely to feature prominently in any shift to technical collection. This may be in the form of audio surveillance (i.e., room listening devices or *bugs*), telephonic intercepts, or Internet-based intercepts. There are other forms of electronic surveillance, such as radio frequency intercepts (i.e., the interception of radio transmissions), but the most commonly used intercepts are from these three methods.

Audio Surveillance

The fundamental principle of any audio surveillance operation is to be able to plant a quality microphone as near as possible to the target and, in doing so, avoid background noise that may render the intercept unintelligible. The types of microphones used in audio surveillance are required by the nature of the work to be very small and are referred to in the trade as *subminiature*. Their minute size allows them to be secretly deployed in the target's environment. Once in place, they can be connected to a high-gain amplifier, then to headphones (for live monitoring), a digital recorder (for listening later), or a transmitter to relay the audio to a listening post. Transmitters range in sophistication from simple FM baby monitors to elaborate frequency-hopping Bluetooth or Wi-Fi devices connected to the Internet that can be monitored by a computer housed a continent away.

If a transmitter is not used to send the intercepted audio, then wires are needed; the wires leading from the microphone to the listening/amplifying equipment must be concealed to prevent detection. In some cases, existing wires such as telephone, electrical, or even, paradoxically, burglar alarm wires can be used instead of running new wires, thus making detection more difficult.

There are also special metal paints on the market which an operative can use to "paint" wires across a room. Once touched up with paint of the surrounding decor, these "wires" are reported to be very difficult to detect (especially if used in an industrial or warehouse setting).

. . . .

Radio transmitters offer an operative a much greater degree of safety from detection because installation requires far less effort than a hard-wired device.

. . . .

There are several types of microphones the surveillant can use, depending on the situation. They are the tube, contact/spike, pneumatic, and directional microphones. Tube microphones are designed to be inserted into a targeted room via a very small drill hole. This species of microphone consists of an element connected to a thin tube. The tube emerges flush with the wall in the targeted room and can only be detected by very close inspection. Tube microphones are likely to be in spots made classic in spy novels—behind a wall, a picture, a piece of furniture, anything that would hinder detection for as long as possible.

Contact and spike microphones, in contrast, require less effort to secure their installation. These microphones do not respond to air vibration as a conventional microphone does but rather translate vibration into sound. Contact microphones are like the "pickups" used by musicians to amplify their instruments, and spike microphones resemble the vintage phonograph needle. These types of microphones are attached to the exterior of a wall, window, floor, or ceiling. Once in place, these devices will reproduce quite clearly the sounds produced within the targeted room. These microphones lend themselves well to permanent installation.

The pneumatic cavity microphone is the electronic version of the drinking glass placed against the wall trick, historically recognized as an effective method for monitoring adjacent room conversations. The pneumatic microphone is substantially superior and operates by using a specially constructed shell which is highly responsive to surface vibrations at audio frequencies found in the range of human speech. This "cavity" is used in conjunction with a conventional microphone element to enhance the device's performance. It also forces audio output to correspond to a wall's surface (or window, floor, or ceiling, depending on the case) vibrations rather than a direct sound output.

Directional microphones are of two types: parabolic and shotgun. Parabolic microphones consist of a "dish" with an inwardly pointing microphone element. The targeted audio is reflected and focused into the microphone element, thus gaining a directional effect. The shotgun microphone (also known as a *rifle* or *machine gun* mic) operates on the same principle but utilizes a long tube, or set of tubes, in a cluster to pinpoint the targeted conversation. The effective range of these microphones is reported to be about 150 meters, and they are known to be able to pick up audio through closed windows at closer distances.

Another area of audio surveillance, discussed briefly above, is that of wireless microphones, also known as miniature radio transmitters. These devices rank further up the hierarchy in surveillance sophistication. These devices do not have any wires or connections to reveal their location. They can be attached to furniture or fixtures by means of a magnet or adhesive surface or concealed in everyday objects such as rings, pens, cigarette lighters, books, ashtrays, or pictures. Transmitters do not require the eavesdropper, or his equipment, to be located nearby. Their range of transmission varies from sixty meters to almost a kilometer. It is directly dependent upon transmitter strength, the thickness of surrounding walls, the sensitivity and selectivity of the receiver, as well as its antenna system.

Body transmitters are generally larger, more powerful, and better constructed than wireless microphones. This is because the chance of detection is slight, and the device is intended to be used repeatedly. These devices are designed to operate from an operative's coat pocket, underclothing, or attached by tape directly to the operative's body.

Akin to the body transmitter is the briefcase transmitter. Not only can this device be used by a "walk-in spy," but it can be conveniently "forgotten" in the target's room or office to obtain ensuing conversations.

Another type of electronic surveillance transmitter operates by broadcasting in the very low frequency range (VLF is between 3 kHz and 30 kHz). This device uses electrical power lines for signal transmission. The signals move along the wire path and, because of the device's very low frequency, very little energy is radiated into space. This method of communication is used by many of the wireless intercoms sold commercially.

Communication equipment that operates outside of the standard FM radio broadcast frequencies tend to be more secure from interception (that is, outside of the 88 MHz to 108 MHz frequency range). This is because the radio receivers needed for this type of radio reception are not sold in regular retail outlets. Nevertheless, they are available commercially at radio and electronics stores and are a common feature in the radio rooms of radio amateurs (i.e., "ham radio" operators).

There is also a cadre of radio enthusiasts in the general community known as "listeners" who make it a hobby to scan the radio spectrum listening for any unusual content or sources (e.g., a shortwave listener). These hobbyists have high-gain antennas and wideband receivers that scan many hundreds of individual radio frequencies each second (commonly termed *scanners*) and, as such, could detect the conversation collected by a bug.

If there is a chance of interception by a casual listener, the radio technician who will oversee the bug installation should consider the use of a scrambler or other form of encryption. Contrast this countermeasure with the failed Watergate political espionage operation of 1972, where the operatives used no operational security to protect their two-way radio conversations.[8]

Some receivers operate in the microwave part of the radio spectrum, such as those used by telephone companies for telecommunications and by private enterprises for computer data transmission (e.g., Bluetooth and Wi-Fi devices). Such receivers are complicated in design and expensive, although military and governmental intelligence agencies would have ready access to these. Units used for intercepting microwave communications can be set up in a van or building anywhere along the path between the transmitter and the receiver, which could be several hundred kilometers long.

Telephone Intercepts

The telephone is a very useful medium for electronic surveillance. Obtaining information using the telephone involves two methods: the first uses devices that intercept conversation directly from landlines or the cellular network and requires no entry into the target's property or access to their mobile device. The second method uses a portion of the telephone system for eavesdropping and usually requires physical access to some part of the telephone system or device.

Wiretapping is the interception of fixed line or cell telephone communications, as well as computer data that are transmitted over landlines. The interception of these signals can take place anywhere between the target's phone location and the telephone exchange. The more difficult parts of the telephone system to install a device are at the target's property—in the case of a fixed landline device—and the lines leading out of that building. Once the targeted line(s) leaves the building and melds with the wider telephone network, interception is less difficult, because with a court-ordered warrant, a surveillant can install unobtrusive equipment with ease.

Internet-Based Intercepts

Apart from some university and government research libraries, the Internet is arguably the wealthiest source of information for analysts. It is a source of not only published material but also the private messages transmitted over the Internet (e.g., e-mail). Businesses, governments, and individuals all create, access, or modify records of numerous descriptions that are located on computer servers connected to the Internet. Because these data exist in digital form on magnetic media, this realm is known as *cyberspace*.

In general, analysts can obtain data without a warrant if the data are placed in the public domain. This is analogous to the physical world where access is not restricted—public libraries, commercially published books and magazines, and newspapers. However, where access could be considered "private" by a court, then some form of legal order or subpoena is likely to be needed. By and large, the laws pertaining to telephonic intercepts apply to intercepting data in cyberspace; in many jurisdictions, laws have been enacted to cover such intercepts. Analysts must always work within the law when formulating information collection plans. When in doubt, obtain a legal opinion about the legality of what is being proposed, especially if it is a new, novel, or previously untested method of data collection. History is littered with examples of people who have succumbed to acting outside the law or outside what the publicly would accept as ethical.

Mail Covers

Postal

A very useful data collection method is the *postal mail cover*. This investigative technique has been used by law enforcement agencies for many decades. It collects information by recording what is printed on the outer covering of an envelope or package via some form of photographic technique—photocopying, digital scanning, or digital photography. For the analyst, it is important to note that a mail cover operation does not involve reading or recording the contents of the postal item (e.g., letter or card); only the data on the outside are recorded. Nonetheless, this simple and effective method of data collection can reap a wealth of information—return address, postmark-related information (date and place of posting), and any description of the contents (e.g., "do not bend—photos enclosed," card). Because the mail is not opened, no search is being conducted, only a form of physical surveillance. The targets will never know that their mail is being monitored, so there is usually no administrative disclosure requirement by the agency that it is conducting surveillance. Postal mail covers are usually bound by the laws or regulations of a nation's postal service, and these governance arrangements dictate how and when this technique can be used as well as how long the collection operation can proceed.

E-mail

In 2013 the American signals intelligence intercept program known as PRISM was exposed. It was alleged that e-mail and other forms of "live communications," such as photographs, video chat, and related formats, were being intercepted by intelligence services since 2007. The arguments relating to the legality of this aside, this type of covert information-gathering operation is a good case in point about the value of the information contained in the metadata of such messages. It is understood that these intercepts were not "reading" the content of the messages but were reading the data contained in the electronic "envelope" that routed the message, as would be done in a postal mail cover.

These metadata are very useful if combined with other data sources (see chapter 5 on open-source information—big data and data mining). With as little as one, two, or three pieces of additional information, these metadata can produce very focused leads or provide insights regarding the target or their activity. The strength of this type of operation is that the interception can be automated so that millions of intercepts can be handled daily. Moreover, these metadata can then be easily queried in a data warehouse environment when they are combined with other pieces of information.

FIGURE 4.3   Unsecured dumpsters like this make for potentially rich sources of information. *Source*: Photograph by author.

Waste Recovery

This is a long-standing law enforcement and private investigator technique that is popularly referred to as *dumpster diving*.[9] Despite the initial aversion to the thought of rummaging around in someone's waste material, this is a potentially rich and valuable source of information (see figure 4.3). Confidential material of all types can be found in waste—manuals, notes, letters, memos, reports, files, photographs, passwords, identity cards, receipts, schedules, itineraries, telephone numbers, and much more (including computer hard disk drives, USB flash drives, and a variety of data that have been backed up onto CDs/DVDs). The reason for this is that most people believe that once a piece of paper (or an old computer drive) is placed in a waste bin, it has "disappeared." They believe that no one would bother "getting dirty" searching through someone else's garbage.

Recovery can take place at any point between where the waste leaves the target's premises to, and including, the landfill/recycling site. If the recovery is to take place on the target's premises, be conscious that there may be legal issues associated with the operation, as a court could find that the material recovered was still in the possession of the target, and hence, a warrant of some kind was required.[10]

Information obtained via waste recovery was at one time considered high-value/low-cost because it yielded more benefit than what it cost to gather it. However, with its popularization in the press and cinema, waste recovery has become more difficult. Government agencies, businesses, and individuals regularly use document shredders and are more conscious of how and what they dispose. Security surrounding waste has improved with commercial-scale confidential document destruction becoming a service that is widely available.

Key Words and Phrases

The key words and phrases associated with this chapter are listed below. Demonstrate your understanding of each by writing either a short definition or a one- or two-sentence explanation.

aerial photography
audio surveillance
clandestine sources
covert photography
dumpster diving
electronic surveillance
fixed surveillance
informants (or agents)
moving surveillance
physical surveillance
postal mail cover

waste recovery
wiretaps

Study Questions

1. Explain the difference between obtaining information by covert methods as opposed to clandestine methods.

2. Explain two different types of covert data collection methods available to the analyst.

3. What are the advantages of covert data, and how could an analyst use these in practice? Give examples.

Learning Activity

Select a public building in your jurisdiction. Use an Internet-based aerial photography facility to create an electronic slide briefing for a notional surveillance team. Provide in your briefing details on access to and from the building, the surrounding terrain, and potential infiltration and exfiltration points. Note any limitations the maps may have as a way of better understanding what can be done with these types of sources.

Notes

[1] J. Kirk Barefoot, *Undercover Investigation* (Springfield, IL: Charles C Thomas, 1975), 4.

[2] Waters, *Class 11*, 118–19.

[3] Richard Helms, *A Look Over My Shoulder: A Life in the Central Intelligence Agency* (New York: Random House, 2003), 33.

[4] Raymond Siljander, *Fundamentals of Physical Surveillance: A Guide for Uniformed and Plainclothes Personnel* (Springfield, IL: Charles C Thomas, 1977), 5.

[5] Monoculars are also popular, as they are smaller and hence more concealable (less than half the physical size of binoculars). They tend to be less obvious when held to the eye because they require only one hand and, in doing so, only one eye is covered, thus making the act of viewing less noticeable to people around the surveillant.

[6] Raymond Siljander, *Clandestine Photography: Basic to Advanced Daytime and Nighttime Manual Surveillance Photography Techniques* (Springfield, IL: Charles C Thomas, 2012), xi.

[7] "Norway Blocks Apple Aerial Photos," *Sky News*, accessed August 18, 2013, http://www.skynews .com.au/tech/article.aspx?id=896524.

[8] Although there is no evidence that their transmissions were intercepted, these operatives took a great risk in making this assumption. G. Gordon Liddy, *Will: The Autobiography of G. Gordon Liddy* (London: Severn House, 1980), 244. For the break-in of Dr. Daniel Ellsberg's psychiatrist's office in California in September 1971, prior to the Watergate black bag operation (Daniel Ellsberg, *Secrets: A Memoir of Vietnam and the Pentagon Papers* [New York: Viking, 2002]), the operatives used four handheld transceivers sold by the Radio Shack electronics retailer—5-watt, 6-channel TRC-100B that operated on the 27 MHz Citizen Band Service (CB). The frequency the operatives used was shared with a local taxi company (Liddy, *Will*, 165).

[9] The term *dumpster* is a genericized name for the trademark Dumpster. In England it is referred to as *skipping*, as these mobile garbage bins are known there as "skips"; John Hoffman, *The Art and Science of Dumpster Diving* (Boulder, CO: Paladin Press, 1993); and John Hoffman, *Dumpster Diving: The Advanced Course: How to Turn Other People's Trash into Money, Publicity, and Power* (Boulder, CO: Paladin Press, 2002).

[10] Rick Sarre and Tim Prenzler, *The Law of Private Security in Australia*, second edition (Pyrmont, Australia: Thomson Lawbook, 2009).

Chapter 5

Open Sources of Information

Unobtrusive Data Collection

Our discussion on open-source information will include an examination of social media and so-called "big data." But to make our way into that discussion, let's first look at unobtrusive data collection and, in particular, indirect information gathering.

Unobtrusive methods attempt to extract data without gaining the target's attention. Unobtrusive methods are conducted without the target knowing about an operation to collect information about him or her.

For intelligence analysts, there are several advantages in using unobtrusive methods in their research. Chief among these is what the analyst observes has taken place—as opposed to self-reporting by, say, agents. These methods are, by nature, intrinsically safe, as they do not place researchers or operations officers (i.e., case officers), agents, or other field operatives (e.g., surveillance teams) in contact with the target or in an environment that could be hostile or dangerous.[1] They are, therefore, discreet and nondisruptive techniques.

Because these methods do not rely on direct contact, they increase the reliability of the study because the research can be replicated, thus allowing checks of the study's reliability and validity to be confirmed. Access does not present a problem because permission is not required, and in the case of a hostile target where permission could not be secured, the analyst does not have to resort to court-approved or executive government–approved covert techniques.

Unobtrusive methods are cost efficient, as undercover operatives do not have to be tasked, nor do surveillance teams or investigators/interrogators have to collect data. Because of its relative economy, unobtrusive methods lend themselves to being used for longitudinal studies where the analyst needs to follow the activities of a target over time.

This, by no means, should underestimate the value of covert and clandestine data collection and data obtained from secret sources, but it highlights the relevance open-source information and unobtrusive analytic techniques have in collection plans. In the years since the September 11, 2001, terrorist attacks, the intelligence services have pointed out many times the problems and limitations that the lack of agents on the ground caused for intelligence.[2]

Although unobtrusive methods are discussed here in positive terms (which they are), covert and clandestine sources of information should never be wholly replaced by unobtrusive methods.

Unobtrusive methods, used astutely, can be a positive boon to information collected by covert and clandestine means. But one method should not replace the other.[3]

Unobtrusive data collection can be used as the analyst's main source of data or used to supplement other forms of data to triangulate results. These indirect methods lend themselves to collection by automated and electronic means. The best way to understand indirect methods is by way of example. For instance, if a study wanted to measure the current interest in neo-Nazi issues in a particular region (e.g., if there was some indication of a resurgence in hate crimes), an intelligence operation could set up a website to gather statistical information about those who log on, with the assumption being that those visiting such a website are either ideological supporters of this form of dogma or participants—potential or otherwise—in the ideology's edicts.

Data, such as the country where the Internet visitor originated, could be tracked along with the day, time, and web pages accessed. How long they stay on the website could be measured and whether they were returning viewers or once-only readers. Depending on the construction of the website, many other types of data could be collected, including provision for interactive input by the website visitor. If the analyst in charge of the operation desired, this data collection method could also be used as part of a sting operation where e-mail addresses are obtained via an opt-in facility or a blog.[4]

TEXTBOX 5.1 | **Case Study**

The study of radio station listening preferences is an example relating to business intelligence that has been cited in the literature from time to time. In this study, the researchers are reported to have conducted an unobtrusive survey of radio stations that were favored by car drivers in a geographic area. The researchers attended automotive repair shops, and, while customers' cars were being serviced, they noted the current radio station displayed on the radio (whether it was in the AM or FM broadcast band and what frequency).

The advantage of this method is that it does not rely on the respondent having to tell the truth. A respondent who admits he or she listens to a radio station that plays music not in popular fashion, or broadcasts certain political messages, or is owned by a religious organization, may feel embarrassed about his or her behavior. Prevention of embarrassment may lead respondents to lying, thereby distorting the data. Some of the limitations are that it only captures those respondents who can afford to have their cars serviced at a garage, thus excluding those who service their cars themselves (out of choice or necessity). It also assumes that the current radio station is the one most often or exclusively listened to.

Nevertheless, if a company wanted to market its goods or services to a demographic consisting of electric car owners, then attending garages that repair and service these types of vehicles would be a quick and inexpensive way of collecting data about which radio station the business should spend its advertising budget with. It could also be used to verify claims by radio stations about what segment of the market they reach.

One consideration that needs to be kept in mind when using this technique is that, because data are being collected without the target's consent, there may be ethical and legal issues to consider. For instance, with the radio station data collection case study, one would need to consider whether checking the car's radio without the owner's permission would violate any state or federal statutes regarding privacy.

There are other sources of indirect information, including monitoring radio and television broadcasts for speeches made by political leaders and field operatives attending public speaking forums. In the case of the latter, intelligence analysts need to brief and debrief operatives regarding the specific information required (as per the information collection plan), as well as any additional information gleaned by observation.

Often, unobtrusive methods will be appropriate because the data sought are readily available. *Reliability* is an estimate of the *consistency* a collection instrument will yield each time employed or the consistency between two or more sets of data that have been collected.

But just as with other data collection methods, analysts will want to assure themselves of the reliability of the collection method. In this regard, indirect data collection techniques can act as a check for the reliability of another data collection method that may be in use (e.g., a direct method) or for estimating the reliability of itself via a test-retest approach. This is done by collecting data at two different points in time and computing the correlation between the two sets of data. If an analyst considers that there is no change in the underlying condition between the two tests, then the data's reliability can be estimated.

Open-Source Data

Open-source data is information available to the public.[5] It requires no special authority or needs no special request to be made to obtain these data.[6] These sources are in direct contrast to covert and clandestine methods, which are, arguably, the methods most commonly associated with intelligence work. In the parlance of social science research, open-source information is categorized as secondary data, and covert and clandestine information are likened to primary data.

Primary data is information collected by the intelligence researcher for their specific project. For instance, an analyst may identify in his or her information collection plan photographs of a bridge over the Orrenabad River. In this case an operative may be sent to the physical site, and, using a cover story, they would obtain the photographs.

In contrast, secondary data is information collected for another purpose (and by others) but usable to answer the intelligence question under investigation. Again, using the Orrenabad River example, secondary data may include commercially available photographs of the bridge from satellites; or photographs of the bridge taken by recent travelers who have posted these on their social media websites; or photographs that related to tourist promotional material (on the Web or in hard copy in libraries); or any number of other publicly available sources.

Although one might assume that because intelligence research is conducted in secret, the sources of information an analyst uses are also secret, as Professor Harry Howe Ransom wrote in his influential work on intelligence: "95 per cent of peacetime intelligence [comes] from open sources."[7] Professor Ransom's own analysis of the U.S. national intelligence collection effort stated that in excess of 80 percent came from "overt, above-board methods [that] would normally be available to anyone with a well-organized information gathering system."[8]

The late Richard Helms, former director of central intelligence, stated that between the end of World War II, when the Office of Strategic Services was deactivated, and 1947, when the CIA was created, the agency responsible for secret intelligence was the Strategic Services Unit (SSU). In conducting its intelligence research on the Union of the Soviet Socialist Republics, the SSU used the Library of Congress as its main source of data.[9] All the Library of Congress's data in relation to the USSR were publicly available.

With regard to business intelligence, it has been estimated that "90 percent of all information that you and your business need to make key decisions and to understand your market and competitors is already public or can be systematically developed from public data."[10] As an illustrative point from history, take this Cold War example. Polish intelligence officer Colonel Pawel Monat, who was a military attaché in Washington, DC, saved his communist government large sums of money, time, and effort by accessing open-source information about commercial aviation "secrets." Regarding one experience in particular—that is, with *Aviation Week* magazine—he wrote: "Very little of this information was of really classified nature. We could have dug up most of it ourselves from other sources. But it would have taken us months of work and required us to shell out thousands of dollars to various agents to ferret out the facts, one by one. The magazine handed it all to us on a silver platter [for fifty cents]."[11]

More recently, Tom Clancy was queried about his infallible knowledge of some of the obscure technical and scientific details contained in his espionage novels. He is reported to have denied having access to classified defense information, but instead pointed out what others have discovered—it could all be found in the open-source literature.[12]

- -

It is estimated that one weekday edition of today's *New York Times* contains more information than the average person in seventeenth-century England was likely to come across in an entire lifetime.[13]

- -

The importance of systematically collecting and analyzing open-source information did not become a priority for the intelligence community until after these attacks. For instance, the effective mining of Internet-based information has enabled the intelligence community to better understand how jihadists use the Internet's Web-television capabilities, chat rooms, and news sites to train their members and raise money.[14]

Social Media

Because we live in an age where information is central to every aspect of life, an astonishing variety of obligations have been placed on individuals to record information about their affairs. The same applies to corporate bodies and governments. It is because of these record systems that society generates what has become known as a *paper trail*.

A paper trail can be described as all records and documents created by an individual or entity during commercial and social interaction with other individuals, organizations, government departments, and businesses (both public and private). These records and documents have the effect of leaving a trail detailing where the individual (or entity) has been, with whom they have had dealings, what goods and services they have purchased, what they own, what their likes and dislikes are, and more importantly, what their intentions may be.

To the analyst, this trail forms a composite picture for any target that comes under surveillance. Uncovering one part of the paper trail can lead the analyst to other sources of information. These sources are not only limited to those on paper but also can be extended to interviews with friends, neighbors, and colleagues of the target, perhaps using a pretext as well as physical, optical, or electronic surveillance.

To the analyst, the paper trail is a valuable set of leads. The value of this information in a collated and analyzed form can be seen in the arrests reported in the media from time to time of influential organized crime members that were, until that point, untouchable by law enforcement agencies.

But a paper trail does not need to be on paper. With social media, what used to be recorded on paper now appears in electronic form. Any form of electronic media where people record social interaction and are accessible to others satisfies this definition. Information about a person's ideology; interests; movements; past, present, and future activities; education; employment; and so on form a long list of the types of data these media record. But unlike the paper trails of the past, these electronic paper trails also hold audio files, video files, and photographs.

Application for Intelligence

The use of social media for intelligence has great application. As people's lives, and the lives of many organizations, are captured every day and in many ways using social media, these data can be incorporated in information collection plans. These data can be collected, collated, stored, analyzed, and shared between intelligence analysts and agencies. Data harvested via online search engines can be done without the knowledge of the person to whom the data relate.

Social networking websites can be used to conduct background investigations on people. Take, for instance, the situation where an operations officer plans to pitch to a potential agent at a public event (e.g., the opening of an artist's recent paintings). An analyst could therefore compile a background file on the potential agent using social media, including social networking, to provide the operations officer with information so they can strike up a conversation with the potential agent.[15]

It would be fair to say that there are few people who do not resent the thought of being surveilled by their government. The thought of a Big Brother society where the state conducts surveillance on everyone conjures up notions of shadowy, sinister, secretive, and repressive regimes. But people around the world now collude with this type of surveillance by willingly posting personal information to social media outlets.

In some regards today's world may have astonished and disturbed George Orwell,[16] but social surveillance is accepted without concern by most of the population, and as such can be and is exploited by intelligence practitioners. Take, as an example, the notorious Jordanian terrorist Humam Khalil Abu Mulal al-Balawi, who began his activities in chat rooms on social media websites. It wasn't long before the world's intelligence agencies began monitoring him through these media and compiling a dossier on him and his activities.[17]

Research suggests that there is a type of person known as a "street stroller." This type of person is said to enjoy being noticed in public, so they openly display themselves—like actors on a stage. If this concept is translated to the world of social media, it could be said that these street strollers have become "cyber strollers." And as such, it would pay dividends for analysts to include these sources of information as part of any information collection plan.

Limitations and Unintended Consequences

As rich as this source is for information, social media has limitations. One example that demonstrates this is the use of *sock puppets*. A sock puppet is a false identity that is created as a deception so that the creator can manipulate the ideas posted on social media websites.[18] This is different from the use of a pseudonym because a sock puppet purports to be another person—a real person, but no such person exists. The person is computer generated with algorithms crafted by the third party. These algorithms are usually based on narrative and statistical probability, as well as other methodologies. Software exists that allows the simultaneous control of numerous false identities.

If used by an intelligence agency, "online operations officers" (like case officers in field operations) can control these "fake agents" for the purposes of, say, penetrating extremist social media forums and sowing information that would lead to an intelligence project's objectives being realized. Such objectives could be wide ranging—from simple disruptive activities aimed at a targeted online community to influencing future actions of these people in the same vein as would an agent provocateur. This is done by what has been described as personality-based social-Web robots (or *bots*). These robots use keywords that define the persona of the fake agent to automate the posting of computer-generated blogs on all the various types of social media that exist.

The implication for analysts who are collecting information from social media is to be mindful that colleagues in their agencies, or allied organizations, could be running sock puppet agents online and they should not mistake this information for genuine information posted by the target group. Likewise, analysts need to be conscious that opposition agents may be doing the same and that such websites may contain misinformation and/or disinformation (see chapter 3 about the issues involved in data evaluation). Further, social activists may be using these techniques, as well as those developed by marketers, to exploit the fundamental flaws in online journalism to manipulate public opinion.[19]

As social media websites are accessible not only to individuals and groups of the target population who may reside outside of the geographic bounds of the analyst's country, citizens of his or her country may also be accessing or participating in these online discussions. As such, another unintended consequence is that the manipulation of this online information may affect public opinion. This issue has consequences in liberal democracies, and it should not be overlooked or discounted. History shows us the ramifications of government officials who have not heeded this lesson. There may also be legal implications in terms of the perennial issue raised by defense counsel—in jurisprudence, it is known as *entrapment*.

A variation of automated creation of fake social media content is the employment of what has come to be called *crowdsourcing*. This is where very large numbers of people, usually in developing economies, are employed to create fake accounts on social media websites and post biased information that supports the "employer's" aims. This could be to add praise to the goals associated with the employer or degrade the opposition, or both. This technique can be used by commercial firms selling goods or services, or security agencies of various nations. In any case, this can be done under the auspices of a "false flag" cover or by way of a company or organization that is set up to isolate the employer, thereby affording deniability. For example, along with personality-based social-Web robots, this technique could be very effective in influencing political change in countries that are the target of intelligence operations.

The Web and the Deep Web

The World Wide Web, or Web for short, has been in existence since 1991. Its purpose is to provide access to information via data stored on servers around the world. Estimates as to the size of the Web vary[20] because information is being added, removed, and changed daily, but, as an indicative number, in 2010 it was estimated that the *surface Web* contained about six hundred billion pages of information (i.e., 600,000,000,000).[21] Other indications suggest that although material is removed from the Web, exponentially more is being added. To access this information, people use browser software and conduct their search via a standard search engine, which has indexed these data.

However, not all information is indexed by these largely commercial search engines. That is because the criteria and indexing algorithms do not capture all the information that exists on the Web. This untapped part of the Web is termed the *invisible Web*, *hidden Web*, or the *dark Web*. Regardless of the term used, they refer to this enormous uncaptured storehouse of online information.

These data are buried in databases and other research holdings on servers around the world. Although they are technically searchable and hence accessible online, they are usually omitted by standard search engines. Searching the deep Web is done through a tailored search interface.

Like the surface Web, estimates of what is contained in the deep Web vary and are based on extrapolations. Some have claimed that it is 550 times larger than the surface Web[22] and contains tens of thousands of terabytes of data. Regardless of the actual size, suffice to say it is a massive amount of information and, to the intelligence analyst, big data represents a potent source of easily accessible material.

Limitations and Unintended Consequences

The thought of searching for intelligence material on the Web or the deep Web might seem, at first glance, a relatively harmless task with little risk, but there are two levels of concern that analysts should bear in mind.

The first is that a visit to a website relating to any issue of concern for a law enforcement or intelligence agency is likely to be monitored by an opposition agency. In the physical world, think of a "trip wire" that triggers an alert once someone steps past a certain point. In cyberspace security and intelligence agencies can install similar trip wires that log the IP address[23] of people visiting certain sites or searching for or downloading information. (Fake websites may also be set up by intelligence agencies as decoys to track people interested in issues of concern to them.)

The trip wire algorithm used to alert analysts will vary from agency to agency and from issue to issue but suffice it to say that searching for material on jihadism or downloading material issued by jihadist groups are likely to trip an alert somewhere with a law enforcement–type agency. There could be other keywords or phrases—for instance, bombs and explosives, weapons, nuclear material, drugs, money transfers, or certain location names, or certain people's names, and so on. If the research project is classified, then searching for or downloading material is likely to leave a paper trail that leads some interested opposition agency to the analyst's desk. If that agency is not an ally, then it is a problem. Even if the agency is a friend, it may not have a need-to-know or there may be no reason to share this information with them, this may again be a problem.

The second level of concern is related to trip wires placed by the targets of intelligence investigations. Like a security and intelligence agency that logs searches and downloads, the targets themselves can log IP addresses and other access information about those who visit their sites. Therefore, an analyst may inadvertently tip off their target if some counterintelligence strategy is not employed.[24]

Data Mining

The term *data mining* conjures up the notion of an analyst "digging" into a number of data sets to extract "nuggets" of informational gold. In a way, this is what the process and practice of data mining is about. At its core, an analyst uses software applications to interrogate several rational databases to discover correlations or patterns in the data that will eventually lead to insightful conclusions being drawn.

Data mining is not new—it has been around for decades. However, it was expensive to perform, and the data sets used were, generally, smaller than those available at the time this edition went to print. The computing hardware was also expensive and less powerful, as were the software applications used to interrogate the databases.

Hardware and software developments, along with data storage devices, have increased processing speed (e.g., multiple processors), sophistication, and capacity, respectively. Moreover, the cost of purchasing and running data mining systems has dropped considerably from its early days to the point where private researchers and contract analysts can afford these systems. Databases comprising many terabytes of information can be accessed for a fee, so analysts do not have to be involved in the collection aspects of the process (which can be considerable).[25] The large data sets themselves can also consist of structured and unstructured data, which was not always the case. Informally these large databases are called *big data*. The computer architectural is referred to as a *data warehouse*. That is, the design of the computer system and its companion technologies.

. . . .

Simply stated, data mining refers to *extracting or "mining" knowledge from large amounts of data*. The term is actually a misnomer. Remember that the mining of gold from rocks or sand is referred to as *gold* mining rather than rock or sand mining. Thus, data mining should have been more appropriately named "knowledge mining."[26]

. . . .

It would be fair to say that originally data mining was used by the business sector to assist its market research. However, once intelligence agencies comprehended the value of this type of analysis, they embraced it, and several large-scale data mining projects were operating post-9/11. Nevertheless, concerns about citizens' privacy and civil liberties soon became a feature of debate because along with data about potential targets were data about law-abiding people who live respectable lives. There were also security concerns about inadvertent access or deliberate "hacking" of the data mining systems by third parties as well as the potential penetration by opposition intelligence services.

The value of data mining is to take disparate data sets and, with a few well-designed software applications, allow analysts to develop complex queries so they can interrogate these databases to see if certain relationships emerge. These patterns are based on association rules which are grounded in logic and/ or mathematical concepts. In a sense, these queries can be likened to hypotheses that are tested against the data to see if they hold true.

Once relationships start to develop, other software applications can be employed to graphically display the results and allow secondary queries to be run. Like finding nuggets of pure gold in a ton of rocks, data mining allows terabytes of information to be processed to find relationships that would be impossible if performed manually (if they could be performed manually, which is not likely).

What does data mining hold for intelligence analysis? Arguably two key strategies are used by intelligence analysts, and these are pattern mining and subject-based mining. With the former, analysts query relationships between variables in the data sets to discover patterns. Because the databases are relational, many more variables can be created by defining them in terms of the existing data items (known as *derived data*). For instance, a new variable may be created by defining it as a data item where attributes A and D were present, but only if these attributes occurred in time before attribute M. By defining new variables this way, data items from many different relational databases can be queried to produce these new variables. These new variables can then be queried in regard to other existing variables or other new derived data items.

About subject-based mining, the analyst starts with subject-specific information items and then mines the data warehouse at his or her disposal to create a profile or dossier of related information to the initiating data. *Profile* and *dossier* are used here to denote a collection of information that may be either narrow or wide ranging, relating to many aspects of the target's life.

Being unchained from having to conduct individual queries on stand-alone small data sets that are characterized by predefined search options is a very powerful method for analysts. When this methodology is coupled with multiple relational databases containing terabytes of information that can be interrogated by sophisticated software using computers with several multicore processors (and distributed across several such servers), data mining becomes the material that Hollywood movies are made of.

By way of example, if a government analyst was looking for a terrorist cell, he or she might, in theory, query several government databases by using existing data items (variables) along with derived data items. These might also be combined with business-related data that are accessible for a fee from the commercial sector. For instance, when considering just these common databases, one can appreciate the power this methodology wields when trying to track down a target, and one can appreciate why civil libertarians recoil with fear about the method's potential misuse:

- address records;
- aircraft registrations;
- airline manifests;
- birth records;
- boat registrations;
- civil court records;
- company and business registrations;
- credit card purchase data;
- credit histories;
- divorce records;
- driver's license information;
- freight records;
- genealogical/family history databases;
- geospatial data;
- hotel/motel reservations data;
- land ownership records;
- marriage records;
- money movement/bank transfer records;
- motor vehicle registrations;
- newspaper archives;
- occupational licensing records;
- police criminal records;
- shipping records;
- Social Security records; and
- social Web, including blogs.

Analytic Software

If an information collection plan includes large data sets that are characteristic of data mining operations, then manual procedures become unrealistic. Analytic software must be used to be able to filter, sort, and collate the raw data, and then to present the findings of various queries. There are several commercially available products on the market. However, it is important that analysts understand research methodologies as well as the nature of the data they are using, along with its limitations. Without this understanding the analyst is not an analyst, but merely a trained collator. There is nothing wrong with having staff trained in the operation of such software programs, but without an understanding of the underlying theory and practice of intelligence research, the risk of errors increases. For instance, incorrect or overextended conclusions could be drawn from the results of queries; "outliers" mistaken for part of a pattern of results; queries could be run against incompatible data sets; or type I or type II errors could be overlooked or not recognized. In short, a wide range of incorrect results could be produced based on a poor or partial understanding of the scientific method of inquiry as it applies to intelligence research.

Analytic software packages are very sophisticated, delivering helpful visual products for briefings and reports. Hollywood movies and television shows have seized on the sophistication of such products and made-for-cinema variants show up in crime and espionage thrillers regularly.

The developers of these software programs license individual workstations as well as server-based applications that run over a variety of networks. Training in how to use these applications is usually provided by the software supplier, though there are many textbooks written by third-party authors about how to use these programs.

. . . .

"We have facts," they say. But facts are not everything—at least half the business lies in how you interpret them![27]

. . . .

Although these products are usually "easy" to use, there are many functions and features, so to become proficient in all aspects of the software a short training course is required. Some operators of these software programs, therefore, confuse this software training with intelligence training—it is not the same. Without demeaning the importance of the role these trained collators perform in intelligence agencies or their skills, this training could be said to be analogous to the training undergone by a butcher when compared to the education undertaken by a surgeon. Given the weight resting on the judgments formed by analysts, it is a compelling argument that an analyst requires at least a bachelor's-level degree, but preferably a master's or doctoral level qualification. On-the-job training is important to operate these software applications efficiently, but this training is not enough to qualify one to become an analyst. *Training* should never be confused with *education*.

Limitations

If open-source information is information available to the public and requires no special operational agents or teams of operatives to collect it, if its collection is not dependent upon a court-ordered warrant or other form of legal authority, if it does not require large operational budgets to support the logistical infrastructure that covert methods require, then one could conclude it is approaching a flawless source of information.

But this is not the case. Open-source data collection has limitations just as covert and clandestine methods do. Although a category of every possible limitation is not possible here, suffice it to say that intelligence analysts who use open-source information need to be mindful of the same issues that are present in obtaining information from other sources. It is worth noting that, because of the nature of open-source data, analysts should be particularly concerned with deception and bias. This is because unlike methods that collect information through some form of secret observation, secondary sources of data are susceptible to intentional as well as unintentional changes. "It is very important to know the background of open sources and the purpose of the public information in order to distinguish objective, factual information from information that lacks merit, contains bias, or is an effort to deceive the reader."[28]

Key Words and Phrases

The key words and phrases associated with this chapter are listed below. Demonstrate your understanding of each by writing either a short definition or a one- or two-sentence explanation.

big data	open-source information
data mining	paper trail
data warehouse	sock puppets
deep Web	surface web
derived data	unobtrusive methods
legend	

Study Questions

1. Explain why intelligence analysts should consider the use of open-source information in their collection plans.

2. Discuss how the use of open-source information might reduce the risk of collecting information using an undercover agent.

3. List at least twelve open sources of information that might be of value to an analyst that are contained in a library.

4. Explain why unobtrusive data collection methods are considered intrinsically safe.

5. Describe what a *paper trail* is and how this concept is projected into the digital world of the Internet.

6. Discuss why it is difficult to estimate the amount of information contained in the Web—regardless of whether it is the surface Web or the deep Web.

Learning Activities

1. Research the different types of tailored search interfaces that are available free on the Internet to query the deep Web. Using one of these facilities, search the Web for information about one of these issues: (1) arms trafficking; (2) Asian organized crime; (3) jihadist ideology; (4) radicalization; or (5) cyber weapons. Then conduct this same search using the surface Web through one of the standard search engines. Compare the findings of the two searches. What differences were noted? From the point of view of an analyst conducting a research project on the issue you selected, argue whether using one or the other, or a combination of both types of searches, would yield the most benefit.

2. Suppose that Country Q has had a sudden change of its leadership regime. As such, the agents who were in place previously have lost access to all secret sources of data. Consider how you as an analyst might use unobtrusive data collection methods in the short term to provide the intelligence needed to monitor the situation until operations officers (case officers) reestablish their agent network(s).

Notes

[1] By way of example, see Joby Warrick, *The Triple Agent: The al-Qaeda Mole Who Infiltrated the CIA* (New York: Doubleday, 2011).

[2] Baer, *See No Evil*; and Mahle, *Denial and Deception.*

[3] Baer, *See No Evil*; and Mahle, *Denial and Deception.*

[4] See, for example, Henry Prunckun, "It's Your Money They're After: Sting Operations in Consumer Fraud Investigation," *Police Studies* 11, no. 4 (Winter 1988): 190–94; Henry Prunckun, "Sting Operations in Consumer Fraud Investigation," *Journal of California Law Enforcement* 23, no. 1 (1989): 27–32. See also, Steven K. Frazier, *The Sting Book: A Guide to Setting Up and Running a Clandestine Storefront Sting Operation* (Springfield, IL: Charles C Thomas, 1994).

[5] Sometimes referred to as open-source intelligence and abbreviated as OSINT.

[6] Although for some agencies—in particular, the military and national security agencies—there may be restrictions imposed by regulations or directives that prohibit the collection, retention, or dissemination of information regarding U.S. citizens. See, for instance, Army Regulation 381-10, *U.S. Army Intelligence Activities*, and Executive Order 12333, *U.S. Intelligence Activities.*

[7] Harry Howe Ransom, *The Intelligence Establishment* (Cambridge, MA: Harvard University Press, 1971), 19. Professor Ransom was quoting Ellis M. Zacharias, a World War II deputy director of the Office of Naval Intelligence. According to Zacharias, only 4 percent of intelligence came from semi-open sources, and a mere 1 percent from secret agents.

[8] Ransom, *The Intelligence Establishment*, 20.

[9] Helms with William Hood, *A Look Over My Shoulder*, 73.

[10] John J. McGonagle Jr. and Carolyn M. Vella, *Outsmarting the Competition: Practical Approaches to Finding and Using Competitive Information* (Naperville, IL: Sourcebooks, 1990), 4.

11   Pawel Monat with John Dille, *Spy in the U.S.* (London: Frederick Muller Limited, 1962), 120.

12   Hitz, *The Great Game*, 86.

13   David Shenk, *Data Smog: Surviving the Information Glut*, revised and updated (New York: HarperCollins, 1997), 25–26.

14   Richard Best and Alfred Cummings, *Open Source Intelligence Issues for Congress* (Washington, DC: Congressional Research Service, 2007).

15   In the counterintelligence context, access to these types of data via social media is a reason why intelligence officers should avoid or restrict the personal information they post to the Web. However, there is a twist to this if the officer is an undercover operative, as having a social media presence may be needed to establish a cover or legend.

16   George Orwell was the pseudonym for Eric Arthur Blair, who wrote the fictional novel *Nineteen Eighty-Four*. In this book Orwell portrays a fictional totalitarian society where government surveillance is omnipresent. Although he describes the system of surveillance that consisted of agents, informants, and two-way "telescreens," the computer monitor, and social media could, by analogy, be considered a manifestation of the latter. George Orwell, *Nineteen Eighty-Four, A Novel* (New York: Harcourt, Brace, 1949).

17   Warrick, *The Triple Agent*.

18   See, also, accounts about how marketers have exploited the online journalism to successfully manipulate public opinion. Ryan Holiday, *Trust Me I'm Lying: Confessions of a Media Manipulator* (New York: Portfolio/Penguin, 2012).

19   Holiday, *Trust Me I'm Lying*.

20   Antal van den Bosch, Toine Bogers, and Maurice de Kunder, "Estimating Search Engine Index Size Variability: A 9-Year Longitudinal Study," *Scientometrics* 107 (2016): 839–56.

21   Mark Levene, *An Introduction to Search Engines and Web Navigation*, second edition (Hoboken, NJ: John Wiley & Sons, 2010), 10.

22   Levene, *An Introduction to Search Engines and Web Navigation*, 10.

23   IP address is the abbreviation for Internet Protocol. It is the logical address assigned to a device, like a computer, on a network. Every computer on the Internet has an IP address, and that address is unique. Therefore, unless a counterintelligence strategy is used to block, hide, or disguise this IP address, its discovery by others can lead them to the intelligence analyst making the inquiries.

24   For a detailed discussion about defensive as well as offensive counterintelligence strategies, see Hank Prunckun, *Counterintelligence Theory and Practice* (Lanham, MD: Rowman & Littlefield, 2011).

25   These would, of course, be unclassified data warehouses, not those of law enforcement, the military, or national security agencies. Nevertheless, these agencies would, no doubt, find some commercial databases very attractive to the types of issues they are probing and hence may have commercial agreements in place to access business-related data sets as any private contractor may.

26   Jiawei Han and Micheline Kamber, *Data Mining: Concepts and Techniques*, second edition (Burlington, MA: Morgan Kaufmann, 2006), 5.

27   Fyodor Dostoevsky, *Crime and Punishment* (originally published 1866), Part II, Chapter IV.

28   Michael C. Taylor, "Doctrine Corner: Open Source Intelligence Doctrine," *Military Intelligence Professional Bulletin* 31, no. 4 (October–December 2005): 14.

Chapter 6

Qualitative Analytics

Oue issue that is common to statistical analyses is "customer accep-
tance." Due to the abstract nature of the mathematical formulae of
these techniques, decision makers can feel troubled when asked to trust
assessments based on such methods. However, this chapter describes several
analytic methods that can be used to make sense of unstructured data in a range
of intelligence settings that are easy to understand by decision makers and easy
to employ by the analyst.

The reason for discussing a variety of methods is that each method tends
to be problem specific. That is, some methods work better with certain types of
issues and data, while others work better in other circumstances. Some qualitative methods are used for strategic assessments, while others are used for tactical or operational problems.

But just because an analyst has examined data using one of these structured
methods does not mean that the results can be taken as absolute—analytic techniques are ways that allow analysts to form judgments (i.e., defensible conclusions) in a way that is transparent to the reader of their reports. Their analyses
can be repeated to demonstrate the validity and reliability of the methods used
(i.e., in keeping with the tenets of scientific methods of inquiry). The point is
that simply using a stepwise analytic method does not replace the application
of sound critical thinking or the application of professional judgment, but they
aid both.

· ·

There is little doubt that the analysis of qualitative data enjoys no consensus about what technique is used.

· ·

SWOT Analysis

Originally devised for corporate planning in the business community, analysis of strengths, weaknesses, opportunities, and threats (SWOT) is one of the most popular analytic methods used by intelligence analysts.[1] This is for two reasons:

1. It can be used with a variety of unstructured data (qualitative data from either primary or secondary sources); and
2. The focus of the research is not variable dependent—it can be either the target or the agency conducting the operation against the target.

The technique was devised for long-range business planning, but it can be applied to a variety of issues in the intelligence realm that are either tactical or strategic. Or, it can be used to analyze information to build a profile or help understand the current situation. A SWOT begins with the analyst defining the *end state*, as it is called in a strategic setting, or *objective*, if it is tactical.

It should be noted that the term *threat* is not used here in the same sense as *threat* is used in chapter 14 when discussing a *threat analysis*. In a security sense, *threat* is a person's resolve to inflict harm on another. However, in a SWOT analysis, *threat* is used to reflect detrimental factors—*risks*, *harms*, *dangers*, or *hazards*—not *threat agents*. This is because SWOT was originally devised by the business community for industrial and commercial forecasting; therefore, businesses use *threat* in the generic sense. In a security environment, *threat* has a different meaning. So, analysts should bear this distinction in mind when working with SWOT.

Using a brainstorming technique, the analyst populates each of the four quadrants of the SWOT matrix with the data (although a matrix typically displays a SWOT, SWOT analyses can be laid out in any way that is suitable for the analyst). For strategy assessments, it is advantageous to have a broad view of the issue and, hence, employ a multidisciplinary team approach (i.e., an ideas workshop) to consider each of the four factors. A tactical assessment could be done by an analysis based on the data collected in the lead-up to an operation or during an operation.

Once this has been done, it is a matter of assessing the factors one at a time and then cross-checking them for agreement (i.e., ensuring there are no contrary or paradoxical positions stated in different quadrants). Assessing can be done by asking hypothetical questions such as:

- In what way can the strengths be used to an advantage?
- How can the weaknesses be shored up?
- What is the best way to take advantage of each opportunity?
- What needs to be done to mitigate the threats (i.e., risks, dangers, or hazards)?

TABLE 6.1 **Example of a SWOT Analytical Matrix**

Analysis of Strengths, Weaknesses, Opportunities, and Threats

	Supportive	Detrimental
Internal	*Strengths* are the attributes associated with the (issue/ problem/agency/etc. under investigation) that are conducive to achieving the end state.	*Weaknesses* are the attributes associated with the (issue/ problem/agency/etc. under investigation) that are detrimental or may prevent achieving the end state.
External	*Opportunities* are the conditions (legal/criminogenic/social/ economic/political/psycholog ical/etc.) that would assist in achieving the end state.	*Threats* are the conditions (legal/ criminogenic/social/economic /political/ psychological/etc.) that might be detrimental to the way the agency carries out its operations.

In a tactical setting, analysts can use the results of SWOT to examine a target's operating structure, method of operating, capabilities, financial base, and so on. A SWOT analysis technique will be used in developing target profiles in chapter 9 (with an example of a target profile involving a notional international criminal enterprise) and chapter 10 ("Operational Assessments") (see table 6.1).

Ways of using the information contained within a SWOT can be generated based on combinations of the factors as follows:

Strengths/Opportunities: ways that will use strengths so that opportunities can be realized.
Weaknesses/Opportunities: ways to address weaknesses to provide relief so that opportunities can be followed.
Strengths/Threats: ways that use strengths "offensively" to moderate threats.
Weaknesses/Threats: defensive ways that will protect weaknesses against threats.

Pest Analysis

If an analytic method could have a "cousin," PEST could be said to be related to SWOT. PEST is an acronym for political, economic, social, and technological factors (social factors could be couched in slightly broader terms, such as sociocultural, if desired; and technological factors can also include policy-related issues). These factors are usually the independent variables that are acting on the dependent variable. This technique has been used by the business community to assess the impact that these external factors might have on the organization or the market in which it operates. But, like SWOT, PEST can be used to an advantage by the intelligence community to assess a variety of issues under investigation.

Because PEST examines external factors, it is essentially half of a SWOT. But where the two differ is in the focus of the inquiry—PEST examines the environment in which the issue is positioned, whereas SWOT examines a dilemma or the actions of, say, a target. Viewed another way, PEST could be the macro scene, whereas SWOT is the micro perspective. PEST is, therefore, used as the main method for analysts when conducting what are termed *environmental scans*. In this sense, PEST is more likely to be used for strategic analysis where the issues are complex.

PEST analysis can be conducted before a SWOT analysis (e.g., via an ideas workshop) to help identify issues, though it is less likely that a SWOT would be conducted before a PEST, as there may be issues raised in a PEST that would subsequently feed into a SWOT.

There are many variations of PEST. Some analysts add additional factors, thus modifying the acronym to variants such as STEP (PEST arranged differently—stay with PEST as it is universally known); PESTELI (adding environmental, legal, and industrial factors); PESTELOM (same as PESTELI, but the industrial factor is substituted by organizational and media factors);

TABLE 6.2 Simple PEST Analysis Template

Political	Economic	Social	Technological
List issues here	List issues here	List issues here	List issues here
A	A	A	A
B	B	B	B
C	C	C	C
D	D	D	D
E	E	E	E
F	F	F	F
G	G	G	G
H	H	H	H
Etc.	Etc.	Etc.	Etc.

Conclusions
Conclusions can be presented here based on the factors above.
These conclusions can be in point form or in narrative.

TABLE 6.3 Detailed PEST Analysis Template

	Comments and Observations	Impact Estimate (High, Medium, Low, or Unknown)	Timing (0–6 months, 7–12 months, 13–24 months, or 24+ months)	Direction (+ Positive, – Negative, or 0 Neutral)	Rise/Fall (> Increase, < Decrease, = Stable, or 0 Unknown)	Import (Critical, Important, Somewhat, Not Very, Not at All, or Unknown)
Political						
Factor 1	Include comments and observations here for each factor	High	0–6 months	+	>	Not very
Factor 2		High	0–6 months	+	>	Not very
Factor 3		Low	7–12 months	+	=	Somewhat
Economic						
Factor 1	Include comments and observations here for each factor	Medium	7–12 months	+	>	Not at all
Factor 2		Low	24+ months	0	>	Important
Factor 3		High	7–12 months	–	<	Critical
Social						
Factor 1	Include comments and observations here for each factor	Low	7–12 months	–	<	Somewhat
Factor 2		Low	13–24 months	–	>	Important
Factor 3		Medium	0–6 months	+	=	Not very
Technological						
Factor 1	Include comments and observations here for each factor	High	24 months	0	=	Critical
Factor 2		Low	0–6 months	+	>	Important
Factor 3		High	7–12 months	+	>	Important

STEEP (social, technological, economic, ethical, and political); and STEE-PLED (social, technological, economic, ethical, political, legal, environmental, and demographic).

There is a view that these variants are not necessary and make the analysis overly complicated. Some scholars have argued that the four factors under PEST cover all the issues that would arise out of an examination of the other subfactors. That is, the subfactors are contained in the main PEST factors. Nevertheless, any of these factors can be mixed and matched to suit the research project.

Finally, like the SWOT analysis, PEST has a simplicity that lends itself to ease of understanding while powerful enough to convey the results to decision makers. There are many examples, but two useful ones are shown in tables 6.2 and 6.3. One is a simple table and the other contains more detail. Both can be modified to suit most intelligence research projects or used according to the analyst's personal preference by adding, subtracting, or blending details found in them.

Force Field Analysis

Force field analysis is a practical technique for examining the pressures that can be applied for or against a policy position, an operational tactic, or any other issue under investigation. It is a method that allows the analyst to form a judgment based on careful weighing of the pros and cons involved,[2] making it transparent to the reader of the report how the conclusions were reached at. This is the technique that underpins what some scholars have referred to as expert judgment.[3] That is, force field analysis requires the subject area expert to commit to writing their thinking on the issue under study, thus laying bare not only the facts that they are weighing up, but the magnitude of influence they have assigned to each factor and why.

For instance, a force field analysis can be carried out to weigh the possible success of a planned operation, or it can be used to gather *driving forces* to overcome or reduce the impact of *restraining forces*. In effect, the force field technique assumes a quasi-stable equilibrium point between these two sets of interests—driving forces and restraining forces—so that this "balancing" can take place. Thought of in another way, a force field analysis is analogous to an assets-versus-liabilities balance sheet.

To illustrate how this works, consider a case of briefing decision makers about the likely impact of a newly proposed law that is intended to curb motorcycle gang violence. Based on the data obtained via the information collection plan, the analyst constructed a force field table that lists the pros and cons. A diagram that shows the conceptual layout of a table is shown in figure 6.1 and a generic table that follows this idea is displayed in table 6.4.

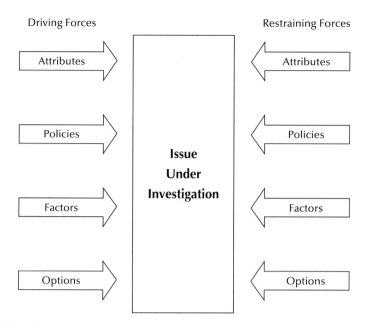

Driving Forces

Restraining Forces

Attributes

Attributes

Policies

Policies

**Issue
Under
Investigation**

Factors

Factors

Options

Options

FIGURE 6.1 Conceptual representation of a Force Field Analysis.

TABLE 6.4 **Generic Force Field Table Showing Pros and Cons**

Why take a stand against international pirates?

Driving Forces	Score	Restraining Forces	Score
Ensure the continuance of the international maritime trade route	+4	Large commitment of warships to interdict and support ships and personnel	−4
Maintain international commerce	+4	Area under pirate control is small compared to navigable sea lanes	−2
Project intolerance for wanton disregard for international law and conventions	+5	Pirates may not be sensitive to such posturing	−3
Ensure safety of crew on-board vessels	+5	Military personnel will be placed in harm's way during interdiction operations	−3

Option total: 18 − 12 = 6, suggesting moderate support for this policy position.

Variations of this table can be made depending on the project and the issue under inquiry.

The analyst sourced her information from a brainstorming workgroup. This approach was particularly helpful, as the time frame of the issue being studied had a horizon of greater than six months. If the time frame was measured in years, then the complexity would have increased and convening a multidisciplinary (and, perhaps, multiagency) group to brainstorm the issues would have been considered instead.

Using this example, then, using a data projector, the analyst displays and addresses the issues raised in the force field diagram, discussing the pros and cons, and, finally, presents the agency's preferred position. The preferred option, whatever it is, must directly address the original research question (i.e., will the proposed new law have an impact on curbing motorcycle gang violence?).

TEXTBOX 6.1 | **Force Field Illustration**

When crafting recommendations, the analyst could also suggest changes to individual factors that, if implemented, could address the issue in favor of the driving forces, for it is the sum effect that the analyst is considering. To illustrate,

- Suppose there was a restraining force like this: new anti-gang legislation could inadvertently contribute to the workload of the court system, which in turn would result in trial delays.
- A recommendation that adds force to the drivers could be crafted: to prevent over listing and trial delays when the new anti-gang legislation is enacted, prosecutors would need to work with the criminal courts' listing coordinators to manage trial lists.

Recommendations formulated in the second item listed above could tip the balance from a position that suggests restraining forces dominate to the one that sees driving forces considered. Viewed another way, force field analysis is a way not only to identify the forces for or against the issue under investigation but also to create a structure that allows the analyst to visualize ways of countering restraining forces. A step-by-step description is as follows:

1. In a few words, describe the issue, plan, proposal, or policy option at the top of the table (see table 6.4). A separate table can be drawn up for each factor, attribute, policy, option, and so on that has been identified. Table 6.4 demonstrates just one such set of factors to illustrate this point.
2. In the left-hand column, list those attributes, options, or factors that can be considered driving forces in relation to the issue under investigation.
3. In the right-hand column, list those factors that are restraining forces.
4. Assign a numeric value to each force factor listed in the two columns. For instance, use an ordinal scale that ranges from, say, weak (+1) to strong (+5) for driving forces and for restraining forces, weak (−1) to strong (−5). In assigning a numeric value to each qualitative factor,

analysts should be conscious that they do not bias the results by assigning values that reflect their own personal views, or the official view of the government of the day, or, perhaps, of one of the key decision makers (e.g., to curry favor). Projecting such bias into the method is unethical because it will artificially manipulate the analysis and use the scientific method simply as a guide for objective research. The safest way to assign the values is to achieve consensus through discussion with, for instance, a few subject specialists that might take the form of a "judgment sample," "convenient sample," or other availability-based sampling technique.[1] If time and resources permit, the nominal group technique can be used to great advantage. Doing so removes any question of bias from the analysts (and the analytic unit that employs them).

5. Tally each column and add the two columns. If the total is a negative number, then the options regarding what the restraining forces are suggesting need to be considered carefully. If the number is positive, then the driving force options need to be considered. There is also the possibility that a zero result could occur or a weak (i.e., +1 or –1) result, suggesting that the direction may, on balance, be the way to proceed. But the analyst needs to apply judgment based on experience in such situations. Remember, this is just a method to guide thinking and reason; it does not reflect an absolute for any given situation.

[1] Gary T. Henry, *Practical Sampling* (Newbury Park, CA: Sage, 1990), 17–20; and Gennaro F. Vito, Julie Kunselman, and Richard Tewksbury, *Introduction to Criminal Justice Research Methods: An Applied Approach*, second edition (Springfield, IL: Charles C Thomas, 2008), 125–28.

Analysis of Competing Hypotheses

Analysis of competing hypotheses is a useful method to think about inductively construed theories in a rational way. It is an important method when the analyst is faced with several plausible propositions to explain the issue under investigation. Rather than being compelled to accept just one theory, analysis of competing hypotheses allows the analyst to evaluate all theories.[4]

Through this technique, the available evidence suggests the most plausible theory rather than having to decide on subjective factors (here, the term *evidence* is a generic term that also applies to arguments and the like). If there are insufficient data to draw a conclusion, the techniques can aid a new (or revised) information collection plan so that further or better data can be fed into the process. Managers of field operatives and other information-collecting assets can use the output of this type of analysis to task their resources more efficiently, saving valuable time.

TEXTBOX 6.2 | Competing Hypotheses Illustration

Here are the steps involved in conducting an analysis of competing hypotheses:

- Draw up a matrix like the one shown in table 6.5, listing the various hypotheses across the top and important pieces of evidence down the left-hand column. Remember that it is not just the appearance of evidence that is always important; in some cases, one might expect not to see a piece of evidence or that key evidence has not shown itself. Each hypothesis and each piece of evidence does not have to be listed in full; a simple abbreviation of H1, H2 and E1, E2 will suffice. The analyst's descriptions in detail can be listed above or below the matrix as a reminder (as has been done in the heroin importation illustration in Textbox 6.3). At this point, the matrix is a quick way of bringing together all the information to form a clear picture.
- Working across the columns, assign a nominal value (+ or –) to indicate if each piece of evidence is consistent with the hypothesis or is inconsistent with the hypothesis.
- Tally the columns and consider whether the column with the most pluses should be advanced as the most likely hypothesis. The caveats placed on the conclusions drawn using force field analysis (see discussion on force field analysis above) apply to this technique also.
- Just because one column may have the most "pluses" does not mean it is the best choice. Some pieces of evidence can and should carry more weight than others. In this regard, the process still requires the analyst to apply some degree of judgment before proceeding to advance this as the course of action.
- If sensitivity is an issue, analysts could consider using another scale, say, the ordinal scale, to attribute weight to each piece of evidence. For example, the use of double pluses (+ +) and double minuses (– –) could be added to the single signs discussed in this section, or a scale like that used in force field analysis could be adapted.

Although the use of the matrix is very useful, it is unlikely that any analyst will include it in the final report or briefing unless the audience is technically oriented (e.g., perhaps, presenting the initial results to a peer group as part of a quality control process or validating the methodology).

To illustrate how this method can be used in practice, take, for example, the study of heroin smuggling into Australia in the early 2000s.[1] At the time it was observed by illicit drug users, police, and drug treatment professionals that heroin at street level was in short supply. There were four hypotheses put forward, and each was plausible. But, which was the actual cause of the shortage?

The study explored four possibilities, and a summary of the analysis appears below.[2] The study's research question is listed along with the various hypotheses and evidence. In table 6.5, the columns H1 through H4 represent the various hypotheses. Evidence for these various propositions is listed in table rows (E1 through E6). At the intersection of each column and row, a sign appears that indicates whether that piece of evidence is consistent with the hypothesis or not.

Although in the study there was narrative discussion regarding each of these points, the table shown here is a convenient way of displaying at a glance the preponderance of evidence for the hypothesis that the shortage was caused by a Taliban-enforced reduction of Afghanistan-grown opium (i.e., H4).

Research Question

What are the likely factors that caused the heroin shortage in Sydney in 2001?

Hypotheses

H1—Recent seizures (at that time) by law enforcement agencies.
H2—The arrest of significant personalities in the supply and distribution chain.
H3—A severe water drought in the poppy-growing regions of Myanmar (Burma).
H4—A Taliban-enforced reduction of Afghanistan-grown opium.

TABLE 6.5 Competing Hypotheses Matrix for Prunckun's Study of Heroin Importation

	H1	H2	H3	H4
E1	+	−	−	−
E2	−	+	−	−
E3	−	−	+	−
E4	−	−	−	+
E5	−	−	−	+
E6	−	−	−	+

Evidence

> E1—Quantitative data about Australian law enforcement seizures.
>
> E2—Elimination of unnamed and unspecified personnel.
>
> E3—Data on crop production and rainfall in Myanmar.
>
> E4—Quantitative data on drug production in Afghanistan.
>
> E5—A 3,000-metric-ton reduction in Afghanistan-grown opium.
>
> E6—Police intelligence of trafficking routes to Europe confirming a diversion of Golden Triangle heroin (destined for Australia) diverted to Europe to fill the Afghan void.

[1] Hank Prunckun, "A Rush to Judgment?: The Origin of the 2001 Australian 'Heroin Drought' and Its Implications for the Future of Drug Law Enforcement," *Global Crime* 7, no. 2 (May 2006): 247–55.
[2] Prunckun, "A Rush to Judgment?" 247–55.

Perception Assessment Analysis

Perception assessment analysis allows the intelligence analyst to demonstrate relationships between actions taken by field operatives and the perceptions of those who will observe or experience those actions.

In psychology and the cognitive sciences, perception is defined as an awareness derived through sensory information. This technique enables operational managers to understand the possible impediments that implementing certain actions might give rise to because of perceptions. A matrix format displays the analytic results so that decision makers can understand how perception may become an impediment to policy implementation.

Taking an example from the military, an assessment might show how others in the operational environment—"enemy, civilian population, multinational, or coalition partners"—could perceive the dealings they have with friendly forces.[5] The matrix is ideal for this, as it lends itself to including other factors, such as criteria for determining "success."

Population size and density, religion, social structure, and ethnic minority groups are important considerations in border security operations. Local customs may vary greatly. Troops must be educated to respect the local customs. Border security operations should minimize disruption of the customs, social activities, and the well-being of the population.[6]

But carrying out this type of analysis requires a more-than-average degree of understanding about the social and cultural issues that dominate the nation, the region, or the locality where troops are operating (as there can be both subtle and noticeable changes from one area to another). Nevertheless, if the analysts do not possess this knowledge, there is no reason why they cannot glean this information from subject experts (e.g., through in-depth interviews or focus groups). This knowledge is then used to assess the likely reactions the observers might have to actions by friendly forces. In a law enforcement context, friendly forces might be translated into a strategy to implement a neighborhood or business watch program, or other community-based crime prevention program.

Measuring perceptions is a difficult science at best. One could argue that there is a relationship between the magnitude of the physical stimuli (i.e., say, actions taken by friendly forces) and how a person perceives these actions. But this may not be the case in a sociocultural setting—what friendly forces view as a positive activity, the local population could perceive as insulting or disrespectful. These actions could cause a backlash against the actions being taken by friendly forces and the forces themselves.

Analysts can measure perception by several methods. The four methods suggested by the U.S. Army[7] are:

- Determine demographic and cultural factors that shape perceptions and reactions;
- Identify patterns and indicators from previous expectations and reactions in a society's history;
- Compare reported reactions to determine if they were based on real or perceived conditions; and
- Monitor editorial and opinion pieces of relevant newspapers for changes in tone or opinion shifts that can steer or may be react to the opinions of a society, organization, or group.

An example of a completed perception assessment analysis is shown in table 6.6. It appeared in the U.S. Army's interim field manual entitled *Open Source Intelligence*[8] and shows across the top the categories that need to be considered before action is taken. In each of the rows are presented the issues relating to the corresponding heading. The first three columns at the right of center are essential factual data, but the three rows to the left of center are interpretations of the data to the right and, as such, require expert subject knowledge in academic disciplines such as history, sociology, anthropology, theology, or political science.

TABLE 6.6 Example of a Completed Perception Assessment Analysis

Condition	Cultural Norm	Friendly Force Action	Population Perception	Cause of Perception	Consequence If Unchanged
Food	Rice	Provided meat and potatoes	Inadequate and inconsistent	Practical (no experience with potatoes and cultural dietary rules on meat)	Starvation and riots
Armed civilian	All men carry weapons	Confiscated all weapons	Unfair and demeaning	Historical (previous experience with Western or military forms of government)	Risk of violence between U.S. forces and armed civilians
Government structure	Tribal	Establish military administration (hierarchical)	Tolerable if the authority fulfills needs		Loss of credibility and eventually control if needs are not met

TEXTBOX 6.4 | **Perception Assessment Case Study**

So, take, for instance, the first condition—food. Here friendly forces are planning to distribute food to the local population who are struggling to feed themselves due to the insurgency. The intention is humane and honorable. However, the likely outcome is starvation due to the perception issues identified in this analysis.

This type of analysis provides transparency and replicability[1] and hence conforms to the scientific method of inquiry. It makes clear the facts and reasoning used to arrive at the final judgments. In doing so, the judgments are defensible.

Although this technique was discussed in a military setting, it can be used in other intelligence contexts—national security, law enforcement, business, and private. Police may use it in neighborhood gang intervention programs; businesses could use it for marketing goods and services in new markets overseas; and private sector intelligence could use it to gauge community reaction to concerns about privacy regarding the use of CCTV surveillance in certain situations.

[1] Some scholars prefer the term *reproducibility*. Both terms are perfectly acceptable, as it is the intent of science to be able to verify research results, detect intellectual fraud, and understand limitations of various research approaches, data, and so on. The view taken here in this book is that both terms reflect this intent.

Network Analysis

If a research question focuses on the need to understand the relationships between two or more individuals, organizations, events, or other factors (or combinations), then network analysis can help make these associations clear. The relationships can be anything—social, business, financial, or even relationships that show abstract concepts such as influence, support, or mentoring.

The origin of network analysis is in the social sciences, where scholars, like Moreno,[9] devised the use of two-dimensional diagrams to display relationships.[10] These were, and are, called *sociograms*, but in intelligence work analysts have called them *network analyses*.[11] Network analysis should not be confused with the closely related analytic technique known as *traffic analysis*.

· ·

Network analysis has a common bond with *traffic analysis*; the latter involves intercepting radio or telecommunications traffic between entities. Using analytic methods, patterns in these communications can reveal inferred meaning in the context of the issue under investigation. It is the exchange of the communication that is the subject of the analysis, not the content of the message. Times, days, frequency, duration, method of transmission, encryption method, and so on are the elements that are studied. As such, traffic analysis is an important methodology for situations where the targets are using encrypted radio transmissions.[12]

. . . .

Network analysis is also called *association analysis* and *link analysis* because, during the process, analysts use a matrix to show associations and lines to shown links.[13] Although these terms are used, this author is in favor of standardization with the term *network analysis*, as the other terms only describe part of the overall analytic technique. Because network analysis has a long history and tradition within the intelligence community,[14] analysts should stay with this term and avoid others.

Network analysis is a structured technique for unstructured data. It consists of plotting nodes that represent entities—circles indicate people, squares indicate companies or businesses, solid lines represent strong associations, dotted lines are used for weak or unconfirmed links, and the numbers along the lines count the number of contacts or interactions each entity has had with the other during the period of the study. Concepts such as *influence* can be represented by using arrows instead of lines.

TEXTBOX 6.5 | Network Analysis Illustration

The individual links that comprise the overall network can be described by the attributes of the associations between the entities. In a criminal context, these attributes might include routine pieces of information, like victims' addresses and phone numbers, their movements prior to the alleged offenses, and the offenders' modus operandi—all of which are analyzed to generate investigative leads, infer an organization's hierarchy (or lack of one), determine points of vulnerability/strength, and so on. A step-by-step description is as follows:

1. Identify all entities. This can be done through other forms of analysis such as telephone record analysis or distilled from surveillance reports, notes or transcripts of interviews, telephone or e-mail intercepts, documents seized during raids, and so forth.

2. Assemble these data in an association matrix (see table 6.7 for an illustration). This is a standard matrix consisting of the same entities listed across the top and down the left-hand side. Where an entity intersects itself, the cell is blanked out. Where there is a known or confirmed association between two entities, a solid dot is entered into the

TABLE 6.7 **Example of a Network Matrix**

	Jack's Restaurant	Giacomo	Elizabeita	Rosa	Vladimir	Ignacy
Jack's Restaurant						
Giacomo	+					
Elizabeita	+	+				
Rosa	+	+	+			
Vladimir				+		
Ignacy	+	+	+			

corresponding cell for the two. If the association is suspected, a hollow dot is used, and a plus sign is used to denote that a person is a key individual in a company or organization.

3. Depict the entities as symbols on a diagram (the diagram can be a marker board, a flipchart, or a computer drawn diagram/document), and draw the relationship lines (i.e., links) between them (see figure 6.2). Common

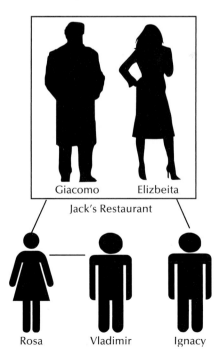

FIGURE 6.2 Example of a simple network diagram showing links between members of a fictitious European criminal enterprise.

symbols are circles for people, squares for corporate entities, and circles within squares for persons associated with an organization; solid lines represent strong associations, dotted lines for weak or unconfirmed links. Influential relationships use arrows pointing from dominant to subordinate. If using a computer program, such as IBM's *Analyst's Notebook* or Palentir's *Gotham*, it will have its own symbols for entities; for instance, a telephone symbol for telephone numbers, a boat for watercraft, a car or truck for motor vehicles, silhouettes for people, and so on. There is no correct way to display the entities on the chart. As intelligence projects differ, so too will each chart. The number and relationship between the entities will vary. As such, analysts will have to use their sense of artistic arrangement to create an exhibit that will clearly and easily show the viewer the relationships. If the graphic is too "busy," it is likely to be confusing. If it is confusing, it defeats the purpose of presenting the data in this way.

Content Analysis

Content analysis is the analysis of text contained in documents. Since these data are usually in narrative form (e.g., transcribed oral speeches, media interviews, or open letters to a public audience), the most common form of analysis is via qualitative methods, but analysis may also incorporate quantitative methods or both qualitative and quantitative methods. The central purpose of content analysis is to develop an understanding of what is contained in the text beyond the superficial message. Some commonly used techniques for content analysis include thematic analysis, indexing, and qualitative descriptive analysis.

Thematic analysis is another form of content analysis where themes are separated like the spectral colors of light as they pass through a prism—red, orange, yellow, blue, indigo, and violet. Themes are separated from text by, not a physical prism, but intellectual prism. This prismatic endeavor calls on the analysts to identify themes using judgments based on knowledge and experience. Being widely read makes thematic analysis a more fruitful enterprise. Ideas that present themselves in the text are identified and given appropriate labels. The passages of text relating to a theme are marked and affiliated to the corresponding theme.

Using a manual system, this could mean photocopying the page text; cutting out the word, passage, or paragraph (i.e., using a pair of scissors); and placing it in a large envelope along with other passages that are identified. Each piece of paper (containing a word, passage, or paragraph) is referenced back to the text as one would do using, say, the Harvard referencing style,[15] so that, when the material is compiled into the final report, the analyst knows where it has come from (like note taking when writing an essay).

This type of analysis can be used in grounded theory research[16] because it ideally lends itself to taking unstructured data and giving it organization. With grounded theory research, these themes then can be interpreted to explain phenomena (i.e., develop a theory about the issue under investigation).

Thematic Metrics

If a computer-based software package is used in connection to thematic analysis, then the same procedure takes place as discussed in terms of the manual system, but the software avoids all the manual cutting, referencing, and storage issues, as this is done electronically. The advantages of using a computer-based solution are great, as the software will have other features, including word count and metrics such as the Flesch Reading Ease and the Flesch-Kincaid Grade Level tests (see "Flesch Reading Ease Illustration" and "Flesch-Kincaid Grade Illustration" sections below). These types of analysis allow the analyst to use a blended approach, incorporating both qualitative and quantitative analysis.

Any number of documents can be analyzed using this technique, and in cases where, say, speeches are delivered by a foreign political figure in the country's local press, these public addresses can be analyzed over time in a quasi-longitudinal study. Alternatively, several author-known documents can be analyzed against a document of unknown or uncertain authorship with this method.

As an illustration, the Flesch Reading Ease and the Flesch-Kincaid Grade Level tests could be used where an analyst wants to gauge whether a speech was aimed at the local population of a developing country or whether its appearance in the daily newspaper was just a vehicle for projecting a message to international leaders. The use of these two tests could quickly yield results that suggest whether the speech under investigation had a reading ease score and grade level commensurate with the country's population or that it was much higher—perhaps, suggesting it was aimed at a better-educated international audience.

Indexing is another way of identifying meaning in the text. Rather than identifying themes, indexing identifies key words in context. This is best done with computer software. An exceptions dictionary is first set up in the software package where words such as *a, an, and, the, is, it, of,* and so on are flagged as exceptions, so when the software searches the text, it does not index these inconsequential words. All other words are then indexed.

These words appear in their context within the document. This allows the analyst to not only count the appearance of certain words—say, a repeated word like "infidel"—but also then tag the sentence or paragraph where these key words appear so that they can be included in further analysis of a wider theme. Indexing is a technique closely tied to quantitative descriptive analysis. Descriptive analysis seeks to describe features of the text quantitatively as is done with numeric data—by describing the most frequently used words or phrases. This type of analysis ideally lends itself to a blended approach of both qualitative and quantitative techniques.

. . . .

Not everything that counts can be counted, and not everything that can be counted counts. (Albert Einstein)

. . . .

Although content analysis has the advantage of having computer-based methods that allow the analysis of very large documents (and multiple documents), the technique is not without limitations. Firstly, the data need to be textual. If there is no source of textual data, no analysis can take place.

Caution must be exercised in terms of sampling bias as with other approaches. In the hypothetical case of the foreign leader's speeches in the local press discussed above, analysis would leave out all the leader's speeches delivered by way of radio or television broadcast or in-person delivery to crowds assembled. The other limitation is that although software packages are useful in automating indexing, counting, and tagging text, these packages cannot interpret what words or phrases mean—it takes an analyst to do this word by word and phrase by phrase.

Flesch Reading Ease Illustration

The product of the Flesch Reading Ease analysis is a rating represented by a number on a scale between 0 and 100. The higher the score, the easier the text is to read. For instance, a document with the following Flesch Reading Ease scores would be interpreted as such:

- 90 to 100—very easy;
- 80 to 89—easy;
- 70 to 79—fairly easy;
- 60 to 69—considered to be what is generally termed plain English;
- 50 to 59—fairly difficult;
- 30 to 49—difficult; and
- 0 to 29—confusing.

The formula for calculating the score is: *readability ease* = 206.835 − (1.015 − *average sentence length*) − (84.6 − *average syllables per word*). Although most word processing packages will have this feature as part of its spelling and grammar checker, it will be of interest to the intelligence analyst to understand how it is calculated. The average sentence length is determined by taking the total number of words in the document and dividing it by the number of sentences. The average number of syllables per word is calculated by taking the total number of syllables divided by the total number of words. A step-by-step description is as follows:

1. Count all the words;
2. Count all the syllables;
3. Count all the sentences;
4. Calculate the average number of syllables per word;
5. Calculate the average number of words per sentence; and
6. Match the readability score.

Flesch-Kincaid Grade Illustration

The Flesch-Kincaid Grade Level analysis converts the Flesch Reading Ease score to a level equivalent to grade school rank (U.S.-based). The formula for calculating the score is *Flesch-Kincaid Grade Level* = (0.39 – *average sentence length*) + (11.8 – *average syllables per word*) – 15.59. For example, a score of 12 indicates that a person who has had a twelfth-grade education could understand the text contained in the document. A step-by-step description is as follows:

1. Count all the words;
2. Count all the syllables;
3. Count all the sentences;
4. Calculate the average number of syllables per word;
5. Calculate the average number of words per sentence;
6. Multiply the average number of words per sentence by 0.39, and add this number to the average number of syllables per word, which is multiplied by 11.8;
7. Subtract 15.59 from the resulting number from step 6; and
8. Match the score with a U.S.-based school grade.

If a word processor or other software package is used to perform these calculations, note any limitations specified in the software, as some results may only report a grade level of 12 even though the grade level exceeds this figure.

Secondary Analysis

Secondary analysis of data is a quantitative approach that is closely aligned to content analysis. Secondary analysis of data relies on information that has already been collected. But, rather than analyzing textual data, secondary analysis analyzes quantitative data for a second time—that is, an examination that is unconnected to the primary collection project.

TEXTBOX 6.6 | Secondary Analysis Case Study

As an example, intelligence analysts used secondary data analysis in the lead-up to the 1973 elections in France. At the time, decision makers in the United States were interested in knowing if a socialist-communist-left radical coalition was likely to form a government in France. Therefore, U.S. decision makers requested an intelligence assessment on the most likely outcome of the election. Intelligence analysts at the CIA were tasked with providing the assessment. Relying on existing data sets, CIA analysts used multiple regression analysis to gauge the impact various historical economic conditions had on the voting patterns of the left.[1]

Based on the results of this secondary analysis of existing data, analysts concluded that economic conditions did, in fact, impact elections but only in the absence of other important political considerations.[2] The use of existing data sets allowed analysts to predict that the domestic political factors affecting the elections would not be as powerful as those in previous elections—therefore raising the potential of a left victory. However, these political factors were also assessed as being strong enough to ensure that the required number of votes would *not* go to a left coalition. Arguably, such analysis was only made possible by using this technique.

Another example is the U.S. Department of State, which has no agents who engage in primary data collection. The Department of State's Bureau of Intelligence and Research therefore relies on data collected by other agencies to undertake its investigations.[3] This has been likened to the research conducted by Nobel laureates Doctors James Watson and Francis Crick, who, in 1953, discovered the double-helix structure of DNA by interpreting secondary data.[4]

[1] Susan Koch and Fred Grupp, "Regression Analysis: Impact of Economic Conditions on Left Voting in France," in *Quantitative Approaches to Political Intelligence: The CIA Experience*, ed. Richards J. Heuer (Boulder, CO: Westview Press, 1978).
[2] Koch and Grupp, "Regression Analysis," 57.
[3] See, http://www.state.gov/s/inr/ (accessed July 16, 2012).
[4] James D. Watson and Francis H. C. Crick, "Molecular Structure of Nucleic Acids: A Structure for Deoxyribose Nucleic Acid," *Nature* 171, no. 4,356 (April 1953): 737–38.

The amount of data collected by governments around the world for social and economic planning is extensive. There are census data, crime statistics, social data, educational data, economic data, and consumer data, just to mention a few broad categories. Data are also collected by private corporations, think tanks, and a variety of nongovernment organizations for their own planning purposes, which are also available to outside researchers. Because these data are stored electronically, they can be imported into the software package being used by the analyst—say, a spreadsheet or a statistical software package such as SPSS. As was seen in the 1973 French election case study, CIA analysts used data from several databases to conduct their multiple regression analysis.

Secondary data analysis is an efficient means of conducting research. Preexisting data sets alleviate the problem of a potentially lengthy collection phase that, in some cases, may have taken months or years to collect. It also means the data may be available at no cost or a modest fee, thus making it inexpensive as well. If a pretext is used to obtain the data set, it will not alert the target (or target country or corporation) that they are the subject of an intelligence operation. For instance, most small intelligence research studies are unlikely to have a budget large enough to conduct a national sample (or international as in the French case cited) because of the cost and time required, but by using a census data set, even a small research budget can gain considerable leverage.

Nevertheless, secondary analysis does have some limitations. In the main, analysts may find it difficult to gain a full appreciation of the problems encountered during the original collection or the errors inherent in the resulting data sets so that these limitations can be considered when manipulating the data during secondary analysis. It may also be a difficult task to link two or more data sets that have little in common—either by the structure of the database, the level of measurement (i.e., nominal, categorical, interval, or ratio), or units of measurement.

Key Words and Phrases

The key words and phrases associated with this chapter are listed below. Demonstrate your understanding of each by writing either a short definition or a one- or two-sentence explanation.

competing hypotheses	network analysis
content analysis	PEST analysis
environmental scan	Secondary analysis
Flesch Reading Ease analysis	SWOT analysis
Flesch-Kincaid Grade Level analysis	

Study Questions

1. What are the four quadrants in a SWOT analysis? Describe each and explain what type of data the analyst would seek to populate each.

2. Compare and contrast SWOT with PEST. Discuss when an analyst might use one technique over the other and why.

3. Describe the variations that can be applied to PEST.

4. Summarize the steps in creating a network analysis.

5. Explain how quantitative analysis can be conducted with unstructured data, say, in the form of a leader of a country's public speeches.

6. List five sources of secondary data.

Learning Activities

1. Suppose you have been tasked to construct a pedigree chart for the dictatorial leader of Country Q. Your findings will form part of a psycholinguistic analysis of him. Using hand-drawn lines or a software package, create a pedigree chart. For this learning activity, use your own family members as a way of indicating your skill in creating the chart. Seek as many different sources of data as possible to simulate a real-world project. If stumbling blocks are encountered in obtaining data about family members (as they would be with a real target), consider how you could collect this information from other sources. List the possible alternative sources and methods of acquiring these data (e.g., using an information collection plan format).

2. Select an editorial containing a few thousand words from a major national or regional newspaper (to ensure enough scope for several themes to be present). Using thematic analysis, highlight the various themes/subthemes discussed in the editorial. Using a pair of scissors, cut out these passages (or alternatively, number the themes in situ, for example, 1 = political; 2 = social; 3 = educational; 4 = emotion; 5 = threats; 6 = lack of logic; and so on. The themes and how they are defined is part of the activity). Now summarize the editorial on two levels—the first being the overt message of the editorial and the second is the result of your thematic analysis. In the case of the latter, you may ask yourself whether the themes suggest anything beyond the simple message contained in the words.

Notes

[1] The technique is sometimes referred to as SLOT analysis because the "L" stands for *limitations* rather than the W for *weaknesses*. In both cases, the same idea is represented.

[2] This technique is based on the method attributed originally to Kurt Lewin's discussion which appeared in Dorwin Cartwright, ed., *Field Theory in Social Science: Selected Theoretical Papers* (New York: Harper & Row, 1951).

[3] Heuer and Pherson, *Structured Analytic Techniques*, 22.

[4] Richards J. Heuer, *Psychology of Intelligence Analysis* (Washington, DC: Center for the Study of Intelligence, Central Intelligence Agency, 1999).

[5] U.S. Department of the Army, *FMI 2-22.9: Open Source Intelligence* (Fort Huachuca, AZ: Department of the Army, 2006), 4–16.

[6] U.S. Department of the Army, *FM 31-55: Border Security/Anti-Infiltration Operations* (Washington, DC: U.S. Government Printing Office, 1972), 7–2.

[7] U.S. Department of the Army, *FMI 2-22.9*, 4–16.

[8] U.S. Department of the Army, *FMI 2-22.9*, 4–16.

[9] Jacob L. Moreno, *Who Shall Survive? Foundations of Sociometry, Group Psychotherapy, and Sociodrama* (Washington, DC: Nervous and Mental Disease Publishing, 1934).

[10] John Scott, *Social Network Analysis: A Handbook* (Newbury Park, CA: Sage, 1991).

[11] Prunckun, "The Intelligence Analyst as Social Scientist," 67–80.

12 U.S. Department of the Army, *Fundamentals of Traffic Analysis (Radio-Telegraph)* (Laguna Hills, CA: Aegean Park Press, 1980). This is a reproduction of original Department of the Army *TM 32-250* (1948) and Department of the Air Force *AFM 100-80, Traffic Analysis* (1946), without changes. However, a glossary and an index were added by Aegean Park Press.

13 International Association of Law Enforcement Intelligence Analysts, *Successful Law Enforcement Using Analytic Methods* (Alexandria, VA: IALEIA, 1997).

14 Francis Ianni and Elizabeth Reuss-Ianni, "Network Analysis," in *Criminal Intelligence Analysis*, eds. Paul Andrews and Marilyn Peterson (Loomis, CA: Palmer Enterprises, 1990).

15 Richard Pears and Graham Shields, *Cite Them Right: The Essential Referencing Guide*, Tenth Edition (London: Palgrave, 2016), 22–90.

16 Uwe Flick, *An Introduction to Qualitative Research, Fourth Edition* (London: Sage, 2009), 427–42.

Chapter 7

Quantitative Analytics

Levels of Data Measurement

When observing variables in intelligence research, these data are organized according to numbers analysts attribute to them. Assigning numbers to represent variables is done as a way of preparing these data for statistical testing. The numbers assigned to the data are the factors that determine the *level of measurement* and, hence, the kinds of statistical tests that can be applied.

There are four levels of measurement: nominal data, ordinal data, interval data, and ratio data. Each level of measurement represents an increase in the type of statistical tests that are permissible. As such, the level of measurement, it could be argued, is the foundational assumption for all statistical testing. That is, the data type determines which statistical test can be conducted. If this assumption is violated, it makes the results of any subsequent statistical test invalid.

For instance, if data were of a nominal scale, then only statistical tests designed to analyze these types of data can be used (say, for example, chi-square analysis). However, if the data were of a ratio scale, then any test at the ratio level and those for lower-level data could be applied. This is because ratio data can be reduced to a lower level of measurement to be analyzed using an appropriate test. If the data are already at a lesser level of measurement, they cannot be converted to a higher level. Likewise, once the data are converted to a lower scale, unless the original data are retained in ratio form, they cannot be disaggregated.

Analysts also use what is termed *derived data*—but this is not the same as a level of measurement; it is information that is produced from combining or interrelating two or more data items to produce a new piece of information.

For example, suppose an analyst has data on several events and has data on when those events took place. Using a computer application, the analyst can produce new data based on an algorithm that, for example, requests "a list of all events that occurred before a certain date but after another specified date, as long as the event was not followed at any time by another type of event."

Nominal Data

Nominal data is the lowest level of measurement and comprises observations that can be placed in a group, for instance, Americans, Australians, Britons, Canadians, or New Zealanders (as such, it is sometimes referred to as a *categorical* scale). The attributes of nominal data are that there is no rank or order to the data—that is, one group is not "greater" or "more" than another group.

By itself, there is no "distance" between the groups as in higher-level data. So, one cannot say that if you are an Australian, you are twice as "ethnic" as a New Zealander. All that can be said in this example is that one is in the Australian group and the other is in the New Zealand group. Also, an observation can only be in one group, not multiple groups.

Ordinal Data

Ordinal data has the same attributes as nominal data, but in addition, it introduces the attribute of rank (sometimes referred to as *rank scale*). Rank, in this sense, suggests that the scale has some direction—say, from less to severe. Take, for instance, the crime of terrorism—three events could be ranked as to their severity: kidnapping, assassination, and bombing. One will note that they have the same attributes as nominal scale data in that observations can be placed in groups, but these groups have a relationship in how they are ranked. Because these observations can be ordered in this way, the level of measurement increases.

Nevertheless, even though there is direction to these data, there is no indication of distance between the data items. For instance, an analyst cannot say that assassination is twice as severe as kidnapping. However, the analysts can say that bombing is greater than kidnapping, that bombing is greater than assassination, and that assassination is greater than kidnapping.

Interval Data

Interval data has the same attributes as ordinal data, but it introduces the dimension of distance or *interval*. That is, data measured using this scale will be able to demonstrate a common unit of measurement for all observations.

Take, for instance, the interval measure of time—a terrorist planted an improvised explosive device in a busy marketplace at 1:00 p.m., and it was detonated by remote control at 1:30 p.m. The analyst can conclude that there were two distinct events (nominal scale), one event was more serious than the other (on the ordinal scale, it could be argued that planting a bomb is serious, but detonating it is far more serious), and the time that elapsed between the two events was thirty minutes (interval scale). Because there is now a measurable distance, the interval scale allows the analyst to conduct arithmetic calculation on the data. One should note that there may be a zero point in this scale (e.g., 00:00 hours) but that zero is an arbitrary notion—it is not real.

Ratio Data

Ratio data is the highest level of data, as it has all the attributes of interval data, but in addition, it has a real zero for the scale's starting point. Having a real zero starting point reference allows the analyst to calculate ratios between any two observations—data can be added, subtracted, multiplied, and divided.

By way of example, suppose the terrorist-improvised explosive device cited above was estimated to contain 15 kilograms of high explosive. Suppose, also, that another explosion that day was due to a device containing 30 kilograms. The analyst can conclude that there were two explosions (nominal scale), one was bigger than the other (ordinal scale), and the larger explosion was 15 kilograms greater (interval scale), as well as having twice the destructive power (ratio scale, assuming, in this example, that destructive power is linear).

Univariate Analysis

Univariate analyses are used when the analyst wants to simply describe a person, organization, location, or object that consists of a single dependent variable. Hence, univariate analysis is also known as *descriptive statistics*. Contrast this type of analysis with bivariate and multivariate analyses where two (bi-) or more (multi-) variables are analyzed (in such analyses, the variables may or may not be dependent upon each other). Univariate analysis can be used with the different levels of data as shown in table 7.1. The descriptive statistics that can be produced are listed in the right-hand column.

Frequencies

Constructing a frequency distribution is often an analyst's first task in analyzing data. This is done by counting the number of observations per category (nominal and ordinal level) or per score (interval and ratio level). The results can be described in the intelligence report's narrative as well as displayed graphically. Figure 7.1 (ordinal level) and table 7.2 (ratio level) are examples of how terrorist event data can be presented. Figure 7.1 shows the number of terrorist events by organization before and after the 1986 U.S. air raid on Libya,[1] whereas table 7.2 shows the number of (notional) bombing events (X) terrorist groups were responsible for in Country Q.

TABLE 7.1 Examples of Descriptive Statistics

Measure Level	Analytic Technique
Nominal	Frequencies
Ordinal	Frequencies, Range, Minimum, Maximum, Median, Mode
Interval	Frequencies, Range, Minimum, Maximum, Median, Mode, Mean, Weighted Mean
Ratio	Frequencies, Range, Minimum, Maximum, Median, Mode, Mean, Weighted Mean

Count

Count is the total number of values in a distribution (i.e., a data set). Using the following distribution as an example, the count would be eleven. These data could represent the number of people killed by roadside bombs or any number of other intelligence-related events:

$$4, 8, 10, 12, 15, 16, 19, 20, 24, 28, 31$$

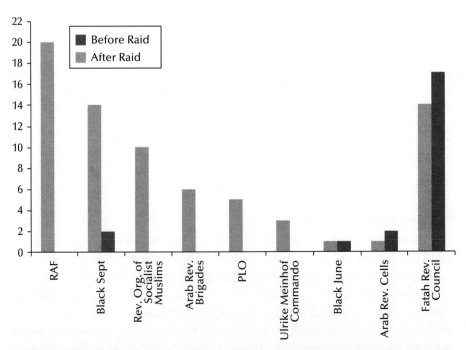

FIGURE 7.1 Terrorist events by Libyan-sponsored groups targeting Americans and U.S. property abroad.

TABLE 7.2 Frequency Distribution of a Series of Notional Bombing Events

X (score)	f (frequency)	fX
5	2	10
4	3	12
3	7	21
2	15	30
1	30	30
	$N = 57$	$\Sigma fX = 103$

Minimum and Maximum

The minimum is the lowest value in a distribution. The maximum is the largest value. For instance, using the same data set representing the minimum number of people killed by roadside bombs as above, the minimum and maximum are 4 and 31, respectively.

Range

The range is the difference between the minimum and maximum values within a distribution. This is calculated by subtracting the smaller value from the larger. Using the same example above, the range would be 27 as calculated here:

$$31 - 4 = 27$$

Mean

The *mean*, also known as the arithmetic *average*, is used to average out quantities. It is calculated by adding all the values of a data set, then dividing the sum by the count of those numbers. Again, take, for instance, the distribution above: the total number of people killed was 187. Divide 187 by 11, and this equals 17:

$$(4 + 8 + 10 + 12 + 15 + 16 + 19 + 20 + 24 + 28 + 31) = 187 / 11 = 17$$

The mean can be used with both interval and ratio data; however, one of the disadvantages of using the mean is that it is affected by extremes at either end of the distribution. For example, if we use the notional roadside bomb data set and substitute 97 for the value 31, the resulting mean would be skewed to 23. Nevertheless, the mean is a useful statistical test, as it can be used to conduct further tests—for instance, an analyst can compare the means of several different samples.

Weighted Mean

Another method used to average quantities is the *weighted mean*. It is used in cases where not all the quantities are of equal importance. The formula for calculating a weighted mean is expressed in the following, where *bar-x* is the mean, w is the weight, x is the number, and Σ is the sum:

$$\bar{x}_w = \frac{w_1 x_1 + w_2 x_2 + w_3 x_3 + \cdots + w_n x_n}{w_1 + w_2 + w_3 + \cdots + w_n} = \frac{\Sigma \, w^* \, x}{\Sigma \, w}$$

Suppose a situation where an intelligence analyst is trying to establish the average price paid for heroin on the street but on a national basis. Data from each state's capital city are compiled and are weighted according to the population of each city (i.e., using census data). This considers the fact that there are price variations at the same point in time between locations because illicit drug prices increase "as one moves away from the drug sources and prices are lower in larger markets."[2]

Suppose that there are three capital cities in Country Q. The price paid for heroin in one city is $148 per gram, another is $256, and the third is $300. The populations of the cities are 5 million people, 2 million people, and 1 million people, respectively. Therefore:

$$\bar{x}_w = \frac{(5)(148) + (2)(256) + (1)(300)}{5 + 2 + 1}$$

$$= \frac{1,552}{8}$$

$$= \$194 \text{ per gram}$$

If the analysts had averaged these data without using a weighting system to consider the price variations caused by distances from the point of importation (the largest city with its port and international airport), then they would have obtained a result of $235 per gram. This is because the state with the smallest population that was far removed from the large port city—and hence had the highest price—skewed the average upward.

Weighted Grand Mean

There may be times when a *grand mean*, or the mean of the sum of all the means, is needed to be calculated. Such cases may arise where, for instance, a mean for heroin in each state's capital city has been calculated, but the national average is needed. To do this, the analyst totals the means for each city and then divides this figure by the number of cities. But because averaging the average can skew the results (sometimes considerably), a *weighted grand mean* is used.

This is calculated by using the same formula for a weighted average; however, instead of using x, the analyst uses *bar-x*, that is, the mean.

Median

The median is the middle value of a distribution. It is, therefore, the halfway point between those values that are greater than the median and the half that are less than the median. Using the following data set, the median is 16:

$$4, 8, 10, 12, 15, 16, 19, 20, 24, 28, 31$$

The median is less susceptible to extremes at the edges of the distribution. Again, take, for example, the notional roadside bomb data set we used previously, and again substitute 97 for the value 31, as was done for the mean, but now the resulting median would be 16, not the skewed 23 that was seen under the mean. Therefore, the median is generally more useful where there are extremes, and the mean most useful when the distribution is absent of such features.

Mode

The mode is the most frequently occurring value in a distribution. However, some data sets do not have a mode, as is evident with the example distribution used so far—there is a single count for each number. If, by contrast, the following distribution was used, the mode would be 12:

$$4, 8, 10, 12, 12, 15, 16, 19, 20, 24, 28, 31$$

Sometimes data sets have several sets of numbers appearing in equal frequency. In such cases, these are referred to as being bimodal (two modes), trimodal (three modes), or, in the case of more modes, multimodal.

Bimodal:

$$4, 8, 10, 12, 12, 15, 16, 19, 20, 24, 28, 28, 31$$

Trimodal:

$$4, 8, 10, 12, 12, 15, 16, 19, 19, 20, 24, 28, 28, 31$$

Of the three measures of central tendency—mean, median, and mode—the mode is the least useful unless the number of values represented by the mode form a large percentage of total distribution. Moreover, no further analysis can be conducted on the mode—an analyst cannot, for instance, compare modes of different samples, as the result would make no sense at all.

Calculating Percent Increases and Decreases

Sometimes an analyst will need to express a number as a fraction of 100. This might be because the analyst needs to show how one quantity is related to another. The mathematical function used to do this is *percent* (meaning, per hundred). As an illustration, 54 percent is 54/100, or, expressed as a decimal, 0.54. When a number increases, an analyst can calculate its percentage increase using the following formula:

percent increase = [(*new figure* – *original figure*) / *original figure*] × 100

When a quantity decreases, the analyst can calculate the percentage decrease by:

percent decrease = [(*original figure* – *new figure*) / *original figure*] × 100

It is important to note that both the formulas exhibit the following principle:

percent increase / decrease = (*change in figure / original figure*) × 100

This is because the analyst is calculating either the percent increase or the percent decrease with the amount of change to the original figure as demonstrated in the following two examples:

1. The number of people attending political rallies in the city of Orrenabad rose from 16,000 to 22,000. What percent increase does this represent?

percent increase = (22,000 – 16,000) /
16,000 = 6,000 / 16,000 = 0.375 x 100 = 37.5%

2. The number of political websites hostile to the new democratically elected government in Orrenabad declined from 930 to 200. What percent decrease does this represent?

percent decrease = (200 – 930) /
930 = –730 / 930 = 0.785 x 100 = –78.5%

Per Capita Calculations

Per capita simply means per person. An analyst can calculate the per capita occurrence of *x*, where *x* is the issue under investigation:

per capita = (*total x / population*) × *rate*

So, using an example of suicides, the per capita figure would be the total number of self-inflicted deaths divided by the total population. In this case, the population could be either the population of the town or city, the region or state, or the country. This statistic can then be used as a means of comparison to other towns or cities or from country to country in a meaningful way.

One of the detractions of per capita calculations is where the figure is very small; in such cases, the ratio becomes meaningless. As an alternative method, the analyst can use per 100,000 in the population, 10,000, or even 1,000.

By way of example, take the notional regional town of Isobel. The town recorded 200 residential burglaries during the year, and it had 100,000 households. Therefore, the burglary rate would be 0.002. This is not a very meaningful figure. However, if it is calculated per 1,000 in the population, then it is 2 burglaries per 1,000 households.

$$(200 / 100,000) \times 1,000 = 2$$

By using a rate per 1,000 instead of a per capita rate, in this example, the figure can more easily be understood.

Rounding Numbers

Rounding numbers is commonly used where the decimal fraction makes little sense or adds to confusion. Take, for example, a hypothetical case where an analyst calculates the average number of rounds fired per soldier during the last six skirmishes with enemy forces to be 194.6342. At four decimal places the result adds no discerning insight to the study's findings, as most people cannot think to four decimal places (we usually can visualize one or two decimal places, but no more—for example, 0.5 is half, and 0.25 is a quarter, and 0.75 is three-quarters). Besides, analysts should be asking themselves what insight this level of detail will add to the conclusions. Sometimes an estimate is all that is needed to demonstrate a point being made or to make a prediction. In these cases, rounding is advisable. A step-by-step description of the process is as follows:

1. Determine the unit that is required to be rounded off—thousands, hundreds, units, or a decimal fraction;
2. Examine the number to the right of the unit to be rounded off;
3. If this number is 5 or more, add an additional unit;
4. If the number is less than 5, subtract a unit.

For instance, using this mathematical convention, if an analyst was rounding 194.6 to the nearest unit, it would be rounded up to 195. If rounding 194.6 to the nearest ten, it would be rounded down to 190. But, if the analyst was rounding 194.6 to the nearest hundred, it would be rounded up to 200.

Bivariate Analysis
Chi-Square

Chi-square is one of the more useful statistical tests for intelligence analysts because it can be used on nominal-level data. It has few assumptions and is, therefore, straightforward to apply and interpret.

Chi-square is a nonparametric test of statistical significance. The term *nonparametric* refers to statistics that deal with variables that are without assumptions as to their form or their distribution parameters. It returns a statistic that reflects the "goodness of fit" or the difference between the observed frequency and the expected observations according to a model hypothesis (H_0—known as the *null hypothesis*).

The power of the chi-square statistic is that it will tell the analyst whether the actual distribution occurred by chance or was likely to be the result of the interaction of the independent variable according to a level of confidence (e.g., 0.01 or 0.05). Later in this chapter, the importance of setting the appropriate level of confidence is discussed in more detail. The following are the only three requirements for using chi-square:

1. Any level data can be used;
2. There must be more than five observations per category (if there are less than five observations, they will be meaningless); and
3. The observations must be independent.

Unlike some other statistical tests, there is no direction indicated by chi-square, so once the result is obtained, an inspection of the data is required to determine the direction (that is, whether it is positively correlated or negatively correlated). Consider the following example of a single sample chi-square: Analysts are concerned about whether the numbers of terrorists in a target organization's cells in North America are equal to those in the organization's Asia region. The observed frequencies are arranged in table form (referred to as a *contingency table*). If the data were represented by two independent samples (that is, in the form of a 2-by-2 contingency table), then the convention is to list the independent variable (x) along the top of the table with the dependent variable along the side (y).

Chi-square can also be used for cases involving two independent samples. For instance, suppose an analyst wanted to know if there were significant differences between insurgents who were young males as opposed to older males and whether these people had previously been involved in criminal activity before joining the insurgency. The null hypothesis (H_0) would be: the number of terrorists in North American cells and Asian cells are equivalent. The alternative hypothesis (H_1) would be: the number of terrorists in Asian cells is more. The observed distribution is:

North America	86
Asia	120
Total	206

The expected distribution under the H_0 is for 50 percent to appear in each:

North America	103
Asia	103
Total	206

The formula for calculation of chi-square is as follows:

$$X^2 = \frac{\Sigma\ ([A_1 - E_1] - .5)^2}{E}$$

X^2 = Chi-square

A = actual or observed frequency

E = expected Frequency

$-.5$ = Yates' correction for continuity

The calculations follow; however, many software spreadsheet packages contain the chi-square function. It is a simple matter of entering the data into the spreadsheet, indicating the degrees of freedom, and activating the chi-square function from the menu options. The spreadsheet will return the chi-square statistic (here it was done manually and is shown in table 7.3).

The degrees of freedom are calculated thus: $df = C - 1$ (where C represents categories). So, in this example it would be $2 - 1 = 1df$.

Yates' correction for continuity is applied in instances where the degrees of freedom are equal to 1 or where the observed frequencies are less than 10. This prevents an overestimation of statistical significance.

In chi-square analysis, the *critical value* is the threshold that determines at what point an analyst would not reject the null hypothesis. Using the critical values contained in the appendix, we observe that a value of 5.28 is greater than the required 3.84 at the 0.05 level ($1df$), so we can reject the null hypothesis—numbers of terrorists that exist in the Asia cell are greater (i.e., we accept H_1—the alternative hypothesis). This means that there would be less than 5 chances in 100 that a result like this would be obtained if random variation was the only explanation.

TABLE 7.3 Manual Calculations for Determining Chi-square

	North America	Asia	Total
Actual/Observed	86	120	206
Expected	103	103	206
$(A - E) - 0.5$	16.5	16.5	
$([A - E] - 0.5)^2$	272.25	272.25	
$([A - E] - 0.5)^2 / E$	3.17	2.27	
Σ	5.44		

Note that the result in this example does not *prove* the alternative hypothesis, it merely *supports* the explanation. However, a hypothesis can be disproven. It is important that these subtleties are understood and reflected accurately in any written report or oral briefing based on such findings. (See also the discussion under "Statistical Significance" below.)

As can be deduced from the formula, the chi-square statistic is the product of each of the individual frequencies. Therefore, each frequency contributes to the final chi-square statistic. If a given frequency is greatly different from the expected frequency, then its contribution to the chi-square statistic can be expected to be large. Conversely, if the frequency closely aligns itself to the expected frequency, then the contribution of that frequency to chi-square will be small.

It is clear that large chi-square statistics indicate that the contingency table contains a frequency(s) that differs noticeably from the expected frequency(s), but the statistic will not be able to point to the frequency(s) responsible for the elevated chi-square. It can only indicate that such a frequency(s) is present. When an excessive result is obtained, it requires the analyst to examine the table to determine which frequency(s) is the cause.

The body of the analyst's report should discuss the conclusions drawn from these results, what they mean, and the implications they have for the study. When discussing these issues, refer directly to the table(s) so the reader is not left in doubt about any aspect of the conclusions.

Statistical Significance
Type I and Type II Errors

The concept of *statistical significance* is important to the analyst, as it makes clear what likelihood there is for an error in judgment. At the center of this process is the *confidence level* chosen by the analyst—this is referred to as the *alpha-level* or *p-value*, for example, 0.05, 0.01 (or another level either higher or lower). Regardless of the level chosen, there is the risk that the null hypothesis could be rejected when it should have been accepted or vice versa—accepted when it should have been rejected. The risk of error increases as the confidence level gets smaller.

For instance, a *p-value* of 0.01 means that there would be less than one chance in one hundred that a result like this would be obtained if random variation was the only explanation (i.e., a 99% chance of being true). A *p-value* of 0.05 indicates that there is a 95 percent chance of being true. And, a *p-value* of 0.001 indicates there is a 99.9 percent chance of being true.

Such errors are referred to as type I errors and type II errors. The former are *false positives*, and the latter are *false negatives*.

As pointed out in the section above about chi-square, these results do not *prove* the alternative hypothesis; they merely *support* it as an explanation. That is to say, with a confidence level of, say, 0.05, there is still a 5 percent chance that the findings may have been the result of another factor(s). However, the hypothesis can be disproven if it fails to meet the confidence level.

By way of example, suppose an analyst has selected a confidence level of 0.05; in this case, the analyst could more easily reject the null hypothesis and declare that there is a statistically significant difference in the data than what would have occurred if he or she had selected the 0.01 level. However, the analyst would be wrong in this conclusion 5 percent of the time. If, however, the analyst selected a confidence level of 0.01, he or she would be wrong only 1 percent of the time.

Type I errors are when some phenomenon is observed, and the conclusion is drawn that there is a difference when in fact none exists—therefore it is viewed as a false positive. A type II error is a false negative—accepting the null hypothesis when it should have been rejected. This is where the analyst fails to observe a difference and accepts the null hypothesis. The relationships between these decisions are summarized in table 7.4.

What is the impact on the analyst's findings of type I and type II errors? A type I error could be described as a "false alarm"—sending a signal that the observed phenomenon is worthy of note (and presumed action) when, in fact, it is a mistaken conclusion. The analogy could be a miner finding pyrite (i.e., fool's gold) instead of gold. In contrast, a type II error could be attributed to a lack of sensitivity of the data collection instrument or an omission of some sort so that the difference was not detected. If the miner analogy is used again, the miner would have thrown out the gold with the tailings from the mine.

From this discussion, the analyst can see that in any research project, they are always at risk of making one of these two types of errors. So, which error is "worse" to make? It depends on the question that has been asked by the decision maker. Both can be equally devastating as can be seen in the following two examples:

TABLE 7.4 Summary of Statistical Decisions

	Where H_0 is true	Where H_0 is false
If H_0 is rejected	Analyst commits a type I error (false positive)	Analyst's decision is correct
If H_0 is not rejected	Analyst's decision is correct	Analyst commits a type II error (false negative)

- If the decision maker asked if there are any weapons of mass destruction in Iraq, then committing a type I error will have serious repercussions if the decision maker is planning a military invasion (i.e., wrongly concluding that such weapons existed when there were none).
- If, however, the analyst is asked whether the United States faces an attack by an international terrorist group, then a type II error needs to be avoided—overlooking a genuine threat to national security could result in another September 11, 2001–style attack.

Displaying Information in Figures and Tables

Figures

Graphs, charts, photographs, drawings, diagrams, as well as other terms are all considered *figures* when writing an intelligence report. The term *figure* is a distillate of all graphical representations into one summary term. The only other term that is used in presenting research results is the term *table*. *Figures* and *tables* are the only two terms that should be used in intelligence writing. However, having said that, we will look at the various lay terms as a way of explaining how results could be presented.

Graphs are used to display numeric data pictorially; in effect, they are symbolic representations. In practice, the term *graph* is used interchangeably with the term *chart*. Intelligence analysts use graphs to display information which would be too complex in narrative form. Therefore, the graph offers the analysts a simple, concise format for conveying the gist of their results to the decision maker.

The most commonly used (and easily recognized by nonanalytic users) are the *pie chart*, *bar chart*, and *line chart*. A pie chart is a circular figure divided into segments that resemble a pie. Each "slice" of the pie represents a data item. The size of the overall pie is 100 percent, with each slice being a representation of a proportion of the total.

A bar chart uses vertical bars (but sometimes they are laid out horizontally) to show the relationship between data across categories. Bar charts are used where the data items are categorical (i.e., independent of each other): for instance, the number of rockets, automatic weapons, and hand grenades that a guerrilla force may have in its possession (a pie chart could be used for the same purpose, as it also represents individual data items). The bars are not drawn contiguously, as in a histogram, but with separations between them to demonstrate they are not related by time or score interval. If, however, the bars are joined in a contiguous manner, then it is referred to as a *histogram* (see figure 7.2). A histogram is a picture of a grouped distribution, which shows the shape of the distribution.

A *frequency polygon* serves the same purpose as a histogram, but it only shows the midpoint of the intervals of the scores. It can be displayed as either bars or dots. If shown as a series of dots, each dot is connected by a line

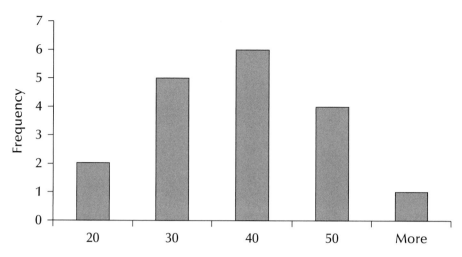

FIGURE 7.2 An example of a histogram.

(see figure 7.3). In this regard, the line becomes a bar chart but with the bar image suppressed—they are merely represented by dots joined by a line.

In contrast, a line chart is used where the data are required to be displayed showing passage of time (e.g., a time-series study)—say, the number of rocket-propelled grenades an insurgent group has held in its cache month by month (see figure. 7.4).

Some forms of graphs use pictures or symbols in place of bars, columns, or lines as a way of reinforcing the message. These are termed *pictographs* and

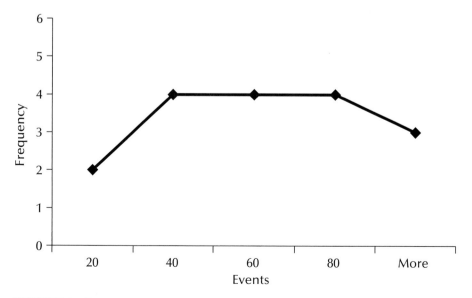

FIGURE 7.3 Example of a frequency polygon.

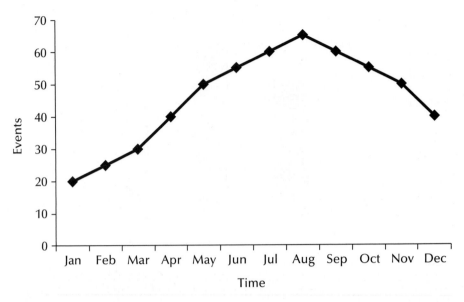

FIGURE 7.4 Example of a line chart.

lend themselves to briefings where the analyst is presenting his or her results via a data projector on a large screen. However, before an analyst uses such a technique, thought should be given to whether the inclusion of pictures will trivialize the presentation. Images that are provided via some commercial software packages could be construed by decision makers as frivolous, and, therefore, their use in a presentation may lessen the impact of the message being conveyed.

Tips for Creating Graphs

- Give graphs captions that reflect the dependent and independent variables being displayed.
- The X axis displays the independent variable, while the Y axis the dependent variable.
- Label both axes and assign an appropriate unit of measurement.

X and Y Axes

Remembering which axis X refers to and which Y refers to is a common problem, even for seasoned analysts. There are many rhymes to help remember, and here is one: "X to the left, Y to the sky." That is, the X axis appears on the left of the figure and runs left to right (i.e., the horizontal axis), whereas the Y axis appears at the base of the figure and runs from the bottom to the top (i.e., the vertical axis).

Traps to Avoid

Here are a few things to keep in mind when constructing graphs:

- Do not be tempted to enhance a graph by using what could be considered a gimmicky feature contained in some software packages—such as three-dimensional charts. Features like this trivialize your research and distract the decision maker's attention away from your study's results and focus too much on the eye-catching graphical image.
- Be mindful of inadvertently distorting chart results by setting the baseline value (i.e., the value at the bottom of the vertical, or y, axis) to a score other than zero.
- Do not mistakenly display categorical data as a frequency polygon (i.e., along the horizontal, or x, axis)—instead, present these data as a bar chart.

Tables

A *table* is a data set arranged in columns. Like graphs, tables make the presentation of numeric data easy for the reader to understand. The information contained in a table needs to be simply laid out and concisely labeled so the reader is clear about the points being demonstrated.

When constructing a table, convention is to only use horizontal lines. Some software packages place vertical lines into tables, but, strictly speaking, this is not correct. An example of a properly laid-out table is shown in table 7.5.[3] Each column has a descriptive header that identifies the data in each column. Each row also has a header, identifying the data in the row. The data appears in the remaining central part of the table. The caption appears either at the top or at the bottom of the table.

Because we read from left to right, it makes sense to lay the table out in that order, as the reader is likely to scan the table beginning at the left and moving to the right; and from the top, moving down to the bottom. Note in the example

TABLE 7.5 Worldwide Terrorist Events by Severity Level Pre- and Post-1986 U.S. Air Raid on Libya

| Severity Levels | Terrorist Events | | |
	Before Raid	After Raid	Percent Change (%)
High	541	458	−15.3
Medium	170	155	−8.8
Low	145	244	+68.3
Totals	856	857	+00.1

in table 7.5 that the "before" data appears to the left of the "after" data for this reason (i.e., in chronological order).

Column and row spacing is important for a pleasing visual presentation as well as for understanding. Columns and rows should be equally spaced with enough "white space" to make reading easy. Large numbers should have commas as separators for thousands and decimal places kept to a minimum. Missing data in table cells should have some explanation, such as "not available," or whatever the reason. Consider rounding large numbers for ease of understanding for those who find dealing with numbers difficult. For instance, if a table contains several columns of numbers, they could be rounded for clarity—for example, 1,239,867 could be rounded to 1,240,000. You can see that rounding makes it easier to understand and compare data within a table. At the same time, doing so does not jeopardize the overall integrity of the information being presented.

Financial Analysis

The single most useful analytic technique for the non-accountant analyst is net worth analysis. In most agencies, financial analysis is conducted by a qualified forensic accountant because of the degree of knowledge it requires to understand the processes and procedures to reconstruct the target's financial position.

Nonetheless, an intelligence analyst can conduct a preliminary analysis of the target's net worth using the method described here. If the analogy of a paramedic and a surgeon is used, the intelligence analyst would be the paramedic performing the first-stage analysis while calling in the surgeon (perhaps a forensic accountant) to perform the more intricate analysis once the central issues have been identified.

Net worth is an indirect method of assessing the target's income and, therefore, is a handy technique in situations where the analyst may have come across information that suggests some form of illegal enterprise or secret deals (e.g., arms trafficking). It could also be used to assess a target's suitability to an approach by a field operative who is hoping to recruit the target as an agent (e.g., an offer of financial assistance).

Net worth is simply the difference between the target's assets and liabilities. If the analyst conducts a net worth analysis over time, say, for the end of each financial year, he or she can compile a picture as to whether the target is growing in worth or is experiencing losses and what the magnitude of these gains or losses might be. The formulas for calculating net worth are as follows, step by step:

1. Assets – liabilities = net worth
2. Net worth – prior year's net worth = increase or decrease in net worth
3. Net worth increase (or decrease) + living expenses = income
4. Income – funds in known sources = funds from potentially illegal sources[4]

Key Words and Phrases

The key words and phrases associated with this chapter are listed below. Demonstrate your understanding of each by writing either a short definition or a one- or two-sentence explanation.

average	minimum
categorical data	mode
Chi-square analysis	nominal data
descriptive statistics	*p-value*
figure	per capita
frequency	range
interval data	ratio data
level of confidence	statistical significance
maximum	table
mean	type I error
medium	type II error

Study Questions

1. What are the four levels of measurement in statistics? Describe the attributes of each level.
2. List the different types of univariate analysis available to the intelligence analyst.
3. Describe the differences between mean and weighted mean. Give an example of how an analyst might use each.
4. What is the difference between a type I error and a type II error? Explain.

Learning Activities

1. Community elders in Country Q are concerned about attacks on street markets—they suspect that they are not random and that this could signify growing factional tensions. The intelligence cell attached to the nation's paramilitary police has divided the country into five equal regions and collated the attack data accordingly. This information is shown in table 7.6.

   Using a chi-square test of significance, determine whether it is likely that this distribution of attacks is by chance (random) or if other forces may be at play. Use a 0.05 confidence level. What can you conclude from these results?

2. Suppose an intelligence analyst is preparing a briefing to industry executives of the occurrences of trademark violations in a major city known for its high international tourist traffic. Over the past year, field operatives have noted the following numbers of individuals trading in counterfeit trademarked goods for each month starting in January and ending in December:

TABLE 7.6 Country Q Street Market Attacks

Region	Number of Attacks
1	26
2	19
3	31
4	17
5	11

27, 35, 17, 13, 42, 37, 52, 48, 20, 24, 12, and 30. Select an appropriate method of displaying these data for an electronic slide presentation, and prepare the slide using a commercial software package.

Notes

[1] Henry Prunckun, "Operation El Dorado Canyon: A Military Solution to the Law Enforcement Problem of Terrorism—A Quantitative Analysis" (Master's thesis, University of South Australia, 1994), 47.

[2] Jonathan Caulkins, "What Price Data Tell Us about Drug Markets," *Journal of Drug Issues* 28, no. 3 (Summer 1998): 602.

[3] Prunckun, "Operation El Dorado Canyon," 52.

[4] Leigh Edwards Somers, *Economic Crimes: Investigating Principles and Techniques* (New York: Clark Boardman Company, 1984), 99.

Chapter 8

Geointelligence

Although geointelligence is seen as a relatively new area of intelligence analysis, it has been around for over a century. As an example, during World War I, military analysts used printed maps, pins, and overlays to assess enemy positions, fortifications, and their order of battle (see figure 8.1[1]). They also used aerial photographs taken from biplanes—"the cameras were bulky and were just handheld by the observer, but they provide their worth in the static warfare of Europe."[2] Analysts used these simple hardcopy graphical representations to plan attacks, build defenses, and launch counterattacks. However, geointelligence is being used in fields other than the world's militaries, and is becoming an important analytic approach with law enforcement agencies, businesses, and the private operators such as NGOs.

Today, commercial software, such as IBM's *Analyst's Notebook* or Palantir Technologies' *Gotham*, have replaced these rudimentary visual aids with real-time representations that collect data from any number of sensors and can then present images of the area under study on wall monitors, workstations, and handheld communications devices. These software applications allow analysts to instantly query the data using a graphical interface in response to, say, a situation commander's request. Geointelligence analysis is a way of displaying information where visualization can show what the information means. Geointelligence software applications "connected network visualizations, social network analysis, and geospatial or temporal views to help [analysts] uncover hidden connections and patterns in data. This insight can help [analysts] better identify and disrupt criminal, cyber and fraudulent threats."[3]

Software applications provide analysts with the ability to customize the data inputs and how these data (or selected data items) are displayed, as well as to change the display parameters to answer a commander's questions as a

133

FIGURE 8.1 First World War military intelligence students studying aerial photographs showing the intricate trench systems used by opposing forces. *Source*: Courtesy of the U.S. Army.

situation unfolds, or to ask "what if" questions of the data as part of planning an operation. Although it is beyond the scope of this book to teach how to use these geointelligence programs, analysts need to understand the foundational concepts on which these automated systems are based (recall that a computer program is only an integrated collection of instructions that replicate what a person would do manually). If an analyst does not know the theory underpinning what the computer program does, he or she is merely a technician, not an intelligence analyst. The three concepts that support the various commercial geointelligence applications are maps, overlays, and mosaics.

Maps

A map is simply a two-dimensional graphic representation of part of the earth's surface. It is drawn to a scale (except for those that are created in the field and termed *mud maps*) by cartographers and is always oriented with a bearing to north. Mapmakers incorporate certain devices into the map to make reading easy—universal symbols for various features in the physical world as well as colors and lines to augment the representations. This concept is then digitized for computer analysis.

While some physical maps are three-dimensional—being constructed out of sand, clay, wood, plastic, paper, or cardboard—3D digital maps can be produced in seconds and, like their physical cousins, rotated to offer the analyst differing views.

Maps are important because they allow an analyst to simultaneously display several pieces of information that may prove confusing in narrative form—recall the adage *a picture is worth a thousand words*. With computer software, many more sources of information can be input, and these data can change in real time if required. Further, through the medium of a map, analysts can conduct their analysis-in-chief—say, comparing distances and lines of sight and evaluating access, travel routes, and so on. Because each map contains numerous data items, it is a self-contained database that shows the existence and location of many ground features as well as the distance between them.

Arguably, the most frequent user of maps in intelligence work is the military. Although some use is made by law enforcement agencies with the mapping of crimes and crime hot spots, their use is not universal. If a map is to be incorporated into an intelligence report, it is imperative that the analyst knows the cartographic skill level of the reader. If, for instance, the reader has no knowledge beyond reading a city street map, then this is the maximum level of sophistication that should be presented in the map. More detail may cause the reader to lose interest, and, therefore, the analyst will lose his or her audience.

Maps can be sourced from many places—from government departments that are responsible for land surveying to commercial companies that specialize in the production of high-quality maps. At the time of this writing, the Internet featured several digital sources of maps, including maps that showed satellite images of the earth. The resolution of these images is good, and the user can select the level of magnification required. These satellite images can also be displayed as a simple map with terrain features or in composite form (i.e., terrain and image). Other Internet-based mapping systems available at the time of writing included those that showed street-level maps (views) of cities around the world and a virtual view of the oceans' landscape.

Using desktop computer workstations and commercial software packages, analysts can convert paper-based maps to digital images for projection in oral briefings, incorporate them into digitally created documents, or save them to a secure intranet site within the host agency (e.g., in some form of electronic knowledge base as part of the agency's *basic intelligence* holdings—refer to chapter 2 regarding intelligence taxonomies.).

Aerial photographs are photographs taken from any of a variety of airborne platforms, such as fixed and rotatable wing aircraft, unmanned drones, gas-filled balloons, and satellites. The aerial photograph can be used as either a supplement to a cartographic map or as a map substitute.

Why would an analyst consider displaying intelligence in the form of aerial photography? On the one hand, a topographic map may have been created some years previously and, hence, could be obsolete. On the other, an aerial photograph taken recently (via the analyst's information collection plan at the start of the research) shows any changes in landscape as they occur.

In this regard, a display of aerial photographs and maps provides more information than either alone. Photographs can be obtained readily, whereas maps can take weeks to be prepared. Changes can be noted and compared daily or even hourly if the issue is that important (e.g., the Cuban Missile Crisis of October 1962). The downside, however, is that aerial photographic interpretation is both an art and a science that takes considerable skill and training. Nevertheless, basic information can be conveyed easily and clearly in this form, even for a generalist analyst.

Overlays

The analytic technique of overlaying information is the second key concept to geointelligence. This method is used to display additional information about the terrain or activities within the area under study. A manual illustration of a map overlay, from the U.S. Army's field manual entitled *Map Reading and Land Navigation*,[4] is shown in figure 8.2.

Physical overlays are usually clear sheets of plastic-like material that allow the analyst to hand draw or annotate the map/photograph with standardized

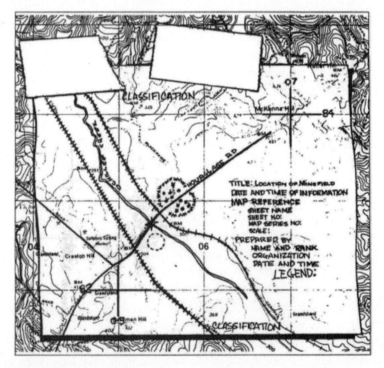

FIGURE 8.2 Example of a military map overlay with notation in the margins. *Source:* Courtesy of the U.S. Army.

symbols or codes. They are most commonly used in operational theaters that are characterized by quick decisions and frequent changes of plans. Marks on the clear sheets can be erased and redrawn as events or plans change. Several overlays can be used to "build" a picture of various activities or present different tactical options.

This type of manual overlay can be presented electronically using a software package. This method is most effective in oral briefings where an image is shown, and with the click of a mouse button, additional information can be overlaid, thus emphasizing the point the analyst wants to make.

Mosaics

Finally, a mosaic is the third keystone to geointelligence. A mosaic is created by combining two or more overlapping graphics in such a way that they form a single picture. Graphical data can be maps, aerial photographs, and vertical photographs (including those taken at low and high oblique). However, many mosaics are of a photographic nature, as they offer operational commanders and field operatives a panorama-like view of an area under investigation.

Since their employ during World War I, mosaics have been useful in displaying spatial data and, hence, vital intelligence. With commercial software packages, photographs can be combined with terrain data so that a digitized image can be constructed to produce a three-dimensional, mosaic-orthogonal map.

These mosaics are valuable in training field operatives in such techniques as border crossing and covert insertions—techniques that require the operative to enter a hostile country (or, in the case of law enforcement, a violent or dangerous neighborhood in an urban area). These computer-generated, mosaic-orthogonal maps can be extensive, covering tens of thousands of square kilometers.

Key Words and Phrases

The key words and phrases associated with this chapter are listed below. Demonstrate your understanding of each by writing either a short definition or a one- or two-sentence explanation.

aerial photograph   mud map
mosaic   overlay

Study Questions

1. Define the term *map* and give three examples of commonly used maps.

2. Describe a situation where an intelligence analyst might use an overlay.

3. List the main features of a mosaic.
4. Using the Internet, search for commercial software applications that can be used in geointelligence.

List two and describe the geographical features each package offers an intelligence analyst.

Learning Activity

Suppose you have been asked to construct a map overlay to assist field operatives in a covert operation. Using a street map for the city in which you live as an example, use your imagination to construct an overlay that shows the following detail: a muster point for pre-operation briefings; the location of a notional target, any potential hazards (countersurveillance points), and an exfiltration route for the covert team. Annotate the overlay with an appropriate security classification.

Notes

[1] John Patrick Finnegan, U.S. Army Intelligence and Security Command; U.S. Department of the Army, *Military Intelligence: A Pictorial History* (Arlington, VA: Department of the Army, 1984), 40.

[2] Harold Hough, *Satellite Surveillance* (Port Townsend, WA: Loompanics Unlimited, 1991), 8.

[3] IBM, *Analyst's Notebook*, accessed September 11, 2018, https://www.ibm.com/au-en/marketplace/analysts-notebook.

[4] U.S. Department of the Army, *FM3-25.26: Map Reading and Land Navigation* (Washington, DC: Department of the Army, 2001), figure 7-2.

Chapter 9

Target Profiles

A *target profile* is a type of an intelligence report that summarizes information about a specific target. It is an operationally focused description that is considered a short-form report.[1] Joby Warrick in his book on a CIA double agent operation describes the role a target profile plays: "Like an artist assembling a giant mosaic, [the targeter can] summon bits of information from wiretaps, cell phone intercepts, surveillance videos, informant reports, and even news accounts [as well as other open sources] . . . to develop a profile that the agency's spies, drone operators, and undercover case officers [can use operationally]."[2]

A target can be an individual or group, but it could also be a company or an organization. In the case of the latter, the report may be titled *criminal business profile*, *terrorist organization profile*, or some similar name. A variation to the target profile is the *problem profile*—this is a report that focuses on an issue, not a person or an organization. An example could be a series of crimes occurring in a geographic "hot spot." In any case, the target can be either the subject of a current inquiry or an emerging target for a proposed investigation. The report summarizes what is known about the target and, in doing so, identifies information gaps, which feed into a collection plan for additional data.

Background

Target profiles often provide field operatives with a range of options regarding possible intents (i.e., hypothesis derived from inductive reasoning) or possible ramifications if the target continues the activity at the center of the report's concerns (e.g., risk assessment). In doing so, a good report will prioritize the need to make further inquiries about the target in ranked order with other targets under investigation so that intelligence unit managers can allocate resources.

A target profile consists of several sections that are arranged to "tell a story": background, personal details, criminal record (in the case of a law enforcement target), physical environment, analysis, and target planning. There may also be attachments appended to the end of the report.

Even though the different components that comprise a target profile are discussed in this chapter, for clarity, an example of a completed target profile appears at the end. This example relates to a hypothetical criminal enterprise that, for the purposes of the exercise, was suspected of operating in several European and Middle Eastern countries as well as in India.

Key Parts of a Target Profile

Introduction

This section provides brief details about the legal basis or agency policy which gives the analyst authority to compile the report and the name of the authorizing officer (e.g., the intelligence unit's manager), date, and file number for audit purposes.

Background

The background section of the profile contains a short statement of the report's aims or objectives, scope, and a brief description of how the target fits into the broader picture—the context (e.g., motorcycle gangs in the region).

> *Context* is the background to a problem or situation. It allows analysts to make sense of why an event is happening by allowing them to explain key contributing factors.

Personal Details

This section provides a descriptive analysis of the target (sometimes referred to as the *person of interest* or abbreviated as POI). It will contain a biography and physical description of the target and, if available, a photograph. Any aliases used by the target are included along with a description of the target's usual or last practiced occupation, business address, business affiliations, and so on. Other pertinent facts, such as driving licenses, trade licenses, and vehicles owned or regularly driven (in the case that they do not own a vehicle), appear in this section.

The personal details section can also contain details about the target's social and/or psychological functioning. This could consider information about places the target frequents, personal friends, family connections, and business associates.

Business Details

A range of information about the target's own business or the businesses they are associated with appears here. Rather than being prescriptive about what should be included in this section, suffice it to say that any detail that bears directly on portraying any of the elements of the *Kipling method*—what, why, when, how, where, and who—associated with the objective of the report should be included. By way of example, in a money laundering case, details to consider are off-shore bank accounts, electronic fund transfer arrangements, businesses and nonprofit organizations in the cash flow chain, key personnel, financial information, and company data from the government agency responsible for registering companies in the jurisdiction, and so on.

. . . .

I keep six honest serving-men (They taught me all I knew);/Their names are What and Why and When and How and Where and Who.[3]

. . . .

Criminal Record

In addition to outlining the target's criminal history, the target profile could contain a list of court appearances, how they responded to previous probation or parole orders, and, if currently on bail, bail conditions and reporting arrangements. There may be intelligence from a prison or jail intelligence unit that could prove insightful—if available, consider including it.

If the target has prior convictions or has been arrested for violence or firearms offenses, these details need to be highlighted as an occupational safety issue for fellow officers who might have to deal one-on-one with the target. Further, the types of crimes or the frequency of offense may be relevant as to why the target profile is being developed, and, therefore, it too should be a feature. If agency records note the target's modus operandi, then this information will be another important aspect for inclusion.

Regarding corporate and private sector intelligence, where practitioners do not have legitimate access to these data, analysts may only be able to obtain this type of information from public databases. Newspapers, both hard copy and online, report on criminal activities that take place at local, state or provincial, and national levels. These reports contain the offenders' names, their offenses, court convictions, and probation and parole details. This is because this information forms part of the public record. These data are suitable for inclusion in this section if it is recorded what is proved as fact (e.g., in a court of law) and what is alleged by a law enforcement agency. Not all criminal matters are reported in newspapers, but public databases like this are important sources of information for corporate and private intelligence analysts.

Criminal Associates

Sections like this can be added to the target profile to provide additional facts about the target. Here details of the target's associates who have criminal records are listed. Information relating to their arrests and/or convictions is listed in reverse chronological order. If the target's associates have a probation record, a prison file, or a parole dossier, those details can be included in this section, or for clarity, they can be provided under a new section heading to correspond to that information.

Physical Environment

Observations made by surveillance operatives appear in this section of the profile. Details about the target's physical space complements what is known about his or her social and psychological makeup (e.g., arrests and convictions can be considered external manifestations of their psyche). Moreover, surveillance operatives may have noted some of the ways the target practices countersurveillance or has put in place other intelligence countermeasures. Surveillance reports may have also commented on whether these precautions are conducted regularly, on an ad hoc basis, and whether they appear to be effective.

Analysis

This is the "engine room" of the report. The material that appears in the sections just discussed is descriptive in nature. However, in this section, the analyst applies one or more analytic methods, so these data provide insight. It is sometimes described as the "so what" section. That is, what do all the previous facts mean, and what implications do they have? Depending on the issue or allegation, it might be as simple as positioning the target within the wider criminogenic landscape, or it might be as sophisticated as detailing where the target fits within a transnational crime syndicate, terrorist group (or offshoot), espionage ring, military establishment, and so on.

This is done via analysis; analysts cannot rely on "a hunch," "gut feel," or base it on "experience" or "belief." If a conclusion is drawn, then analysts must be able to demonstrate how they arrived at the finding. For instance, if a profile focuses on the risk the target poses to the community (or field operatives, etc.), then a risk analysis must be conducted.

How elaborate this analysis is depends on the facts and issues surrounding the target as well as the aim of the report. But generally, for the purposes of a target profile, it can be a simple, straightforward table examining the likelihood and consequences of key hazards (i.e., the sources of risk).

If business and financial information is presented in the business section of the report, the analyst could then present some form of financial analysis or network analysis of the key personnel involved.

Even if the data are "thin," at a minimum an analyst can conduct a SWOT analysis that examines the strengths, weaknesses, opportunities, and threats posed by the target. Such an analysis can highlight missing data (i.e., intelligence gaps) and form the basis for recommendations for additional data collection via a new information collection plan.

The analyst can insert additional analyses depending upon what data were described in the preceding sections, but one important analysis that the analyst should always include is that of countermeasures (if any). A simple force field analysis of the precautions taken by the target when using landline and mobile telephony, voice over Internet (VOiP) communications, data transmission (including e-mail), two-way radio, or satellite telephony would be helpful for planning how field operatives are tasked in the future. If these are missing, it needs to be highlighted.

> It's no sin to admit an intelligence gap. . . . By admitting to the unknown, we may get someone's attention and initiate some seriously needed collection action. Your work might make a positive contribution by calling someone's attention to an intelligence gap of possible consequence.[4]

Include also observations made when the target makes face-to-face contact with "significant others"—for instance, does the target practice countersurveillance techniques in these situations? Are codes, ciphers, or encryption used when they communicate?

Target Planning

Having presented the facts and analyzed these to gain an understanding into the target's activities, the planning section takes the insights developed and answers the question of "where to from here?" or "so what do we do now?" The planning section usually starts off with a short narrative summarizing the findings in the context of the objective and then discusses practical and realistic ways of addressing the problem.

This can be done by providing a range of policy or operational options—from the "do-nothing" option to an option that could be described as a "gold standard." Unless there are large political pressures being applied because of the actions of the target, the Rolls-Royce option is normally outside most agencies' budgets, so one of the middle options is going to be more attractive (acknowledging that there will be some trade-offs in effectiveness and/or efficiency that should be noted in the report). The bottom line is to present decision makers with a way of stopping, disrupting, or reducing the illegal, harmful, or otherwise detrimental effects of the target's activities.

The do-nothing option, although at first glance appearing to be one that would be dismissed outright, could be a viable choice either where further time is required to gather critical pieces of information or where all necessary data are in hand and arrest, capture, or seizure is the next and final step. If more information is required, then the analyst must be mindful of the costs that will be incurred in gathering these data and the likelihood that such intelligence gathering will benefit the analysis and improve the recommendations of the report in a material way.

Attachments

Because a target profile is usually a short, sharp, and focused report, attachments should be kept to a minimum. A few examples of what might appear in an appendix are a map, a photograph, or an organizational chart showing complex relationships that would be confusing if they appeared in the body of the text as narrative.

Terminology

In practice, some terms used in the intelligence arena are applied inappropriately. As practitioners, it is important that we use the key terms correctly; otherwise, our reports will lack credibility. Following are a few words that typically cause difficulties. Next to each term appears a definition. No doubt there are other definitions, but what is important in considering these is that analysts focus their thoughts on writing precisely.

- **Allegation:** An accusation yet to be substantiated.
- **Analysis:** Systematic examination that follows some scientific, mathematical, or logical procedure or process.
- **Assumption:** Something that is true without proof.
- **Believe/Belief:** Synonymous with *faith* and, hence, not a recognized intelligence methodology. I suggest that the word *consider* be used. *Consideration* is based on fact and reason.

- **Conclusion:** A judgment or finding.
- **Consideration:** Deliberation, a process of long, careful thought.
- **Evidence:** Something (e.g., data) that indicates that something exists or contributes to the process of proving the truth of something.
- **Fact:** Something that can be observed or experienced through one of the five senses and is verifiable.
- **Hypothesis:** A theory, an explanation for something, which is then used as the basis for examination or investigation—speculation, conjecture, guesswork.
- **Inference:** A theory constructed from data that have been subject to analysis.
- **Intelligence:** "Insight" expressed in the form of a product (e.g., report, target profile, target assessment, estimate) and the process that produces such a product.
- **Investigation:** The assembling (i.e., pre- or peri-) or reconstruction (i.e., post-) of facts surrounding an event.
- **Postulate:** Something that is true and forms the basis of a theory.
- **Probability:** Likelihood, chance of something happening. Statistical confidence is the probability that a statement is true. If probability is not based on analysis, it is conjecture. (The use of words such as "will" conjure the idea of 100 percent certainty—avoid saying something "will" unless probability analysis can confirm this.)
- **Proof:** The legal process of introducing a fact into evidence with the intent to establish the truth of something.
- **Standard of proof:** Beyond reasonable doubt (criminal) and on the balance of probabilities (civil).
- **Suspected:** Alleged.
- **Truth:** A somewhat subjective notion. For instance, it was once viewed that the earth was flat, and this was the accepted truth at the time. To have questioned this truth was heresy. In the criminal justice setting, truth is derived via a judicial process of proofing evidence in accordance with the rules of evidence, criminal procedures, and precedent.

Finally, different words mean different things to different people. Adjectives that invoke some level of sensationalism should be avoided in an intelligence report. The best way to do this is to "describe" or "explain," but do not excite. For instance, what an analyst might see as "extreme" may be "insignificant" to the reader.

· ·

Avoid the use of personal, subjective, or unproved ideas and ambiguous language in intelligence reports. Statements made need to be supported by evidence.

· ·

TEXTBOX 9.1 | Example of a Target Profile

~Secret~

Date: February 28, 2019
Authorizing Officer: Director, Criminal Intelligence Analysis Organization (CIAO)
Crime Analysis: Organized Crime Group (Delta X-Ray Analytic Team)
In the matter of: Section 50, Anti-People Smuggling Act, 2002
File: I-0043/2019

Background

Interpol has requested the CIAO to assist it in its investigation of an allegation of people smuggling and it is suspected that Lucien DEJAY may be implicated in this criminal enterprise. The alleged criminal enterprise is suspected to operate in several countries, including France, the United Kingdom (UK), the United Arab Emirates (UAE), and the Republic of India.

Personal Details

Name: Lucien DEJAY (AKA "Disco")
DOB: April 1, 1988
Born: Grenoble, France
Citizenship: French
Marital Status: Divorced
Occupation: Owner of A2B Transport, Abu Dhabi
Distinguishing features: 6'1" tall; full facial beard

Lucien Dejay

Business Details

- 2005 to 2007—telemarketer
- 2007 to 2010—insurance salesman
- 2010 to 2013—used-car salesman
- 2013 to 2015—printing-industry salesman
- 2015 to present—partner and co-owner of a trucking company in Abu Dhabi, UAE, that trades as *A2B Transport*

Criminal Associates

1. Alain PRESSCOT (AKA Albee PRESS), French national and a person friendly with the Mignon Syndicate (Marseilles, France). The Mignon

Syndicate is reported by Interpol to be involved in people smuggling into the UK. PRESSCOT meets socially with members of the Syndicate when he visits Marseilles. University educated with a Bachelor of Business Degree. He currently owns a fleet of container trucks in Abu Dhabi. No criminal record.

2. Gunther LETZ (AKA "Grunter"), German national, antecedents consisting of arrests for assault with a deadly weapon (switchblade knife) and possession of an illegal firearm (M1 assault rifle). Ex-German soldier with combat experience in Afghanistan (reconnaissance) and has trained "security guards" (described in the press as "mercenaries") throughout Africa for various mining companies. He is reported by Interpol to be a member of the Mignon Syndicate but owns a charter boat company in Port Sudan and has two oceangoing vessels. Interpol reports that it is investigating him for people smuggling (table 10.1 in chapter 10 gives a brief list of pros and cons of the alleged smuggling process).

Physical Environment—Surveillance

Interpol Information Report—#01/2019

A meeting took place between LETZ and PRESSCOT in Dubai, UAE, on January 25, 2019. LETZ used a convoluted travel route to and from the meeting at the Intercontinental Hotel.

Indian Bureau of Immigration Report—#02/2019

An application lodged at the Indian embassy in Abu Dhabi by Lucien DEJAY for a business visa to travel from UAE to Hyderabad, India, on February 12, 2019. DEJAY has requested the visa for multiple entries over a six-month period.

TABLE 9.1 Criminal Record

Year	Offense	Penalty
2010	Arrested for alleged money laundering $80,000	Charges dropped, insufficient evidence
2008	Convicted for possession of printing equipment restricted by law	Fined $20,000 plus court fees
2006	Convicted for possession of forged artworks	Fined $5,000 plus court fees
2004	Convicted for aiding and abetting forgery of religious artifacts	Sentenced to 6 months prison, suspended under a good behavior bond for 6 months
2002	Convicted for passing forged checks with a total value of $10,000	Sentenced to 3 months prison, suspended under a good behavior bond for 6 months

Abu Dhabi Police Information Report—#03/2019

Information received from the Abu Dhabi Police advises that DEJAY attended the Abu Dhabi Export Trade Office on February 1, 2019. His inquiries raised some concerns. He is reported to have asked questions about what documentation was required to enable the move of merchandise from Sudan into UAE by ship and what documentation was required to transship that cargo to the UK via truck. He wanted to take away the forms needed and asked to see an example of a completed form. When questioned, DEJAY stated that he just wanted to make sure he filled in the forms correctly.

Interpol Information Report—#04/2019

Surveillance of LETZ indicated a meeting took place in the Intercontinental Hotel on January 30, 2019. The meeting was between LETZ, PRESSCOT, and another European male that fit the description of DEJAY.

Interpol Information Report—#05/2019

An influx of displaced persons has taken place in suburbs close to Port Sudan. The people are known to be staying in shanties on the outskirts of the port city. It is not known at this time why these people are gathering at this location.

Indian Bureau of Immigration Report—#06/2019

Lucien DEJAY entered India from Abu Dhabi on February 12, 2019. He flew to Hyderabad.

Central Bureau of Investigation Report—#07/2019

DEJAY received a male visitor at about 19:00 hours on February 12, 2019, at the Hyderabad Novatel. The visitor carried a black briefcase in and out of the meeting. Surveillance could not determine what was in the briefcase. Surveillance, however, followed the male visitor after the meeting to an address in Hyderabad, and from that they identified the person as Ramesh GUNTUR. Surveillance established that GUNTUR is a twenty-one-year-old software engineering student at a university. A check of police records showed that he had NO criminal record.

Internet Search—#08/2019

A search of publicly available information on the Internet (e.g., on Facebook and other social media websites) revealed that a Ramesh GUNTUR stated that he lived in India and is offering to sell "custom-designed" certificates and identification papers (i.e., custom design is considered code for fake and forged documents). His Web posting claims that his documents are of the highest standard.

Analysis

Interpol has requested the CIAO to assist it in an investigation it is conducting into an allegation of people smuggling. The allegation is that Lucien DEJAY may be implicated in this criminal enterprise.

At present, the CIAO has some data that relates to DEJAY, and this is in the form of his personal details, employment details, details of countersurveillance practiced by the target and his associates during clandestine meetings, criminal record, criminal associates, and surveillance reports.

An analysis of the strengths, weaknesses, opportunities, and threats (SWOT) of these data is summarized in table 9.2 in matrix form.[1]

Examining two factors of the SWOT analysis,[2] there are four key strengths, but eight important threats. There are several ways that police can use these strengths to "offensively" moderate the threats. The ones that present themselves include:

TABLE 9.2 **SWOT Analysis**

		Pros	**Cons**
Internal		Strengths	Weaknesses
		• NCAA's involvement in this operation is not known to target	• International locations of target and associates
		• Ability to provide close surveillance domestically	• Possible legal jurisdictional issues
		• Can build a dossier on domestic associates quickly	• Difficulty in conducting overseas surveillance
		• Ability to monitor *GUNTUR's* Indian activities	• Reliance on INTERPOL and other agencies for intelligence on movements (e.g., ships and trucks)
External		Opportunities	Threats
		• Can work closely with INTERPOL	• Data indicates possible people—smuggling operation from Port Sudan through Abu Dhabi via ship, then to (possible) UK via truck
		• Access to open-source intelligence on Sudan	• Data indicates *DEWIRE* likely obtained false passports and other documents via Hyderabad forger (*GUNTUR*)
		• Access to open-source intelligence on associates and business associates	• Large numbers of unidentified people already gathered near *LETZ's* shipping port in Sudan
		• *DEWIRE* nonviolent "con man" travel	• Being businesspeople and with links to a crime syndicate, they have potential to access large amount of money to facilitate illegal operations
		• *PRESSCOT* nonviolent businessman	• Target and associates appear to practice countersurveillance during clandestine meetings
			• Increased involvement with other law enforcement agencies increases risk of "leaks"
			• *LETZ* has history of violence and is military trained
			• *LETZ* and *PRESSCOT* are linked to France-based crime syndicate (Mignon Syndicate)

1. As the target's associate LETZ is trained in military reconnaissance and has practiced countersurveillance while conducting clandestine meeting, the CIAO can use this knowledge when tasking surveillance units and during other data-gathering operations to ensure CIAO's involvement remains undetected.
2. CIAO's ability to provide domestic surveillance can be concentrated on the only known Indian associate, GUNTUR.
3. CIAO's domestic surveillance capability can be used to monitor any other associates who may become involved in the alleged criminal enterprise.
4. The CIAO can construct dossiers on the target's Indian associate and the target's Indian activities from the information of Interpol.

Target Plan

The results of this analysis support the hypothesis that there is a criminal enterprise operating to smuggle many people from Port Sudan on the Red Sea to Abu Dhabi via ship and then transport these people in containers overland via truck to the UK. To facilitate this, these findings suggest that the target, DEJAY, has procured the services of a Hyderabad-based forger (GUNTUR) to provide the critical travel documents for the people being smuggled.

As it is not known whether the documents have been provided (e.g., electronically via e-mail) and because Interpol reports that there are many unidentified people camped on the outskirts of Port Sudan, it is prudent to assume that a people-smuggling operation may take place soon.

If these propositions hold true, then the following recommendations would place the CIAO in a good position to assist Interpol should the operation escalate into a full criminal investigation. In order of priority these actions include:

1. Place immigration alert on DEJAY, LETZ, and PRESSCOT.
2. If the target or his two associates visit India, consider immediate surveillance.
3. If LETZ visits India, ensure all surveillance operations are aware of his propensity for violence.
4. Ensure all surveillance operatives are aware that the target and his two associates are surveillance conscious and that they practice countersurveillance.
5. Compile a dossier on GUNTUR, his associates, and his activities.
6. There may be enough probable cause to suspect a crime has been committed between DEJAY and GUNTUR regarding forged travel documents—legal advice should be sought.
7. If legal advice supports a charge of false documentation regarding people smuggling, GUNTUR should be arrested, and a search warrant obtained for his abode and his computer.
8. If legal advice does not support this, a search warrant for electronic intercept should be considered for his Internet connection to gather

evidence regarding the likelihood of imminent supply of forged travel documents.

Oliver Yardley

Oliver Yardley
CHIEF SECURITY ANALYST

---

[1] Although many types of analysis can be used, the use of a simple SWOT analysis (i.e., strengths, weaknesses, opportunities, and threats) is often the most effective and easiest to conduct—no special training is required, just critical thinking skills.

[2] For brevity, only two factors were considered. Other SWOT factors could be listed in a similar fashion. For instance, there are several combinations that can be used as the basis for formulating the "Target Plan" section:

- Strengths/Opportunities—Ways that law enforcement can use strengths so that opportunities can be realized.
- Weaknesses/Opportunities—Ways law enforcement can address weaknesses to provide relief so that opportunities can be pursued.
- Strengths/Threats—Ways law enforcement can use strengths to "offensively" moderate the threats.
- Weaknesses/Threats—Are there defensive actions that law enforcement can implement that will protect against threats?

Key Words and Phrases

The key words and phrases associated with this chapter are listed below. Demonstrate your understanding of each by writing either a short definition or a one- or two-sentence explanation.

person of interest   target profile
Kipling method

Study Questions

1. List the key parts of a target profile and briefly explain the types of information that would appear in each section.

2. Explain why analysts need to be conscious about the use of intelligence-related terms in their reports.

Learning Activity

Research an organized crime–related issue that is currently receiving public attention—this could be state/province-based or it could be national or international. For instance, issues like drugs or arms trafficking, people smuggling, money laundering, racketeering, outlaw motorcycle gangs, and so on, are topical. Now, with this information, select a target profile type (e.g., target profile of an individual, problem profile, criminal business profile, gang profile, terrorist organization profile) and then create the profile. Refer to the example target profile provided in this chapter and endnote 6 for guidance.

Notes

1. Contrast the reports discussed here with the national security policy assessments (i.e., strategic intelligence assessments) or long-form report, discussed in chapter 15.
2. Warrick, *The Triple Agent*, 69.
3. Rudyard Kipling's poem, "I Keep Six Honest Serving-Men." See, for example, *Animal Stories* (Cornwall, UK: The House of Stratus, 2011), 134. The method is also known by journalists and law enforcement investigators as the *Five Ws and H* (and is sometimes abbreviated as 5W1H).
4. James S. Major, *Writing Classified and Unclassified Papers for National Security* (Lanham, MD: Scarecrow Press, 2009), 8.

Chapter 10

Operational Assessments

An operational assessment is a type of intelligence report that takes a wider view of a situation than does the target profile, which is tactical in its scope. Although not in the league of a strategic assessment, the objective of this type of report is to shift the emphasis away from being reactive to being anticipatory. Whereas the target profile focuses on an individual (or company or organization), the operational assessment looks at the problem in a broader way. The audience for an operational assessment would be a whole-of-agency group that deals with tasking or an interagency group responsible for coordinating assets across several organizations (which could include agencies at different levels of government, or sectors—for example, military and law enforcement).

For example, if a target profile examines Jack KNIFE, who is involved in drug trafficking, then an operational assessment may look at not only where KNIFE fits into this picture but the extent to which the drugs are trafficked, those involved (buying and selling), the social and economic impact on the community from the direct effects of the illicit drugs, and the indirect and consequential effects of the ill-gotten profits on, say, corrupting legitimate business, political, or regulatory officials.

Operational versus Strategic Assessments

Although an operational assessment has the hallmarks of a strategic assessment that will be discussed in chapter 15, it falls short of its companion because it focuses on short-term objectives that would result from immediate action to prevent further illegal or otherwise unwanted activity. A strategic assessment looks at a longer time frame and usually features several recommendations that, in combination, need to be put in place to defend against the threat, or to neutralize it, or to treat a risk.

Agencies will have their own house style for this type of report (and it may even be known under a variation of this name), but it will follow this template to a large degree. Analysts may optimize the sections and format to suit the intelligence project they are working on. Because the life span of an operational assessment is short, a new or revised report may have to be required to be produced weekly or monthly, whereas a strategic assessment is a unique report on a specific topic.

Operational or Tactical Assessments

Although these analytic reports are termed *operational assessments*, they have been referred to as *tactical assessments*. If the issue under investigation is broader than what is happening at the tactical level (e.g., investigation and apprehension), but not prognostic as strategic intelligence would be (i.e., long-term implications), then it is operational. However, some agencies have used the term *tactical*,[1] and in previous editions of this book that term was used. This anomaly has been corrected here to avoid confusion.

It is worth being mindful that, like a target profile (discussed in chapter 9), other names can be applied to operational assessments depending on the issues under investigation. Take, for instance, these examples: *criminal business assessment*, *terrorist organization assessment*, or a name relating to a specific crime problem, like a *stolen vehicle assessment*. Variations and adaptation can be applied to suit the topic being studied. But whatever is used, it needs to be clear what type of report it is and that it is different from a target profile or a strategic assessment, which are at the other two ends of the report continuum.

. . . .

The value of [operational assessments] to law enforcement administrators beyond the immediate arrest and prosecution can be extremely important in determining how, where, and with what degree of intensity resources should be allocated.[2]

. . . .

Key Parts of an Operational Assessment
Introduction

This section provides brief details about the legal basis or agency policy which gives the analyst authority to compile the report, and the name of the authorizing officer (e.g., the intelligence unit's manager), date, and file number for audit purposes.

Background

The report's introduction section will contain a statement of the assessment's objective as well as a description of how the problem or issue under investigation arose. Like a target profile, this section needs to provide an acknowledgment of the legal basis or agency policy that provides the authority for compiling the report and the name of the authorizing officer (e.g., the chair of the tasking group or the officer in charge of the interagency committee).

Aim

The aim is the report's research question. It acts to guide the research and keep the inquiry focused on a specific issue (as well as what is in scope, and what is not). This helps keep the investigation from "wandering" into areas that could be interesting but not relevant to the outcome of the issues being perused.

Current Situation

This section is comparable to the various descriptive sections that appear after the background section but before the analysis section of a target profile. In fact, this section may comprise several subsections of descriptive data about the problem. These data can come from other intelligence reports (e.g., target profiles); open sources (e.g., library reference books and Internet searches); academic studies (PhD dissertations and master's theses); or articles in scholarly journals, books, or government publications (e.g., bureau of statistics), to cite a few.

In addition to describing the phenomenon, the analyst can explain the ramifications of the problem in its historical, social, economic, political, religious, cultural, or anthropological context and its extent in the jurisdiction (e.g., the region, the nation, or around the globe). But it is important not to interpret the information here in this section—that comes after analysis, in the prognosis section. The analyst could explain any progress being made, pitfalls encountered during the investigation, or the implementation of interventions to date. This information sets the scene for the next section, which is the analysis.

Analysis

As in the analytic section of the target profile, this is where analysts present the results of their analysis using techniques such as statistical analysis, network analysis, force field analysis, SWOT, PESTO, or others depending on the scope of the research question.

Prognosis

The prognosis section is essentially a discussion of the analysis but extrapolates from the findings to assess what is revealed about the activity under investigation and what can be done to provide relief. The analyst may consider a change in focus from what is or was being done to a modified or new approach, or a shift in priorities using the same interventions, and so forth.

It is common to present this discussion within the frame of the results of the analysis. Although framed in the logical order of the analysis, this is an exercise in deductive reasoning in a narrative form—or "thinking out loud" about each of the issues discovered in the analytic process that preceded it.

To produce a range of options for decision makers to consider, this section talks about the agency's strategic mission/goals or key performance indicators (KPIs) and how possible interventions may impact these benchmarks. Decision makers around the conference table can then argue priorities and resources according to "what works," "best value," or "best practice." Issues that might be discussed in the prognosis section could be generated from any one (or more) of the topics contained in the *five Is model*:

- Intelligence: Issues relating to information gathering, collation, and analyzing (past or future);
- Intervention: Tactics to block, disrupt, weaken, or eliminate "the problem";
- Implementation: Translating the goal of the proposed intervention (theory or principles) into practical methods in the field;
- Involvement: Ways to get other agencies (or companies, organizations, and individuals) to contribute somehow to being part of the implementation of the intervention(s); and
- Impact: How the problem will be evaluated and by whom. The evaluation may be simple or complex, but as the problem is one of an operational nature, a basic evaluation is most likely all that is needed (i.e., an output-based evaluation rather than one that is outcome focused).

Recommendations

Intelligence managers dealing with operational issues that are within the scope of this type of assessment will require options for consideration. Stemming from the previous section, the analyst needs only restate the range of options available. This can appear in the form of a bulleted list to simplify what is possible. If there is a preferred option, this can be highlighted in some way—for instance, appearing first in the list with the other options appearing in a list below in diminishing order, with the least preferred at the end.

To help frame a set of recommendations, you can use the straw man technique discussed in the text box below. This technique allows decision makers to understand the strengths/benefits of a goal-orientated option when contrasted with other options. In doing so the sage words of former U.S. director of National Intelligence—Lieutenant General James Clapper (USAF retired)—should be heeded: "There is an unwritten, almost sacred writ of intelligence professional that we in intelligence should avoid engaging in policy formation or execution. We support policy makers by providing them with timely, accurate, relevant, even anticipatory intelligence, but we don't participate in making the policy sausage."[3]

Straw Man Technique

One method to help decision makers make astute decisions is to use the straw man technique. The way this is done is to draft a goal-orientated proposal or solution (i.e., the straw man) and place it among a range of alternative options (this can range from the gold standard through to the do-nothing option). The analyst then discusses the relevant option by pointing out the shortcomings of the alternative recommendations. That is, by discussing how parts of the various options do not meet the goal of the operation/project. It is important that the shortcomings of the alternative options are discussed in relation to the operation/project's goal. The critiquing process should not be steeped in manipulative or emotional language or done by selectively choosing points to be discussed because this will undermine the credibility of what should be a timely, accurate, and relevant report.

In this way, the straw man technique is a beneficial process as it can provide a springboard for exploring other operational possibilities. Presenting recommendations in this way allows the decision maker to understand the strengths/benefits of the goal-orientated option when contrasted with other possibilities. It can also facilitate some idea generation by the decision maker who may then request modifications to the preferred option based on considerations that were beyond the privy of the analyst (e.g., political, social, cultural, historical, economic, or other factors). Regardless, the straw man approach to making recommendations increases the chances that the decision maker will be more comfortable with and, hence, "own" the final choice.

Appendixes

Because an operational assessment is a focused report like the target profile, the attachments that may be included need to be kept to a minimum. Examples might include a map, a photograph, or an organizational chart showing complex relationships that can be more helpful than a drawn-out narrative.

General Considerations for Operational Reports

While writing the intelligence report, avoid placing facts, inferences, recommendations, and analysis within the same sections. Consider using a *funnel approach* to write the report. That is, start from the general, work to the specific—like the shape of a funnel.

Each section needs to help explain the "story" so the narrative flows logically. If a section of the report discusses the current situation, it could contain the facts that are known. The analysis section that follows takes these facts and subjects them to one or more analytic techniques so that insight can be developed. This analysis should also place some level of likelihood/probability on these scenarios (or hypotheses) with discussion about the limits (e.g., based on, say, a risk or inferential analysis). This narrative would then lead the reader to the plan/recommendations section—like a funnel. Or simply, it's a story that has a beginning, middle, and an end.

Unlike fictional stories, the beginning of an intelligence story contains facts—what, why, when, how, where, and who (following the Kipling method). The middle tends to contain analysis, and the end contains the report's conclusions, recommendations for action, or policy options, all of which can appear in a variety of forms (often prescribed by the employing agency in a standardized template).

Analysts should resist the temptation to append their analytic results at the end of the report, as it could mean they failed to refer to them in the narrative (i.e., to help explain the story). Alternatively, referring the reader to peruse the appendices is getting the reader to do the job of the analyst.

In the same vein, tables of data or matrices should not be simply dropped into the analysis section of the report, as a lot of detail is often contained in these. It is better to summarize the key aspects of these analyses and, in case the reader wants to see the big picture or how you arrived at your conclusion, place the diagram or other figure/table in an appendix.

The reason for suggesting this writing approach is that the key points become the basis on which the analyst will make recommendations. Presenting the assessment's recommendations as a set of options is an important aspect of the report. Couching the options in terms of a threat assessment, a risk assessment, a budget, or the human resources available are excellent approaches. To the reader, such features make the recommendations actionable.

These guidelines are not hard-and-fast but following them will increase the likelihood that the message contained in an intelligence report will be understood by decision makers and, if so, acted upon.

| TEXTBOX 10.1 | Example of an Operational Assessment |

~Secret~

Date: April 1, 2019
Authorizing Officer: Director, Criminal Intelligence Analysis
                             Organization (CIAO)
Crime Analysis: Organized Crime Group (Delta X-Ray Analytic
                             Team)
In the matter of: Section 50, Anti-People Smuggling Act, 2002
File: I-0038/2019

Background

Six weeks ago, the International Organized Crime Group (Delta X-Ray) was tasked with developing a target profile on Lucien DEJAY in relation to an allegation that he was involved in a criminal enterprise to smuggle people. This criminal enterprise was alleged to have been operating in France, the United Kingdom (UK), the United Arab Emirates (UAE), and the Republic of India. The results of the target profile analysis supported the hypothesis that there is a criminal enterprise in operation that is smuggling groups of people from Port Sudan on the Red Sea to Abu Dhabi via ship, and then transporting these people in cargo containers over land via truck to the UK. The report's findings suggested that DEJAY procures the services of a Hyderabad-based forger (GUNTER) to provide the critical travel documents for the people being smuggled.

Aim

The aim of this operational assessment is to assess whether the matter involving DEJAY is an isolated case of people smuggling or whether there are other criminal enterprises operating in this illicit industry.

Current Situation[1]

People smuggling is the illegal transportation of people across international borders. This happens either in secret (covert) or clandestinely (openly under deception). It usually requires some false travel and/or identity documents and involves a person or group that facilitates the operation. The facilitator is paid for their services, which include the obtaining of the false documentation.

It is important to note that people smuggling differs from *people trafficking*, which has been described as modern-day slavery. People trafficking is characterized by force and coercion, sometimes coupled with deception, where the subject people are deprived of freedom and placed in a position of debt bondage. The most common forms of people trafficking involve sex exploitation and labor exploitation. People trafficking is not the subject of this assessment.

Research shows that there is no one single reason why people consent to being smuggled across borders, but the chief reasons include new social or employment opportunities or reuniting with family in the destination country.

The fees paid to people smugglers can be many times the cost of legitimate travel, and there is no guarantee that the smuggler will fulfill their promise to carry out the smuggling operation or, if they do, there is no assurance the operation will be successful. Anecdotal evidence shows that people pay smugglers between $4,000 for a wholly land-based infiltration to $75,000 for an operation involving sea travel. Case studies show that seaborne attempts at people smuggling end in capsized boats and sometimes mass drowning. The rescue and hospitalization of people overboard (see figure 10.1) and the subsequent investigations into the incidents are costly and time consuming for authorities. Land-based smuggling cases show that people have been killed through asphyxiation and heat—again, consuming large amounts of public resources to deal with the aftermath of the tragedy.

FIGURE 10.1 Rescue of a woman overboard by Hong Kong police.

People who contract the smuggler's services can be subject to physical and/or sexual violence en route. These people can also be subject to blackmail by the smugglers once they enter the destination country for fear of exposure of their illegal residence status, though this is not universal and appears to be in a small number of cases.

The current case involving DEJAY has the hallmarks of a classic people-smuggling operation. The target profile compiled by the Delta X-Ray analytic team of the Organized Crime Group supports such a hypothesis, and its report provides compelling evidence to back this proposition. Since the target profile was developed, Interpol has communicated its intent to conduct a criminal investigation into the matter.

Because people-smuggling operations are conducted in secret, it is difficult to know the exact scale or number of criminal enterprises involved. However, researchers studying this phenomenon estimate that as many as 800,000 people may have entered the European Union in the last calendar year. This estimate is based on a UN methodology that highlights its tenuous conclusion but considers it a reasonable approximation. This indicates a very low risk of capture, and official statistics support this.

Studies show that nearly all countries are affected by people smuggling by being either a country of origin or a destination country. This has the effect of increasing the chances of crime and corruption in countries touched by the smuggling operations because of the large profits that are generated from the enterprise.

Analysis[2]

The purpose of this operational assessment was to assess whether the DEJAY matter is an isolated event or whether this activity is likely to involve other criminal enterprises. When the facts presented above were weighted in a pros-and-cons analysis (see table 10.1), there was an overwhelming amount of evidence to support the conclusion that the DEJAY matter is not isolated.

It could be concluded that there is a strong probability that other smugglers are operating in or through the jurisdiction overseen by the CIAO.

TABLE 10.1 Summary of Pros and Cons

Pros	Cons
• Smuggling is performed covertly and clandestinely.	• Disproportional cost when compared to legal travel.
• Participants are willing subjects.	• Dangerous.
• The rewards are very high.	• Possibly of being caught (low).
• High likelihood of success (low risk of being caught).	• Possibility of being hurt or exploited (low).
• Enforcement agencies cannot cover all the ports and border crossing effectively due to the numbers involved.	
• Payment to corrupt officers lessens the likelihood of detecting smuggling operations.	

It could also be concluded that, given the geographic location this jurisdiction plays in a seaborne transportation route, the amount of money involved is at the higher end of the UN estimate and this, in turn, increases the likelihood of fueling graft and corruption within the jurisdiction. For instance, if the UN estimate of the number of people smuggled into the European Union at 800,000 is reflective of the magnitude of the problem, and a conservative estimate for the cost is calculated at $10,000 per person, then this equates to a $8 billion per year industry.

Prognosis

Although the director of the Criminal Intelligence Analysis Organization has authorized CIAO to join the task force probing the DEJAY allegation (tactical goal), the priority question for the agency is whether the current matter is isolated or is the issue wider spread (operational objective). This assessment concludes that the problem is more than likely to be far greater than a single criminal enterprise, and, given the potential scale of this illicit industry, it is likely to be an ongoing problem that will have implications for other crimes faced by the community.

Recommendations

At this juncture it is important to understand the extent of the people-smuggling business within the jurisdiction. This is an intelligence issue, and, as such, the Strategic Analytic Team (Delta Bravo) of the Organized Crime Group should be tasked to develop a strategic assessment.

The strategic assessment should describe the role the jurisdiction plays in the smuggling process—source, destination, transshipping, facilitating, or other. It should also include an estimate of the size of the problem in terms of number of crime enterprises, the volume of people being trafficked, as well as the ramifications in terms of secondary forms of crime or crimes committed consequentially within the jurisdiction. Finally, the assessment should provide a range of options for addressing each of the issues raised in the report.

Oliver Yardley

Oliver Yardley
CHIEF SECURITY ANALYST

---

[1] This section of the sample report has been abbreviated to demonstrate the type of information that could be presented and the way it should be written. If this was an actual case, this section might be two or three times the length it is, and the narrative would be supported by actual references to the scholarly literature that supports the facts or assertions made. Regarding in-text referencing, it is suggested that the author-date (Harvard) style of referencing be used. This is one of the easiest to use and produces an uncluttered appearance in the text. This has the effect of not slowing down the reader while still offering substantiation to claims and assertions made. There are many free guides that explain the Harvard method of referencing on the Internet.

2 Like the abbreviated "current situation" section of the example report, the analysis section may be longer and contain a more detailed summary of the analysis. But, for the purposes of demonstrating how such a section might look, the information provided here is enough.

Key Words and Phrases

The key words and phrases associated with this chapter are listed below. Demonstrate your understanding of each by writing either a short definition or a one- or two-sentence explanation.

Five Is model   operational assessment
funnel writing approach

Study Questions

1. List the key parts of an operational assessment and briefly explain the types of information that would appear in each section.

2. Explain why using a "funnel" approach to writing reports is a useful method.

Learning Activity

Using the target profile developed in chapter 9's learning activity, continue your research on the issue you selected. Using that target profile and the additional information you have discovered on your topic, create an operational assessment. Refer to the sample operational assessment provided in this chapter and endnotes 3 and 4 for assistance.

Notes

1   See, for instance, the United Kingdom's *National Intelligence Model*.
2   Justin J. Dintino and Frederick T. Martens, *Police Intelligence Systems in Crime Control* (Springfield, IL: Charles C Thomas, 1983), 114.
3   James R. Clapper with Trey Brown, *Facts and Fears: Hard Truths from a Life in Intelligence* (New York: Viking, 2018), 49.

Chapter 11

Vehicle Route Security Report

Although the concept of vehicle route analysis will be discussed here in terms of military and paramilitary operations, the concepts apply equally to those operating in other security environments. For instance, an analyst could carry out such an analysis regarding, say, a threat of kidnapping or vehicle hijacking, or by prison intelligence regarding breakout/escape attempts during transport.

It is an invaluable way of thinking for those who recognize that preparation is the best form of defense, and in relation to forces operating in zones that are engaged in the Global War on Terror, it is vital. People are vulnerable while traveling between secure locations.[1] Nevertheless, for personnel who are operating in "zones of dispute"—say, urban areas of industrialized countries where gang violence is prevalent—a vehicle route security report will be important. As history attests, many political assassinations have taken place while the target was in a vehicle; "Archduke Francis Ferdinand, King Alexander I of Yugoslavia, Pancho Villa, John F. Kennedy, Anastasio Somoza, and Rafael Trujillo were all killed while in automobiles."[2]

The analytical process for considering vehicle route security is not only a structured way of thinking but a practical skill for security operatives. Although this analytic method will have primacy with military audiences, it will also be important to security personnel who work in close personal protection. Moreover, it will be vital to intelligence officers engaged in the planning of vehicle or convoy travel through questionable safe areas. Arguably, this is because vehicle route analysis is at the heart of all vehicle movement—whether it is a single one-off passenger "pick-up and drop-off" or a multivehicle motorcade carrying VIPs to various meetings over several days.

Planning Framework

In the 1960s, Brazilian communist revolutionary Carlos Marighella, wrote a handbook that is one of the watershed texts for terrorists. In his *The Mini-Manual of the Urban Guerrilla*, Marighella asserted that superior security forces can be defeated if the attacker can compensate for their weaknesses. To do this, Marighella's strategy was fivefold: (1) take the enemy by surprise; (2) know the terrain better than the enemy; (3) have greater speed and mobility than the enemy; (4) have better information (i.e., intelligence) than the enemy; and (5) be in command of the situation.[3] Knowing how outlaws set up an ambush, the planning framework for route analysis takes into account nine interrelated mitigating plans. These plans, in turn, form a stepwise method for how an analyst or operative conducts vehicle route security analysis.[4] Step by step, an analyst conducts:

1. map reconnaissance;
2. travel surface analysis;
3. hazard analysis;
4. attack site analysis;
5. attack type analysis;
6. vehicle hardening plan;
7. countersurveillance plan;
8. crisis response planning; and
9. communications plan.

This framework needs to be placed into a geography-independent context—that is, these steps apply regardless of whether the vehicle under protection is traveling through one of the world's major cities or through a war zone.

FIGURE 11.1   Hyderabad, as well as other large cities around the world, poses a challenge for vehicle route analysis.

But, the geography context will be different—vehicles carrying VIPs through, say, Amherst, Massachusetts, will be different from the same convoy traveling through Hyderabad, India (see figure 11.1).

Key Process in a Vehicle Route Analysis
Map Reconnaissance

So how does this analytic process work? First, map reconnaissance is conducted, which enables analysts to determine several alternative routes to and from the destination.[5] Having more routes introduces an unpredictable variable to help foil a hostile threat. Route data can be gleaned from a variety of maps—publicly available street directories, government-produced topographical maps, commercial or classified satellite photographs, and maps used by utility companies (yes, Internet-based mapping facilities[6] can be used, but the limitations regarding accuracy/currency of the maps used must be considered in the conclusions that are drawn).

This approach is encouraged because it combines data to gain a greater understanding of the route's total features. Ideally, if some form of geospatial mapping system is available, this would be the analyst's best method. If not, the time-honored overlay mapping system will perform adequately (whether this is via flipcharts or electronic presentation using computer projection software).

Travel Surface Analysis

Considering road surface options is an important part of the overall analytic process, because driving conditions differ for the same road surface. For instance, an otherwise perfectly passable dirt road in the dry season could present a very difficult hazard if only a few centimeters of rain fell by turning the top part of the road into a slippery sheet of mud, slowing vehicles or causing them to lose a substantial measure of maneuverability. This road condition could create a perfect killing zone for attackers.

Having analyzed several alternative routes, the safe havens associated with each, route hazards, and road surfaces features, the next aspect of the overall route plan is to analyze where each attack is likely. This is a more specific type of analysis based on the results of the other contributory analyses. It produces a set of descriptive narratives (or diagrammatic figures) that identify the most probable kill zones—where on the route an attack might start and finish, and the areas likely to conceal the threat.

Hazard Analysis

Hazard analysis identifies any areas along the travel route that might pose a direct danger by, say, placing a restriction on a vehicle's movement (choke points) or providing cover for a person or group who may threaten an attack (i.e., *threat agents*, as will be discussed in chapter 12). It also identifies any areas along the route that might present an indirect hazard by providing support to the danger posed, thus allowing a threat agent to use an open area for the attack. For instance, a restriction could be as simple as a traffic light, stop sign, or highway under/overpass—anything that gives a potential threat agent the ability to control the area as the vehicles pass. The route should be considered from both directions—to the venue, which represented the vehicle's perspective, and from, which will require the analyst to think like an attacker.[7]

Examples of indirect hazards could be a highly built-up urban development along an otherwise clear stretch of roadway. Although the roadway would not be a good place to launch an attack, the attackers could launch a hit-and-run attack and then quickly disappear into the adjacent "urban jungle," thus avoiding identification, capture, or engagement with the vehicle security detail. Travel hazards are features that either impede a vehicle's ability to change course or impose control over a vehicle, restricting its movement to a course that makes it more vulnerable.

Attack Site Analysis

The analyst needs to research the groups that operate in the areas the vehicle or convoy will travel and apply these data in the context of the route's vulnerable points and surface conditions. Whether this process is via scenario building or the analyst's agency's preferred method of theorizing is not critical. What is important is to acknowledge that there are several possible attack variants and that each should be considered—urban static attacks, urban moving attacks, rural static, rural moving, and attack sites for stand-off weapons.

In conducting this type of analysis, it is important to distinguish whether the threat agents are insurgents or guerrillas, or if they are regular military forces. This is because the sites they select may be vastly different. Take, for instance, an attack by regular military forces—this might include ambush via air using helicopter gunships or mortars, whereas a group of local insurgents may select sites where they can use an improvised explosive device, a rocket-propelled grenade launcher, or sniper fire using small arms.

Attack Type Analysis

The type of attack that is likely is based largely on experience. Research shows that attackers tend to use methods that they are at ease with; hence it is likely that the threat will employ weaponry and tactics they have used before. For example, there are groups that have used improvised explosive devices, while others prefer stand-off attacks using sniper weapons or rocket-propelled grenades.

There are many possible types of attacks, from roadblocks to set up a hit-and-run ambush to assaulting an entire convoy in one kill zone. It is important to canvass all possibilities using an idea generation technique, such as brainstorming, and then assess the results using a technique like competing hypothesis (see chapter 6).

Vehicle Hardening Plan

If attack issues are found to present a danger to the vehicle or convoy through one of the proceeding analyses, then the vehicle or convoy may require hardening to mitigate the risks. As there are as many methods of adding protection to vehicles as there are vehicle types, the specifics will not be discussed here. Nevertheless, it is adequate to say that an automotive engineer or mechanic should be consulted to determine the type of armament that can be installed to afford the level of protection required.

Adding protective shielding is not a simple matter as the vehicle's capabilities need to be factored into the fortified design. Factors such as the vehicle's weight-carrying ability and its steering, accelerating, and braking performance need to be carefully considered.[8]

Countersurveillance Planning

To draw all this thinking together is to assess the advantages of using countersurveillance operative(s) at fixed location(s) along the route. This countermeasure is contingent upon the analyst's assessment of not only the overall travel risk but a realistic assessment of how much benefit countersurveillance will have.

Remember that deploying covert field operatives may place these personnel in harm's way, creating an even more dangerous situation—they may be kidnapped, tortured, or killed. Clearly this decision would need to be done in consultation with the leaders of the countersurveillance team and the vehicle security detail.

Analysts should also consider camouflage, concealment, and deception as a means of foiling surveillance. Camouflage, of course, is designed to help the vehicle blend into the surroundings. Traditionally, this is thought of as snow, woodland, jungle, or desert camouflage. However, if the vehicle or convoy is operating in the urban area of a foreign city, it may mean making the vehicle look like those of the local inhabitants that are traversing the city's streets.

Concealment can be as simple as covering the load of a vehicle with a tarpaulin to conceal the goods being carried. And deception can be any tactic that diverts the attention of a threat agent away from the vehicle or convoy—for example, a dummy convoy that leaves minutes early so the attacker's surveillance team sends the assailants in a different direction.[9]

Crisis Response Plan

Having done this, the next step is to develop a crisis response plan for each choke point or route hazard. It is a predetermined set of guidelines that provides the driver with the procedure to be followed if attacked at each vulnerable point. It provides options for the best direction for exiting, how far the next safe haven is, whom to call for assistance, and, most importantly, which roads not to take.

In planning for calls for assistance, the proposal should allow for handheld radio transceivers to be carried in the vehicle. Should the occupants have to abandon the vehicle and prepare for escape and evasion on foot, a handheld radio will be invaluable for providing details of the situation and coordinating a rescue (see communications plan below).

Scheduled halts need to be factored into these plans if the vehicle or convoy will be traveling for several hours. A stop of about fifteen minutes after the first hour is required to help maintain concentration and alertness. Thereafter, a stop of about ten minutes every two hours is required. When these stops are planned, location, cover, rapid egress, and provisions for human comforts need to be considered regarding the overall safety concerns.

In determining the travel hazard options and crisis response plan, an analysis also needs to be conducted of the surfaces the vehicles will be traveling over. This analysis will need to consider conditions for various seasons (if the passengers will be transported over a long period of time) or for the different conditions that are likely during the season the route is used (for shorter-term taskings).

Communications Plan

Providing a situation report (sitrep) on the progress of the vehicle or convoy is fundamental. Usually these reports go to some form of operations center. Therefore, the two-way radio equipment needs to be robust. It needs to be manufactured to military specifications—it cannot include the off-the-shelf commercial-quality radios that are sold through retail outlets. This is because "mil-spec" (or "mil-std" for short) equipment is designed to tolerate dust, heat, cold, and vibration to much higher levels than common commercial-grade radios. Mil-spec radios are sold on the commercial market but are advertised as "public safety" radios and marketed to police, fire, and emergency services.

The type of radio needs to be determined in this plan too—UHF[10] radios do not have the range of HF[11] sets. Such a consideration is a critical factor if the vehicle or convoy is traveling several hundreds of kilometers as opposed to traveling ten kilometers to the next township. UHF radios may also suffer in deep ravines, during thick sandstorms, or if there is dense smoke, whereas VHF[12] radios may perform somewhat better in these conditions. A radio engineer needs to be consulted to help determine the most suitable equipment as well as the frequencies for the operation. It might be determined that a transceiver for each band (i.e., HF, VHF, and UHF) should be installed in the vehicles. Procedures for each band and frequency can then be selected for either the entire mission, parts of the mission, or in emergency situations.

Once equipment requirements have been determined, a set of radio call signs needs to be established, with check-in times and frequencies specified. Moreover, code words for emergency and routine events need to be understood, and all radio operators need to be briefed on the times/areas where radio silence is to be maintained, if required.

If vehicles are traveling in a convoy, then the communications plan needs to specify the frequencies and procedures for intra-convoy communications, perhaps using UHF frequencies, as these lessen the chance that these signals can be intercepted at distance, as discussed in endnote 5. These radios will usually be secondary sets mounted in the vehicle and operating on different frequencies than that being used for communications back to the operations center (i.e., on HF[13] and/or VHF).

Handheld radios also need to be incorporated into the plan as part of the crisis response plan. If personnel need to evacuate the vehicles in an emergency, then the vehicles' mounted radios will be of no value for providing details of the emergency, location status (locstat), or situation report (sitrep).[14]

Supplements

While developing the various analyses that contribute to the overall vehicle route analysis, analysts are likely to consider it necessary to append material that does not fit neatly into the narrative of the body of the report. Maps, diagrams, and aerial photographs immediately come to mind, but there could be other material too: for instance, photographs of safe houses, threat agents, route hazards, and so on. If there is such material, these pieces of information can be appended to the end of the report and referred to in the appropriate section. This type of information can help aid understanding and provide reference in case of emergency—an example could be a list of emergency frequencies.

| TEXTBOX 11.1 | Example of a Vehicle Route Analysis |

~Secret~

Date:	February 28, 2019
Authorizing Officer:	Director, Criminal Intelligence Analysis Organization (CIAO)
Analysis:	Anti-Terrorist Strike Team (Uniform X-Ray Bravo)
In the matter of:	Section 43(c), Countersubversion Act, 2012
File:	I-0092/2019

TASK

The Assault Unit for the Neutralization of Terrorism (AUNT) has requested the Criminal Intelligence Analysis Organization (CIAO) to provide a route plan for the April 1 meeting between Police Colonel Omar Rahman, who will oversee the surrender of arms by the Omen Martyrs Faction in his country, and Director General AUNT. The meeting will be in Tunisia, a neutral country to the dispute. The venue will be the Le Golf Restaurant, located less than 15 kilometers (<9.3 miles) for the Tunis–Carthage International Airport.

STUDY FINDING

The investigation into this issue concludes that the route Director General AUNT will take will be safe and poses negligible risk to the security of her convoy on the day of the meeting.

ANALYSIS

Map Reconnaissance

There are two possible routes that the director general's convoy can take and are shown in figure 11.2.[1] The first is the shortest and most direct route (approximately 7.8 kilometers/4.8 miles), and the second is slightly longer at 13.5 kilometers (8.3 miles). The first route departs the airport's main entrance, tracks north and then east to the destination. The second route tracks south after leaving the airport entrance, then heads east, with a final turn to the north. The northern route is estimated to take 16 minutes in normal traffic and the southern about 20 minutes.

Travel Surface

The roads of both possible routes are, for the most part, dual carriageways with sealed surfaces that are suitable for all-weather conditions. There are neither road works in progress, nor any route planning at the time of the meeting. Neither road presents an issue with traversing the distance to the meeting location.

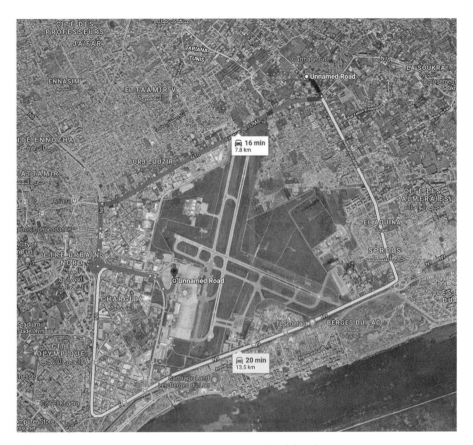

FIGURE 11.2   Two possible routes—north and south of the airport.

Hazards

Choke points accrue at each turn in both routes. In this regard they both have three hazardous points where the convoy will need to slow to negoti-ate the turns. The other hazard encountered in both routes is the urbanized streetscapes because the airport is located within the metropolis. In com-parison, the northern route presents numerically less built areas, and hence poses less of a risk. It is also the shortest distance to cover.

Attack Sites

Two attack site scenarios are possible—the first is for a static attack from a fixed location and the second, a mobile attack using some type of motor vehicle. Because the Omen Martyrs Faction has no ties to any protest groups in Tunisia, and intelligence reports confirm no past or present affiliation between any in-country parties, it is hypothesized that if an attack were to take place, it would be from a mobile platform. This is because, to execute a static attack, an attack site overlooking the route would need to be procured. But, without in-country assistance, this lessens the likelihood. It is more plausible that assailants would steal or hire a motorcycle, or other vehicle, and attack the convoy en route.

Attack Type

With no in-country support, the most likely type of attack is from handguns, shoulder-fired small arms, or a hand-thrown explosive device. This is because any plan to import more lethal stand-off weapons, or to purchase them in-country, is beyond the means of the Omen Martyrs Faction since it is a domestic group with no international connections.

Vehicle Hardening

Given that an attack, if it occurs, is likely to be a mobile attack using a handgun, a shoulder-fired small arm, or a hand-thrown explosive device, any of the Tunisia tactical police vehicle will provide more than adequate protection without shipping AUNT's armored car or making improvements to in-country vehicles.

Countersurveillance

To help deceive any possibility of an armed attack, it is recommended that a deception plan be incorporated into the convoy's route. This will take the form of a dummy convoy waiting at the airport's main terminal exit to present the impression that the director general of AUNT will be departing there ("B" in figure 11.3). However, the director general will mount the Tunisian tactical police vehicle at the aircraft and the vehicle will drive through the airport grounds to the northern utility vehicle access gate and enter the Avenue de L'uma (shown as "A" in figure 11.3). From there, the director general's vehicle will make its way to the meeting venue while the director general's executive officer and advisor will walk to the convoy. They will present to the public that the executive officer is the director general. This convoy will then travel the northern route to the meeting. On the return trip, the same procedure will be followed, with the convoy and executive officer departing first, then the director general. Each will follow the route that they used to arrive. To add authenticity to the "ghost" convoy, a National Guard Special Unit helicopter will shadow at about 300 feet to and from the meeting, leaving the director general's tactical police vehicle to appear as a support vehicle making its way independent of the convoy.

Crisis Response

A police command vehicle will be set up at the National Police club grounds on Avenue de L'uma ("C" in figure 11.3). This will also be the muster point for all convoy vehicles should there be an emergency. The police commander will be the net controller of all radio communications. Paramedics and advance first-aid facilities will be there, and there will be a temporary

FIGURE 11.3 Route deception gates "A" and "B." "C" police command vehicle.

helipad constructed. A medivac helicopter will be on the ground with its pilots ready. A unit of the Anti-Terrorist Brigade will be on standby within the compound, and an armed member of the unit will be aloft with the National Guard Special Unit helicopter.

Communications

Convoy vehicles will use the police unencrypted VHF frequencies to help with the counterintelligence deception (Tunisian police will program these radios for this task). However, the director general's police tactical vehicle will use encrypted mobile cellular telephony to communicate with the command vehicle. Should an emergency occur, a portable UHF repeater station will set up to pass emergency traffic, thus isolating all who may be listening to the frequency. All units will switch to this encrypted UHF frequency and respond to the instructions of the police commander.

Oliver Yardley

Oliver Yardley
CHIEF SECURITY ANALYST

---

[1] This photograph, as well as the two that appear in figure 11.3, are used with the permission of Google LLC.

Summary

Although we have examined the analytic considerations of route analysis, a more thorough understanding of other aspects of driving in high-risk areas would round off the discussion—whether it is driving in Hyderabad, Harare, Hartford, or Helsinki. The technical content of that discussion is likely to be based on real-life experiences. Therefore, if analysts and operatives can gain an understanding of the allied issues of route analysis, it would assist them in performing the various sub-analyses just outlined—for instance:

- vehicle dynamics;
- evasion maneuvers;
- pros and cons of vehicle armoring;
- motorcade defensive tactics;
- effecting an en route rescue;
- vehicle safety equipment; and
- conducting vehicle bomb searches.

Although the basics of how to conduct a route analysis were reviewed, doing so assumes a good deal of subject knowledge that is beyond the scope of this book. Nonetheless, understanding the theoretical framework suggests to those who are interested in performing this type of planning that they should acquire knowledge about such things as the history of where VIPs have been ambushed using explosives or small arms; where they have been kidnapped en route; or where they have been overrun during the attack; and so on.

Also, the interested analyst would benefit from seeking out books that discuss vehicle dynamics, evasion maneuvers, and armoring of a vehicle.[15]

Key Words and Phrases

The key words and phrases associated with this chapter are listed below. Demonstrate your understanding of each by writing either a short definition or a one- or two-sentence explanation.

attack site   hazard
attack type   reconnaissance
countersurveillance   travel surface
crisis response

Study Questions

1. Outline the seven steps for conducting a vehicle route analysis.
2. List three potential sources of geospatial information for a map reconnaissance.
3. Discuss why it is important to conduct a travel surface analysis.

Learning Activity

Suppose you have been asked to help construct a plan for a visiting VIP. The person will travel from the airport nearest to where you work and go to a meeting in a covert location 5 kilometers away. Using a map from one of the sources you identified in study question 2 above, draw a circle around the airport with a 5 kilometer radius. Now select a populated street somewhere along that radius line and, using the seven steps of vehicle analysis, create a plan. The plan need not be immensely detailed. What you are trying to achieve is an understanding of each of the elements that comprise the plan. Once compiled, reflect on these issues: Were you able to populate each sub-analysis to your satisfaction? If not, what was lacking—subject knowledge? More information about the area? Where might you find those details if you were to conduct this exercise as a real-world event? What subject knowledge might you want to feel confident in completing this type of analysis if it were not an exercise?

Notes

1   Anthony J. Scotti, "Defensive Driving Techniques," in *Providing Executive Protection*, ed. Richard W. Kobetz (Berryville, VA: Executive Protection Institute, 1991), 132.

2   Leroy Thompson, *Dead Clients Don't Pay: The Bodyguard's Manual* (Boulder, CO: Paladin Press, 1984), 57.

3   Carlos Marighella, *The Mini-Manual of the Urban Guerrilla* (Boulder, CO: Paladin Press, 1985), 13–19.

4   See, for instance, Robert H. Deatherage Jr., *Survival Driving: Staying Alive on the World's Most Dangerous Roads* (Boulder, CO: Paladin Press, 2006).

5   For more details on practice of reconnaissance, see Henry Prunckun, *How to Undertake Surveillance and Reconnaissance: From a Civilian and Military Perspective* (South Yorkshire: Pen & Sword Military, 2015).

6   If using a commercial mapping facility, analysts need to honor the terms of use that are stipulated by the map's copyright owner.

7   Benny Mares, *Executive Protection: A Professional's Guide to Bodyguarding* (Boulder, CO: Paladin Press, 1994), 38–39.

8   As an example, see U.S. Department of the Army, *FMI 3-07.22, Counterinsurgency Operations* (Washington, DC: U.S. Department of the Army, 2006).

9   For more on countersurveillance, see Prunckun, *Counterintelligence Theory and Practice, Second Edition.*

10   UHF is the abbreviation for *ultra-high frequency*. Frequencies in this part of the radio spectrum range from 300MHz to 3GHz (i.e., 3,000MHz). They exhibit line-of-sight (i.e., point-to-point) propagation and are an excellent choice if the signal needs to be "contained" so that it does not "stray" beyond the operational area. This could be important if the vehicles' signals may be monitored by third parties at some distance. If the monitoring station is not within line of sight, it reduces the chance of interception. Communications security can also be enhanced using voice encryption. Even commercial-grade encryption units provide a very high level of security, though it may not be to the classification of Secret or Top Secret. Nevertheless, if communications security is required for a short period of time (i.e., a matter of hours or a day), then any intercepted encrypted signals may not be able to be unencrypted in that time frame, and if they are eventually unencrypted, the operation would be over and the convoy safely at its destination. A radio engineer needs to be consulted about the technical specifications of such equipment and what it can offer the mission in terms of communications security. Signals in this band are affected by variables involving atmospheric conditions at ground level and terrain. However, because UHF possesses line-of-sight propagation properties, it is ideally suited for communications through satellites because these signals pass directly through the ionized layers of the upper atmosphere. If a communication satellite is available, UHF equipment may be suitable for intra-convoy communication (i.e., using a simplex frequency) as well as long-range communication (i.e., using duplex frequencies). See Martin Davidoff, *The Radio Amateur's Satellite Handbook* (Newington, CT: American Radio Relay League, 1997).

11   HF, or *high frequency*, spans from 3MHz to 30MHz, and it is a band that can deliver reliable communications that range from several kilometers to transcontinental distances. It is also known as the *shortwave* band. But because of the great distances these signals can travel, interception by third parties increases. See, for instance, Harry L. Helms, *How to Tune the Secret Shortwave Spectrum* (Blue Ridge Summit, PA: Tab Books, 1981), and Oliver P. Ferrell, *Confidential Frequency List*, fifth edition (Park Ridge, NJ: Gilfer Associates, 1982). Intelligence agencies continually monitor these bands, so if the convoy's radio traffic is sensitive in any way, one should assume some intelligence agency somewhere in the world may be monitoring (James Bamford, *The Puzzle Palace* [Boston: Houghton Mifflin Company, 1982]).

12   VHF refers to *very high frequency*. This band encompasses frequencies between 30MHz and 300MHz. It lies in between the HF band and the UHF band and is a useful band, as it is not as susceptible to atmospheric conditions and ground terrain as are signals in the UHF band.

13 Because of the nature of HF communications, it requires a large antenna. For instance, at 27MHz a quarter-wave antenna is 9 feet (2.6 meters). At 14MHz, this would be approximately 16 feet (5 meters). And at 5MHz, a vehicle-mounted quarter-wave antenna would be about 47 feet long (14 meters). Granted, HF antennas are usually "shortened" by the addition of loading coils and tuned via automatic tuning devices built into the radio sets, but the antennas are still very large. Their size makes the vehicle stand out and can act as a beacon calling attention to it and the convoy it is in.

14 The basics of emergency communications are covered in such texts as American Radio Relay League, *Emergency Communication Handbook*, ed. Steve Ford (Newington, CT: ARRL, 2005); and Michael Chesbro, *Communications for Survival and Self-Reliance* (Boulder, CO: Paladin Press, 2003).

15 See, for example, Ronald George Ericksen II, *Getaway: Driving Techniques for Escape and Evasion* (Port Townsend, WA: Loompanics Unlimited, 1983). This is an excellent slim-volume paperback that focuses on practical skills and realistic vehicle modifications.

Chapter 12

Threat Assessments

The purpose of a threat assessment is to identify problems that personnel and physical assets may face.[1] A *threat* is a person's resolve to inflict harm on another. It is important to note that a threat cannot be posed by a force of nature or a natural event—these are *hazards*. Only people can pose a threat because they need *intent* and *capability* (or organizations, associations, businesses, or other forms of corporates bodies because they are controlled by people), which will be explained shortly.

Threats can be made against most entities—people, organizations, and nations—by a *threat agent*. The potential harm can be in many forms and can be suffered either physically or emotionally/physiologically. Threat agents do not have to openly declare their resolve to cause harm to constitute a threat, though explicit words or actions make it easier for field operatives to identify the threat agent and for analysts to assess the level of threat.

Threat analysis acknowledges two key factors—that there needs to be a threat agent (which could be anything from a person to a group of people, or a body corporate/organization) and an object of the threat (i.e., the target, which does not have to be a material target such as a shopping mall or an individual; it can be intangible, such as the threat to the ability of a nation to govern, or the security of a particular venue or event). Stated another way, a threat agent who has intent and capability must be able to harm something. By way of example, a threat agent could be a drug trafficker who is intent on and capable of illegally importing, say, heroin; or a group of insurgents who have an intent and capability to destroy a bridge.

When analysts assess a threat agent, they are gauging whether the agent has *intent* and *capability* to produce harm to a target (therefore, naturally occurring phenomena cannot be threats). Intent can be defined as the optimism a threat agent has about successfully attacking a target; and capability as the amount of force a threat agent can bring to bear on a target.

To weigh whether the agent has intent and capability, analysts need to establish two essentials for each of these factors: *desire* and *expectation* (or *ability*) for intent, and *knowledge* and *resources* for capability. These considerations are shown diagrammatically in figure 12.1. As an equation, threat is expressed as:

$$(desire + expectation) + (knowledge + resources) = threat$$

Desire can be described as the threat agents' enthusiasm to cause harm in pursuit of their goal. Expectation is the confidence the threat agents have that they will achieve their goal if their plan is carried out. Knowledge is having information that will allow the threat agents to use or construct devices or carry out processes that are necessary for achieving their goal. Resources include skills (or experience) and materials needed to act on their plan.

A fishbone analysis could be used to show the factors that contribute to each of these factors in a cause-and-effect relationship. In a fishbone analysis the so-called fish's head lists the problem to be investigated—in this case, it is "threat." The major bones of the fish constitute the important categories of information concerning the problem—desire, expectation, knowledge, and resources. From each of these major bones, minor bones sprout, comprising the contributing factors that constitute each of the four categories. Other collection methods can be used depending on the analyst's personal preference—like mind mapping.

Analysts need to consider the context of the threat, their agency's mission, and the list of potential targets when adopting a model to aid them in determining the threat environment. A generic model for calculating threats might look something like the example summary shown in table 12.1. This model can

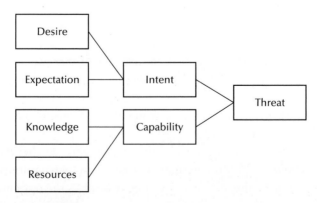

FIGURE 12.1   Threat analysis.

TABLE 12.1 Threat Posed to the Orrenabad Community by the Omen Martyrs Faction

Scale	Scores	Tally
Desire		
Negligible	1	
Minimum	2	
Medium	3	3
High	4	
Acute	5	
Expectation		
Negligible	1	
Minimum	2	
Medium	3	3
High	4	
Acute	5	
Total Intent		**6**
Knowledge		
Negligible	1	
Minimum	2	
Medium	3	3
High	4	
Acute	5	
Resources		
Negligible	1	
Minimum	2	
Medium	3	3
High	4	
Acute	5	
Total Capability		**6**
Threat Coefficient		**12**

be modified to suit the specific requirements of individual agencies or research projects.

Though models do not eliminate subjectivity, using a model requires analysts to be transparent in how they calculate threat and, in doing so, be able to defend their conclusions. You will note that there is no weighting attached to what constitutes, say, an acute or high level of intent. That is because one cannot say how many media announcements it would take from a newly constituted terrorist group to constitute such a level of intent. Ideally, some form of conditioning statement would be attached to each of these scale categories so that decision makers know what is meant by high intent, low intent, and so forth. An example of how a threat coefficient reference table could be constructed is shown in table 12.2.

In addition, models do not eliminate miscalculations because of inadvertent skewing. Note in table 12.1 that intent is calculated by adding desire with expectation, and, in turn, this sum is added to the sum of knowledge and resources (and will range from a low of 4 to the maximum of 20). The process of adding limits the spread of values, whereas the process of multiplying any of these scores would increase the values. For instance, if all scores were multiplied—that is, substituting multiplication for addition—as per the equation, the range would be spread from 1 to 625.

The precision of this wide range of values diminishes the analyst's ability to accurately determine either intent or capability. Therefore, it is suggested that adding all values, rather than multiplying them, will reduce the spread and, therefore, maintain the threat coefficient as an *indicator* rather than promote it as a reflection of its absolute condition. Even if the analyst multiplied desire and expectation and knowledge and resources but added the resulting sums, it would still yield a very wide spread (from 2 to 50)—as would the opposite, that is, multiplying the sums that comprise intent and capability, from 4 to 100.

TABLE 12.2 Examples of a Threat Coefficient Reference Table

Threat	Coefficient	Qualifier (i.e., conditioning statements)
Negligible	1–3	Threat has little or no desire, expectation, knowledge, and/or resources to carry out an attack; or, the threat possesses some of these factors but is missing several.
Minimum	4–6	Threat has some level of desire, expectation, knowledge, and/or resources to carry out an attack or is missing one factor.
Medium	7–9	Threat has demonstrated it has a modest level of desire, expectation, knowledge, and/or resources to carry out an attack.
High	10–12	There is evidence that the threat has an elevated level of desire, expectation, knowledge, and/or resources to carry out an attack.
Acute	13–15	The threat has attempted or carried out an attack before, or evidence shows that the threat possesses a very high level of desire, expectation, knowledge, and/or resources to carry out an attack.

Having said that, two additional issues need to be noted: (1) there is still a need to provide conditioning statements so that the reader of the intelligence report understands what is meant by a medium threat intent and capability (e.g., along the lines of table 12.2); and (2) "unknowns" are not accommodated in this model. Analysts should always be cognizant of unknowns in the form of what are termed *black swans*[2]—unexpected and unforeseeable events or, in this context, threat agents.

The threat coefficient obtained from this analysis is then compared against a reference table to gauge where it sits on the continuum of danger of attack. The scale suggested in table 12.3 can be varied with additional qualifiers, or it can be collapsed if the number is deemed too large. Likewise, how the incremental breakdown of coefficients is determined will depend on whether the agency is willing to accept the risk that a threat agent may slip under its gaze by raising the categories of negligible and minimum. In the end, the number and their descriptors need to make sense in the context of the asset being protected. That is, each of the descriptors needs to have a conditioning statement attached to it to define what is meant by negligible, minimum, medium, high, and acute (table 12.2 is an example).

Threats are context dependent, and what forms a threat in a business setting does not necessarily form a threat in a military setting or national security setting (though the opposite may be true). Bearing this in mind, an example from the military will be discussed to illustrate the threat analysis method. In a low-intensity conflict, threats can range from spontaneous street demonstrations by the local population at one end to terrorist bombings and confrontations with insurgent or guerrilla units at the other end. The techniques for assessing the threat factors can vary depending on the issue under investigation and the analyst's personal preference or the agency's policy.

Nevertheless, the approach is to weight each element using some verifiable means that is open to third-party scrutiny. For instance, an analyst may use a

TABLE 12.3 **Threat Coefficient Scale**

Threat Level	Coefficient
Negligible	4–6
Minimum	7–10
Medium	11–15
High	16–18
Acute	19–20

force field analysis to judge whether there are threats in Country Q associated with a low-intensity campaign being prosecuted by friendly military units. Likewise, the nominal group technique could be employed not only to assess the four factors of a threat (i.e., desire, expectation, knowledge, and resources) but also to generate a list of possible threat agents (i.e., belligerents) to compare the factors against each other. Participants for such a group could be drawn from subject experts or operational specialists or a mixture of both.

There is no firm rule on how this analysis should be done. One way of contextualizing threats is to see them as *threat communities*. Some examples of threat communities pertaining to malicious human threats include:

External

- Competitors;
- Common thefts;
- Conspiracy theorists and other advocates of pseudoscience beliefs;
- Local gangs;
- Organized criminal groups;
- International or transnational terrorists;
- Domestic terrorists (including offshoots);
- Insurgents and guerrillas;
- Anarchists;
- Domestic anarchists;
- Cyber criminals and cyber vandals;
- Radical political groups;
- Rights campaigners;
- Single-issue lobbyists;
- Spies-for-hire (i.e., former law enforcement, security, military, or intelligence personnel who have turned private operatives); and
- Foreign government intelligence services.

Internal

- Principals of the business or corporation;
- Associates;
- Current employees;
- Former employees;
- Temporary staff; and
- Contractors.

These threat communities can be subdivided into more distinct groups if there is a need—for instance, extremist rights campaigners could be classified into the following extremist subgroups: political extremists, religious extremists, single-issue extremists. But bear in mind that membership in one threat community (or subcommunity) does not exclude that person being a member of another or several other threat communities.

. . . .

When compiling a threat assessment, targets can and should be considered in terms of their criticality, cost (either as a direct loss or as an indirect or consequential loss due to disruption), or sensitivity (e.g., compromised information). This is because targets that do not possess any of these attributes may not be considered by threat agents with the same weight.

. . . .

Strategic, Operational, and Tactical Threats

Threats of a strategic nature could be argued to be potential *hazards*, not threats. This is because such issues have not manifested themselves into an expression of intent. Take, for example, a less than friendly country that might be constructing a nuclear facility that is several years away from completion. This construction project, the country explains, will be for peaceful purposes—electric power generation. However, given the construction design, nuclear subject experts have concluded that the facility and/or the material produced could also be used to make a nuclear weapon. So, in this case it would be correct to term this country's nuclear project a strategic hazard rather than a strategic threat; the government authorizing the project (and/or its military) would be the threat. The nuclear facility would be a factor in calculating capability (knowledge and resources).

In this regard, analysts should note that some scholars use the term *harm* instead of *hazard*. This is not the view adapted by this book because harm is seen as the result (real or potential) of some event or action (*harm* is also referred to as *impact* or *consequence*). Because harm is what has, will, or is likely to occur, it is viewed here as incorrect in this context. *Impact* (i.e., harm) is discussed in the next chapter on vulnerability analysis, and it is explained why that term is not correct in this context. It is recommended that analysts make themselves aware of the liberal use of these other terms but use the term *hazard* in intelligence briefings and reports.

The concept of a threat is normally reserved for matters that are either operational or tactical. For instance, an operational threat is an entity, such as an organization that is waging a campaign that is widely spread—like an organized crime group that is involved in the rebirthing of stolen motor vehicles. An example of a tactical threat is an individual or group who is the target of immediate action. Such actions might include prevention, detection, or enforcement. In some cases, actions taken to deal with tactical threats might impact an operational level threat. Using the rebirthing of stolen motor vehicles example, if law enforcers in, say, the New England area raid several individuals who are dismantling cars in their garages in adjoining states, these actions might impact organized crime in that area (an operational threat).

Threat assessments need to be adequate; perfection is rarely, if ever, obtainable. Consider the threat assessment example shown in table 12.4. It discusses the four factors that comprise a threat for a fictitious threat agent. The format of the assessment is not critical as long as the reader can understand the report's message. In this example, the assessment is presented in a table form, but it could also be presented in the form of a memorandum, narrative report, pro forma report template (i.e., "tick-box"), or a digital slide presentation.

TEXTBOX 12.1 | Example of a Threat Assessment

~Secret~

Date:	February 28, 2019
Authorizing Officer:	Director, Criminal Intelligence Analysis Organization (CIAO)
Crime Analysis:	Anti-Terrorist Strike Team (Uniform X-Ray Bravo)
In the matter of:	Section 43(c), Countersubversion Act, 2012
File:	I-0082/2019

Threat Assessment for the Omen Martyrs Faction

The Assault Unit for the Neutralization of Terrorism (AUNT) has requested the CIAO to help understand the threat the Omen Martyrs Faction presents. An investigation into the group's intent and capabilities was carried out and a summary of the study's findings are presented below in table 12.4.

Desire: The Omen Martyrs Faction operates as an autonomous entity that targets Western representations in its country as well and people who do not ascribe to the group's interpretation of its faith. Being educated, the group exhibits the attributes of having more than an average level of desire to inflict harm, estimated to be approximately 8 or 9 on a scale of 1 to 10.

Expectations: The group subscribes to a radical religious ideology that is not shared by the wider community in Orrenabad. It considers its mission to destroy objects that run counter to its dogmatic philosophic outlook; hence, it is targeting objects that can be physically destroyed. Being an educated group, its view is that self-sacrifice is accepted but only when need be (e.g., armed combat with its opponents). The reason for this approach is that the group expects to be successful in carrying out attacks and therefore wants to retain its valued members. These factors present to the study's analysts as reflecting a more-than-average level of expectation to succeed in an attack, estimated to be 7 or 8 on a scale of 1 to 10.

Knowledge: The group develops its attack plans based on target acquisition intelligence obtains from fixed and mobile surveillance that members conduct (to maintain operational security), as well as paid informants. Although the members are educated, they hold a low level of computer savvy,

TABLE 12.4 Threat Assessment for the Omen Martyrs Faction

Summary	Observations
Desire	
Targets	Objects that represent Western values or people who do not ascribe to their interpretation of their faith (including other believers)
Affiliation	Totally autonomous
Recruitment	Educated local ethnic population
Target characteristics	Symbolic and iconic objects with some level of visibility and, hence, media coverage
Tactics	Targets mass gathering, critical infrastructure, communications, mass transport, and distribution chains
Expectation	
Motivation	Radical religious ideology
Intent	Destruction
Tolerance to risk	Medium
Self-sacrifice	Somewhat accepting
Willingness to inflict collateral harm	Extreme
Knowledge	
Planning	Based on target acquisition intelligence through fixed and mobile surveillance, informants
Information	Open-source data collection as well as access to declassified military manuals
Training	Low-grade, informal facilities, though training standards are crude, knowledge transfer is effective
International	Training and ideological support, connections
Resources	
Financing	Extortion and kidnapping the wealthy
Weapons	Although it is adept in constructing improvised explosives and small arms, intelligence reports show it has recently acquired a numbers of anti-tank rockets
Skills	Attack vector dependent: • Computer-based—very low; • Electronic/communications—moderate; • Small arms—high; and • Explosives—very high.

so the group has access to open-source data, rather than to data obtained from computer penetrations. Training is effective, and the group has ties with international terrorist organizations. The study concluded that these factors reflected an average level of knowledge to conduct an attack, estimated to be between 4 and 6 on a scale of 1 to 10.

Resources: The group finances its operations by extortion and kidnaping wealthy people, mostly local businessmen. This tactic has yielded the group an estimated $3 million in the last financial year. It has access to small arms on the local black market, and its members have been trained in making improvised explosives. Although it has no demonstrated skills in computer hacking, the group has been monitored using encrypted two-way radios during operations. Using encryption suggests a high level of sophistication, but radio engineers were able to decrypt the signals because the device used by the group was only an off-the-shelf proprietary product. Recently, the group has acquired an unspecified number of anti-tank rockets that were smuggled across the Orrenabad border. Such factors reflected a very high level of resources available to the group that were estimated to be approximately an 8 or 9 on a scale of 1 to 10.

In conclusion, the Omen Martyrs Faction poses a level of threat that warrants both surveillance and police interdiction. This is because the group exhibits high levels of desire to cause harm and high levels of expectations that it can carry out attacks. The evidence gathered by this study makes the report confident in putting forward the proposition that the group has intent.

The Omen Martyrs Faction has an average level of knowledge to plan attacks, but from past operations this level of knowledge has not been an impediment since its intent is so strong. However, the group's resources are at a very high level and the fact that it now has stand-off weapons in the form of shoulder-launched rockets makes the group one of the more formidable groups in the region.

Oliver Yardley

Oliver Yardley
CHIEF SECURITY ANALYST

Key Words and Phrases

The key words and phrases associated with this chapter are listed below. Demonstrate your understanding of each by writing either a short definition or a one- or two-sentence explanation.

capability	knowledge
coefficient	resources
desire	threat
expectation	threat agent
intent	threat communities

Study Questions

1. List the factors that comprise a threat analysis. Explain why each is important to understanding a threat.

2. Explain why a threat cannot be a force of nature or a natural event.

3. Explain why it is important to have qualifiers, or conditioning statements, that define what is meant by the four threat factors, such as negligible, minimum, medium, high, and acute?

Learning Activity

It is unlikely that an actual threat assessment can be completed as a student assignment, but given that a threat assessment comprises four factors, it is possible to craft an abridged assessment using one or more of these factors to be able to gain an appreciation of what is involved in writing a threat assessment. So, for this learning activity, select one of the external threat communities discussed earlier in this chapter to focus your assessment. Using credible open-source information, obtain data about this possible threat that will help you analyze if any one of the four factors (desire, expectation, knowledge or resources) is present. Present your findings in a table format.

Notes

[1] James F. Broder and Gene Tucker, *Risk and the Security Survey*, fourth edition (Waltham, MA: Butterworth-Heinemann, 2012), 316.

[2] See, for example, a discussion of such unknowns in several contexts: Nassim Nicholas Taleb, *The Black Swan: The Impact of the Highly Improbable* (New York: Random House, 2007).

Chapter 13

Vulnerability Assessments

Vulnerability can be described as a weakness in an *asset* that can be exploited by a threat agent. The term *asset* is being used in this context to denote a resource that requires protection.[1] A resource can be a person or group of people or a physical entity (e.g., a piece of critical infrastructure). Viewed another way, vulnerability is an asset's capability to withstand harm inflected by a threat. Harm can be anything from experiencing a minor nuisance event to a situation that is catastrophic.

Vulnerability is a function of several factors—attractiveness of the target, feasibility of carrying out an attack, and potential impact (i.e., potential *harm* as discussed in the previous chapter). This model is shown diagrammatically in figure 13.1. Usually these factors entail such considerations as status of the target, potential for the attack to succeed, potential for the threat agent to get away with the attack, and potential for inflicting loss. These factors can be weighed against measures to mitigate loss and to deter or prevent attack on an asset (e.g., through, for instance, a force field analysis—see chapter 6).

Formulae-based analyses are common among law enforcement and security agencies engaged in counterterrorism because they offer a transparent way to calculate vulnerability, and, although the methods vary from agency to agency, they usually follow a basic stepwise method. Figure 13.1 shows a generic approach.

1. Define what constitutes an asset (critical infrastructure, transport network, food chain, distribution hubs, or any of the essential services—for example, electric power, gas, potable water, sewerage);
2. Sort these assets into categories;
3. Assign a grade or level of importance to each asset; and
4. Identify potential impact on the asset if it suffers harm.

193

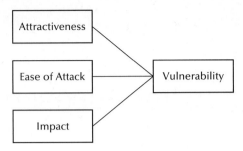

FIGURE 13.1 Vulnerability analysis.

As there is no one single criterion for calculating vulnerability because each class of asset may require special considerations to be considered (and there may be agency protocols that take precedence also), one general approach is to use a model such as:

target attractiveness + ease of attack + impact = vulnerability

To operationalize *attractiveness*, the analyst could ask questions along the following lines and tabulate the results to insert into the model:

- Is the target readily recognizable? Rather than answer this question in a dichotomous way (i.e., using nominal data—yes/no), the analyst could use ordinal data to give greater precision to the overall vulnerability indicator—for example, is the target recognizable internationally in the same way the Empire State Building, St Basil's Cathedral, or the London Bridge are; or is it recognizable only nationally, or statewide, or just locally?
- Is the target the subject of media attention/coverage? Again, an analyst could construct a scale of attention from rarely to frequently/weekly. Coverage could be in the local press or by global newscasters.
- Does the target have a symbolic status in terms of historical, cultural, religious, or other importance (e.g., the Dome of the Rock in Jerusalem)? The analyst could assess this type of factor as having, on one end of the spectrum, no symbolic status to the other end as having multiple imports.

Attractiveness needs to be placed in context with the threat agent. For instance, some scholars are of the view that some Islamic extremist groups see assets that represent Western culture or symbolize Western values as attractive.[2] To operationalize the concept of *ease of attack*, the analyst could ask these types of questions:

- How difficult would it be for the threat agent to predict the peak attendance times at the target? Establish a scale from certain (as in the case of published opening hours) to very difficult (in the case of a training center located in a remote area and opened only for ad hoc lectures).
- Are there security measures in place (e.g., calculated on a scale of low to high deterrence or low to high prevention)?

Questions that probe the existence and extent of controls (or lack thereof) can also be asked to gauge ease of attack. On the one hand, if there is a high degree of control effectiveness, this will usually reduce ease. On the other hand, if there is a low level of control effectiveness, it will increase ease. Analysts should be mindful that, with some targets, even a small reduction in control effectiveness can result in a disproportional increase in ease of attack. *Impact* could be operationalized by questions like:

- What are the numbers of people frequenting the target? Establish a scale ranging from a few daily/weekly/monthly to hundreds or thousands daily/weekly/monthly. Are these same people attracted from the local community, or are they international tourists?
- In dollar terms, what would the financial impact of an attack be if the asset was disrupted, incapacitated, or destroyed? Or it could be put in terms of hours without operation, units of production, and so on.

Impact is predicated on an assumption that terrorists want their attacks to result in large numbers of deaths. This may have been true at the time of this

TABLE 13.1 Vulnerability of the City's Main Bridge over the Orrenabad River

Scale	Scores	Tally
Attractiveness		
Negligible	1	1
Minimum	2	
Medium	3	
High	4	
Acute	5	
Ease of Attack		
Negligible	1	
Minimum	2	
Medium	3	
High	4	4
Acute	5	
Impact		
Negligible	1	
Minimum	2	2
Medium	3	
High	4	
Acute	5	
Vulnerability Coefficient		**7**

writing when there was an Islamic State–focused climate, but such an assumption may not always be valid; for instance, there may exist a nationalist-focused group that seeks to destroy infrastructure rather than kill people. In such a case, these terrorists may view heavy public traffic as an inhibitor to ease of attack. The two paradigms could be described as *effect-based attacks* versus *event-based attacks*.[3]

TABLE 13.2 Examples of a Vulnerability Coefficient Reference Table

Vulnerability	Coefficient	Qualifier (i.e., conditioning statements)
Negligible	1–3	• Can only be attacked successfully if the threat agent has an acute threat coefficient; or • Has little or no importance; or • The range of security measures makes attack very difficult; or • If attacked, the information has little utility to cause harm.
Minimum	4–6	• Can only be attacked successfully if the threat agent has a high coefficient (or greater); or • Has limited importance; or • The range of security measures makes attack difficult; or • If attacked, the information has only some utility to cause harm.
Medium	7–9	• Can only be successfully penetrated if the threat agent has a medium coefficient (or greater); or • Has reasonable amount of importance associated with it; or • The range of security measures makes penetration moderately difficult; or • If attacked, the information has a moderate level of utility to cause harm.
High	10–12	• Can only be successfully attacked if the threat agent has a minimum threat coefficient (or greater); or • Has a sizable amount of importance associated with it; or • The range of security measures makes penetration undemanding; or • If attacked, the information has a high degree of utility to cause harm.
Acute	13–15	• Can only be successfully attacked if the threat agent has a low threat coefficient (or greater); or • Has a very high level of importance associated with it; or • The range of security measures is nonexistent; or • If attacked, the information will cause immediate and/or extreme harm.

A template for calculating vulnerability looks like the table shown in table 13.1. The vulnerability coefficient derived from this analysis is then compared against a reference table to gauge where it sits on the continuum of susceptibility to attack. The scale can be increased with additional qualifiers (i.e., conditioning statements), or it could be collapsed if the number is deemed too many. In the end, the number and the qualifiers make sense in the context of the asset being protected (the left-hand and center columns of table 13.2). Qualitative descriptors (i.e., conditioning statements) can be added for each category as shown in the right-hand column of table 13.2. Note that *consequence* is not a factor that is considered in a vulnerability assessment. It is, however, considered in a risk assessment in chapter 14.

TEXTBOX 13.1 | **Example of a Vulnerability Assessment**

~Secret~

Date:	February 28, 2019
Authorizing Officer:	Director, Criminal Intelligence Analysis Organization (CIAO)
Crime Analysis:	Anti-Terrorist Strike Team (Uniform X-Ray Bravo)
In the matter of:	Section 43(c), Countersubversion Act, 2012
File:	I-0078/2019

Vulnerability Assessment—Orrenabad River Bridge

The AUNT has requested the CIAO to assist it in determining the vulnerability of the Main Bridge spanning the Orrenabad River. The bridge has been identified as a potential target of attack by the Omen Martyrs Faction.

Bridge Details

Name:	Gate to Heaven Bridge (referred to by locals as the "Main Bridge")
Built:	1978
Construction:	Wood and steel
Purpose:	Foot and light vehicle traffic
Traffic:	On average, daytime traffic is about 60 people and 120 small vehicles per hour.

Main Bridge

Attractiveness

From a range of perspectives—economic, social, militarily, and symbolic—bridges have been attractive targets for conflicting parties throughout history. But historic cases show that not all bridges are of equal attractiveness. A bridge offers an attractive target if it is viewed as a strategic asset, as in the case of an airport or a seaport. These types of bridges are usually internationally recognized and are highly attractive. However, in the case of the Main Bridge, its purpose is to carry foot and light vehicle traffic between the eastern and western suburbs of Orrenabad. All heavy vehicle traffic as well as commuter bus traffic are carried by the two bridges to the north and a bridge to the south. In this regard, its attractiveness was assessed to be "negligible."

Ease of Attack

The Main Bridge, although located centrally in the metropolis of Orrenabad, is surrounded by undeveloped land that has been reserved as a nature sanctuary, and hence its light construction which limits the type of traffic it carries. The areas at each of the bridge's approaches are tree lines with an understory of bush and high grass. These factors have been assessed as being able to hide insurgents' infiltration and exfiltration. The number of kilometers of the sanctuary-suburban interface is beyond the city's police force to patrol. This is because there are many dozens of formal and informal paths leading into the sanctuary for the city's residents to enjoy. This means that, although a light defensive ring can be established around the edge of the sanctuary, the bridge's defense-in-chief would have to be established closer to the bridge. But given that AUNT's target profile for the Omen Martyrs Faction indicates the group has acquired stand-off weapons in the form of anti-tank rockets, ease of attack has been assessed as "high."

Impact

Because the Main Bridge is only able to carry foot and light vehicle traffic, the impact has been assessed as being "medium." There are three other more substantial bridges (two to the north and one to the south) that will be able to carry all the traffic if the Main Bridge is destroyed. Traffic engineers with the city's Bridge Maintenance Department have advised that there will some moderate delays if all traffic from the Main Bridge was diverted, but for only an hour at the start of business and an hour at close of business. Otherwise, only a slight delay will result. As such, impact has been assessed as "minimum."

Conclusion

Bridges have been important targets for insurgents and AUNT's request reflects its concern for the Main Bridge over the Orrenabad River. The bridge's attractiveness, ease of attack and the potential impact were assessed. Table 13.1 summarizes the findings of this vulnerability assessment. Attractiveness was assessed as negligible (coefficient of 1); ease of attack as high (coefficient of 4), and impact as minimum (coefficient of 2). The combination of these factors drew a coefficient of 7, which translates to a vulnerability of "medium." However, 7 is at the lower end of the medium ranking scale, and as such, targets in this category are usually only able to be successfully attacked if the range of security measures makes penetration moderately difficult (table 13.2). Therefore, if the local police were able to increase the level of security to include the two layers of surveillance/defense discussed in the ease of attack section of this report, it is considered that this would be enough to deter attack by the Omen Martyrs Faction.

Oliver Yardley

Oliver Yardley
CHIEF SECURITY ANALYST

Key Words and Phrases

The key words and phrases associated with this chapter are listed below. Demonstrate your understanding of each by writing either a short definition or a one- or two-sentence explanation.

attractiveness

ease of attach

impact

vulnerability

Study Questions

1. Explain why attractiveness is an important element in determining vulnerability, that is, would a venue still be vulnerable if it lacked attractiveness?

2. List at least three considerations that might affect how a threat agent views how easy it would be to attack a target. As your target, choose one of the following: a large city office building, a sports stadium, or a cruise liner.

Learning Activity

If impact can be operationalized using metrics such as the number of people frequenting the target and what the financial toil might be if the target is attacked, then brainstorm possible sources of information for each of these types of data. For your target, use the example you selected in study question 2 above—a large city office building, a sports stadium, or a cruise liner.

Notes

1 See for instance, Mary Lynn Garcia, *Vulnerability Assessment of Physical Protection Systems* (Burlington, MA: Elsevier Butterworth-Heinemann, 2006).

2 Carl Hammer, *Tide of Terror: America, Islamic Extremism, and the War on Terror* (Boulder, CO: Paladin Press, 2003).

3 Henry Prunckun and Troy Whitford, *Terrorism and Counterterrorism: A Comprehensive Introduction to Actors and Actions* (Boulder, CO: Lynne Rienner Publishers, 2019), 141.

Chapter 14

Risk Assessments

A risk assessment can be carried out in relation to almost any situation; it is not just for issues of grave concern. Although, risk assessments are key features in the field of counterterrorism, risk analysis techniques can be applied to situations that may be the target of criminals or criminal organizations (e.g., criminal gangs) not associated with terrorism. Risk is a function of *likelihood* and *consequence*. The term *probability* is sometimes used instead of *likelihood*. Both are acceptable. Analyzing risk allows analysts to recommend measures that provide field commanders with the ability to

- accept the risk as is; or
- treat the risk (which includes such decisions as to avoid the risk altogether, mitigate the risk, or defer the risk to another person or agency).

In intelligence research, analysts can focus on a wide range of risks. These can vary from minor ones—say, a noncritical local facility—to risks that liberal democratic nations face from the likes of weak and corrupt governments; rogue states; sub-state and trans-state actors; organized criminals, radical ethnic, racial, and religious groups; and far-right-wing political groups.

Internationally, a risk analysis follows a standardized model. The Swiss-based International Organization for Standardization (ISO) has published a document that puts forward a common approach for dealing with risk by providing generic guidelines in relation to the principles of managing risk.[1] In Australia, as well as in New Zealand, uniformity in risk management is specified by AS/NZS 31000:2009. This document is published through a joint venture by these two organizations: Standards Australia and Standards New Zealand. AS/NZ 31000:2009, along with the ISO:31000, can be applied to several activities, decisions, or operations in the private and public sectors as well as the military and law enforcement agencies. They can also be applied by nonprofit organizations, businesses, community groups, and individuals.

According to AS/NZ 31000:2009, risk is "the effect of uncertainty on objects."[2] Risk assessment is "the overall process of risk analysis and risk evaluation,"[3] and risk management is "the coordinated activities to direct and control an organization with regard to risk."[4] Understanding these terms helps distinguish the process of managing risk from the analytic process of assessing risk using the equation:

risk = likelihood + consequence

Likelihood refers to the probability of "a specific event or outcome, measured by a ratio of specific events or outcomes to the total number of possible events or outcomes." *Consequence* is defined as "the outcome of an event affecting objects."[5]

TEXTBOX 14.1 | Risk Analysis Illustration

Likelihood and consequence are evaluated in the analysis phase of the risk management cycle. This analytic cycle comprises phases shown diagrammatically in figure 14.1.[1] A step-by-step description is as follows:

1. Use two analytic aids—in the form of scales—to evaluate a target's risk rating (i.e., the asset under consideration). These two scales consist of a likelihood scale (see table 14.1) and the consequences scale (see table 14.2).
2. The results of these two assessments are then fed into a risk rating matrix (see table 14.3) that returns a risk rating coefficient.
3. Finally, the analyst looks up the risk rating coefficient on the risk evaluation scale (see table 14.4) to determine what actions (if any) are required.

Examples of low-risk events include:

- An event that would occur rarely and would result in insignificant consequences (reflected in table 14.3 as E1); or
- An event that is unlikely to occur and would result in minor consequences (reflected in table 14.3 as D2).
- Examples of high-risk situations include:
- An event that would occur rarely but would result in catastrophic consequences (reflected in table 14.3 as E5); or

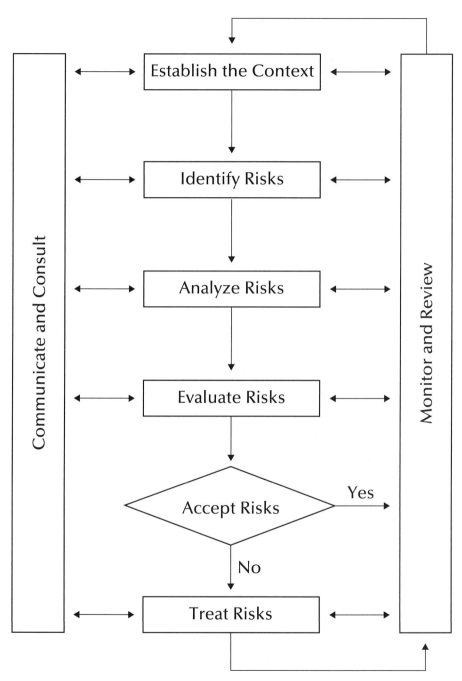

FIGURE 14.1 Risk management cycle.

TABLE 14.1 Example of a Likelihood Scale

Rank	Likelihood	Descriptors
A	Almost Certain	The situation is expected to happen
B	Likely	The situation will probably occur
C	Possible	The situation should occur at some time
D	Unlikely	The situation could occur at some time
E	Rare	The situation would only occur under exceptional circumstances

TABLE 14.2 Example of a Consequences Scale

Rank	Consequence	Descriptors
1	Insignificant	Will only have a small impact
2	Minor	Will have a minor level of impact
3	Moderate	Will cause considerable impact
4	Major	Will cause noticeable impact
5	Catastrophic	Will cause systems and/or operations to fail with high impact

TABLE 14.3 Example of a Risk Rating Matrix

	Consequences				
	1	2	3	4	5
Likelihood	Insignificant	Minor	Moderate	Major	Catastrophic
A Almost Certain	Moderate	High	Extreme	Extreme	Extreme
B Likely	Moderate	High	High	Extreme	Extreme
C Possible	Low	Moderate	High	Extreme	Extreme
D Unlikely	Low	Low	Moderate	High	Extreme
E Rare	Low	Low	Moderate	High	High

- An event that is likely to occur and have minor consequences (reflected in table 14.3 as B2).

Source: Queensland Government and Local Government Association, *Local Government Counter-Terrorism Risk Management Kit* (Brisbane, Australia: Queensland Government and Local Government Association, 2004), 16.

[1] International Organization for Standardization, *ISO 31000*, 2009, 14.

Treating Risk

Once each risk is assessed in this way, they can be positioned on the risk rating matrix (see table 14.3) so they can be compared with each other to prioritize treatment options. Take, for instance, the following events considered by troops stationed in Country Q:

- The risk posed by a person-borne suicide bomb to a public meeting place could be located at C5 (possibly with catastrophic consequences—therefore, it is an extreme risk); or
- Violence because of a street demonstration could be located at B3 (likely with moderate consequences—so the risk is high).

The scale provided in the risk rating table (see table 14.4) is useful for judging whether the analyst recommends accepting the risk or treating the risk (and, if so, to what extent). Without the risk assessment process, the recommendations of the analyst could be called into question as an overreaction or, equally, deemed an underestimate of the seriousness of the situation. These models curb subjectivity to some extent by providing transparency about how analysts make their calculations.

Although the risk rating (see table 14.4) shows what is a generally accepted distribution of risk levels,[6] analysts will need to make their own judgments as to where these transition points take place. Many times, this will be a topic for discussion with the employing agency or a matter set by policy. Yet, by using a

TABLE 14.4 Example of a Risk Evaluation Scale

Risk Rating	Suggested Actions for Treatment
Low Risk	Manage using standard operating procedures.
Moderate Risk	Outline specific management actions that need to be taken.
High Risk	Create a business contiguity plan and a response plan (test frequently).
Extreme Risk	Urgent actions are necessary (in addition to those per high risk).

systematic approach to risk management, analysts can reduce the likelihood and lessen consequences through the application of technology, science, or personal or collective effort.

· ·

According to Emergency Management Australia (EMA), some treatment options for critical infrastructure include awareness and vigilance, communication and consultation, engineering options, monitoring and review, resource management, security and surveillance, and community capability and self-reliance.[7]

· ·

A systematic way is by developing a treatment plan. There are four elements to a logical approach that is transparent and defensible: developing a plan that addresses prevention, preparation, response, and recovery (PPRR).

Prevention considers the risk and tries to implement ways that could stop it from happening. Preparedness acknowledges that despite preventative measures, the event may still occur, so one should prepare for it. If it does occur, response is that part of the plan that deals with how agencies will mobilize and act (and what type of action they will take, etc.).

The final element provides guidance for recovery operation. This aspect of the plan anticipates the worst-case scenario: preventative measures have failed and, although preparation measures may have mitigated the impact to some degree, the event has still occurred; response has contained and brought the event to an end, but it is now time to recover from the event's effects.

PPRR plans can be used in a range of issues, from national security applications to law enforcement and industrial/economic issues. But it should be borne in mind that when planning for one type of event, it is prudent to consider actions to cover what is termed *all hazards*. For instance, if an analyst is considering the impact of a terrorist event, then he or she should consider the event occurring because of nature—fire, flood, wind, tsunami, earthquake, or storm surge.

When compiling a PPRR plan, try to avoid constructing the plan in such a way that elements form either conceptual or real barriers between them—there is usually no clear delineation between the elements, though they may be expressed in these terms. Also, bear in mind that not each element will carry the same weight of importance—the four elements may not be equal. In fact, some elements may not have any strategies or treatments, or, if they do, they are few in number or minimal.

Further, although the elements are cited in a sequence—P-P-R-R—they may be put into action at the same time; for instance, response and recovery

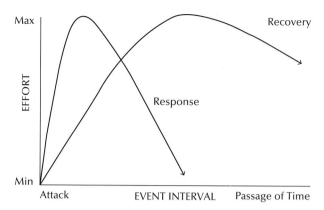

FIGURE 14.2 Comparison of response and recovery efforts.

can, and, in most cases, should, start at the same time, as they are inextricably linked. Figure 14.2 demonstrates this in graphic form. As it is arguable that, until recovery starts, the target of attack cannot function, recovery should be considered at the earliest opportunity.

Finally, though the language appears to contain action-oriented terms, the treatments do not have to be physically based options. Options involving social dimensions are also needed. Take, as an example, a terrorist attack where people are the target and the first pillar of the doctrine is *kill one, frighten ten thousand*.[8] Analysts should try to keep their thinking about treatments broad and innovative.

Key Words and Phrases

The key words and phrases associated with this chapter are listed below. Demonstrate your understanding of each by writing either a short definition or a one- or two-sentence explanation.

all hazards   risk
consequence   treatment
likelihood

Study Questions

1. List the elements that comprise a risk analysis. Explain why each is important to the understanding of risk.

2. List the elements that comprise a PPRR plan. Describe each and explain why these elements are important to counterterrorism.

Learning Activity

Suppose the agency in your jurisdiction that is responsible for monitoring threats of subversion and terrorism has assessed that the water pipeline that connects the city's drinking supply (e.g., a reservoir) to your city's population is at risk to attack by the Omen Martyrs Faction. Using PPRR, devise a plan that considers each of the elements. Although the terrorism group is fictional, use the information about your city's water supply to formulate your PPRR plan.

Notes

[1] International Organization for Standardization, *ISO 31000: Risk Management—Guidelines on Principles and Implementation of Risk Management* (Geneva, Switzerland: ISO, 2009).

[2] International Organization for Standardization, *ISO 31000*, 2009, 1.

[3] International Organization for Standardization, *ISO 31000*, 2009, 4.

[4] International Organization for Standardization, *ISO 31000*, 2009, 2.

[5] International Organization for Standardization, *ISO 31000*, 2009, 5.

[6] Queensland Government and Local Government Association of Queensland, *Local Government Counter-Terrorism Risk Management Kit*, (Brisbane: State of Queensland and Local Government Association of Queensland, 2004), 16.

[7] Emergency Management Australia, *Critical Infrastructure Emergency Risk Management and Assurance*, second edition (Canberra, Australia: Attorney General's Department, 2004), 43.

[8] Sun Tzu, cited in Richard Clutterbuck, *Terrorism in an Unstable World* (New York: Routledge, 1994), 3–4.

Chapter 15

National Security Policy Assessments

Strategic Intelligence Research

Strategic intelligence is considered a higher form of intelligence research because it provides a comprehensive understanding of the target or the activity at the center of the investigation. It is related to operational assessment discussed in chapter 10, but this type of inquiry provides insights into future possibilities—that is, implications for longer-term policy or ramifications for practice. As such, a strategic intelligence report has more details than an operational assessment. It is usually the result of many weeks, months, or even years of research. Not surprisingly, the analysts who work on strategic research projects are often topic experts with extensive knowledge of a specific subject area and, usually, hold advanced degrees.

Because this type of report provides options that will aid planning and policy development, as well as the allocation of a range of resources (including, perhaps, human resources who will be placed in harm's way), the report takes on a different form from the short-form reports that are common in operational and tactical intelligence.

· ·

Strategic intelligence analysis can be considered a specific form of research that addresses any issue at the level of breadth and detail necessary to describe threats, risks, and opportunities in a way that helps determine programs and policies.[1]

· ·

The end of the intelligence cycle, or what is now being termed the *intelligence process*, is to produce a *report* of some description for dissemination.

Often termed an *intelligence product*, the central purpose of the report is to inform the decision maker about the problem, how the analyst approached the inquiry, what was learned, what the information means, and what implications the findings might have for the future. Reports take two forms—written reports and oral briefings. Each may take on a variation, which is characterized by graphics or illustrations. These types of reports are summarized in table 15.1. This chapter will examine the strategic *intelligence assessment* or *intelligence estimate* or, as it is sometimes known, the *long-form report*.

Rare is the analyst who can produce a word-perfect report in one draft. Writing an intelligence report is a formative process, not summative. The analyst should not feel discouraged if it takes several passes at redrafting before arriving at the final version. During the process, the analyst should seek feedback and advice from colleagues—doing so can only strengthen the document's message.

The objective should be an error-free report with no awkwardness that can distract the reader from the content. A good approach is to read the text through the eyes of the intended audience. Will they understand what is being said? Can they follow the thought sequence? Is it well laid out, and is the organization logical? The length and format of reports vary according to the agency, the type of information the audience wants to know, and the message that is trying to be conveyed.[2]

On the point of academic rigor, analysts should ask themselves: Does the intelligence assessment reflect sound research and analysis? The research methods and the analytic techniques used need to be thoughtfully considered as to their appropriateness for the research question or hypothesis. Put another way: Will the assessment and its findings withstand critical appraisal by peers? Reading widely and having a substantial personal library that contains texts on applied research methodologies are key to being successful as a scholar-spy.

TABLE 15.1 Summary of Report Types

Products	Form
Operational Reports, Target Profiles, Operational Assessments, Reports, Memos, Minutes, Strategic Assessments, Strategic Studies, and National Estimates	Written
Briefings	Oral
Charts, Overlays, and Situational Maps	Graphic/Illustration

. . . .

Precision is a hallmark of the intelligence profession. The term itself is synonymous with accuracy and exactness. Say precisely what you mean. Check your facts to be sure they are facts, and if possible, that you have evidence from more than one source.[3]

. . . .

Although intelligence agencies are likely to have their own house style for writing strategic intelligence reports, below is an illustrative example that will give new analysts an idea of what might be asked of them in developing a strategic assessment or estimate. The length of the various sections and subsections are likely to vary depending on the target/subject/topic, urgency of the report, and production requirements specified by the intelligence manager. For instance, some sections, such as that of methodology, may be condensed to a few paragraphs or a page. Some sections may be omitted altogether. Nevertheless, this example shows what strategic reports are likely to include and what information is expected to be contained within the individual parts.

TEXTBOX 15.1 | Illustration of a Strategic Assessment

Title

The purpose of the assessment is to inform decision makers who authorized the intelligence research project or key personnel who receive such reports as a matter of course (e.g., routine briefings). Therefore, the assessment's title should capture the reader's attention but, at the same time, accurately reflect the essence of what's contained in the report without sensationalizing the matter. It should not be a long-winded description of the project. A title is short and concise.

Executive Summary/Key Judgments

An *executive summary* is like an *abstract* in an academic study and serves the same purpose—it is a summary that provides the reader with an overview of the study's purpose and findings. It can be called "key judgments" or similar and appears at the start of the report, before the introduction and background. In the open-source literature, indexing services will often use this information as a way of cataloging the report for other researchers to find.

Table of Contents

A table showing the major section titles and the major headings within each of the sections makes for a convenient way to help the reader find information. If subheadings and other minor headings are incorporated into the table, the added details may make the presentation "busy" and therefore confusing to read. This is true in cases where reports total hundreds of pages. The number of headings and minor headings can therefore fill several pages of a table of contents. However, if it is a shorter report, and the inclusion of minor headings in the table will not take the presentation beyond a single page, it might be worth including them.

List of Tables and Figures

If the tables and figures contained in the report are numerous, this section can be separated into two—a list of tables and a list of figures.

Glossary/List of Acronyms

This is a helpful addition for readers who are not familiar with intelligence or industry-related terms. Even if they are, it is worth including this section, as it helps avoid confusion—for instance, the abbreviation *CI* could mean *counterintelligence*, *competitor intelligence*, or *critical infrastructure*.

Introduction

This section contains several sections that lead the reader through the different aspects of the issue under investigation—from the general to the specific.

Background
This is a short, concise section that sets the context of the issue under study by providing an account of the issue surrounding the events or circumstances. It needs to contain enough information, so the reader understands the main or central ideas about the issue. It should not repeat what will appear in the literature review (below), but it sets the scene for the more detailed discussion that will appear there.

Rationale
The rationale section presents the reader the motivation, reasoning, or justification for undertaking the research: Why was it considered important to conduct the study into the events/situation that were described in the background section? What were the expected benefits of the research? The material in this section should flow logically from the previous section and not repeat the information that appears in the background.

Theoretical Base (Optional)
Even though intelligence research is applied research with a practical outcome, there is usually some theory tied to it. If this is the case, this section, therefore, lays out the theoretical base on which the study was grounded. The analyst needs to outline the theory, its assumptions, and so on, and how it relates to the study. This section leads the reader into the next section, which states the research question. This section needs to be concise and to avoid overly complicated explanations or discussions on the theory—just

state it in simple terms so that the reader knows how the research question relates. Being concise is the key here—expansion of the theory and its application can be done, if needed, as part of the literature review.

Research Question or Statement of Guiding Purpose

Having presented the reader with the background of the issue under investigation and the reasoning for undertaking the study, the analyst now needs to state what the research question will be. State the research question in terms of, for instance, "the purpose of the study was to . . ." or "the matter under investigation can be stated as follows . . . ." If the analyst is testing a hypothesis, it can be stated here also.

As the research question is the study's "compass," it needs to be clear and precise. Do not be tempted to explain the methodology or repeat the importance of doing the study (i.e., rationale); just state the research question. One paragraph of about sixty words will do. Note that a research question is just that—it is a question, not many, nor is it a series of related aims or goals. Having a short lead-in to the question is fine, but, then, state the question, perhaps, like this: "In summary, the matter under investigation can be stated as follows: An increase of police on the street will lead to a reduction in victim-reported crime."

Dissemination (Optional)

This section may or may not feature in the final assessment depending on the agency's in-house report style. However, dissemination should be considered, as this is the object of the strategic intelligence project. So, considering the intended audience is important. To some degree, the analyst should have discussed this in the section on rationale, so this could be incorporated into that section if desired. But dissemination needs to be spelled out—will the results be circulated directly to decision makers under some security caveat, or will it be a highly classified report for operational commanders who may use it to initiate a, say, counterintelligence investigation, or to guide/focus an existing covert or military operation? This section, if not incorporated into the rationale, needs to be short but clear—who is the readership?

Literature Review or Context (Optional)

This section can consist of one main section or several sections, depending on the complexity of the study. The literature review is the section where the analyst "tells the story" about the issue under investigation.

Even though information is collected, this should not be confused with the data collection phase of the study-in-chief. The literature review simply provides an overview of the issue. In this regard, it provides the context for the research, and, in a sense, this section could be referred to as *background* rather than literature review.

So, this section should provide a summary (i.e., in proportion to the overall length of the intelligence assessment) of the research that has been conducted to date and where your proposed study fits into this picture (i.e., the "gap" that this research has bridged). Having said that, it should not be an annotated bibliography—the analyst needs to synthesize the key literature in the field, define the variables, and explain how these variables were operationalized and what theory was used to test the hypothesis or explore the research question. This section can also contain a discussion about the study's theoretical base (if used) and the presumed relationship between the variables.

A good way to begin writing this section is to mind map the concepts related to the issue; then arrange these concepts into a series of headings that form a logical order that "tells the story." The end of the section should lead the reader into the method section.

Methodology (all or parts optional)

This is an important section of the intelligence assessment. If the analyst has carefully crafted the study's research question and placed it in its theoretical framework, it will guide the reader through the overall design, providing understanding of what was done and why. Designs might include:

- Evaluation (to plan intervention programs/operations);
- Case study (what is going on?);
- Longitudinal study (has there been any change over time?);
- Comparison (are A and B different?);
- Cross-sectional (are A and B different at this point in time?);
- Longitudinal comparison (are A and B different over time?);
- Experimental and quasi-experimental (what effect does A have on B?); or
- A combination of the above.

In the methodology section, the analyst needs to define the concepts he or she will study so that they can be operationalized and observed, and then measured. The analyst also needs to identify what data will be required (whether these data will be from primary or secondary sources; whether they will be qualitative, quantitative, or both; if the data will come from open sources, empirical observation, or via covert sources, etc.) and how these data will be collated and analyzed (e.g., statistically or thematic analysis) to test the hypothesis.

The analyst needs to turn his or her mind to the related issues of sample size, how confounding variables will be controlled (i.e., the potential that observations are due to something other than what is being measured), and what limitations these extraneous influences might present for the research (e.g., possible alternative explanations for the relationship between A and B) or the limits inherent in the data (e.g., missing or incomplete data), and so forth.

Data Collection (Optional)

In this section, the analyst needs to think carefully about what data will be needed to answer the research question (or hypothesis) and how these data will be collected. Because what is being described in this section is based on the scientific method of inquiry, it needs to be transparent, with enough detail to allow the reader to replicate the study, should this be desired. Even if the study is not replicated (few intelligence studies ever are), having a transparent and potentially replicable method allows the reader to critically evaluate the robustness of the method. In academia, this is known as peer review, and it is the highest form of assessment for research, whether it is secret or not.

To start with, a data collection plan should appear in this section (e.g., it could be in the form of a stepwise narrative or outline). The following points are suggestions to consider when writing the data collection section:

1. What data will answer the research question, where are these data held, and what is the best way of obtaining them? Answers to these questions will help the reader understand why primary data (from sources such as observations or informants/ agents) or secondary data (from open sources) was chosen for the study.
2. What are the theoretical roots for the decisions that were made in (1) above (they cannot be the analyst's opinion—references to scholarly authority is required to support these decisions)?
3. What is considered the best methodological framework to undertake the study (e.g., quantitative, qualitative, or mixed methods), and what is the scholarly thinking that supports this choice (i.e., the analyst will need to support this with references)?
4. If the study is using samples, the analyst will need to ground this in theory that supports such aspects as the sample frame and sample size (e.g., via references to the literature on methodologies).

Data Collation and Analysis (Optional)

In this section of the methodology the analyst needs to reflect on the type of data they have decided to collect so that he or she can explain how it was collated and then analyzed. Like the stepwise data collection plan, the analyst needs to explain to the reader how the analytic methods that were used produced the results that were reported (i.e., how these analyses answered the research question). For instance, if the study looked for correlations or relationships between variables, what statistical test(s) were used? If the study examined themes or patterns in unstructured data, what methods were used? Remember, the decisions that were made to use certain processes and/or methods in the study need to be supported with references to the theoretical literature—they cannot be just the opinions of the analyst.

Limitations

If any major limitations were noted, they need to be discussed in this section. It is important that the procedures and methods discussed here link to how the study went about answering the research question or hypothesis. The reader needs to be able to understand what was done (i.e., transparency) to be able to replicate it. However, the analyst does not need to list every single possible limitation—just list any limitations in the data or the method used to analyze the data. This is done to demonstrate that these shortcomings were taken into consideration when the conclusions were drawn. The need for temperament becomes clear when one considers intelligence advise such as "I've been told all this intelligence about WMD and this is the best we've got" or "Don't worry, it's a slam dunk!"[1]

Legal Authority (or Ethical Considerations)

If the research being undertaken is classified, then authorization is presumably based upon some legal framework. This legal foundation thus grants the analyst the authority he or she needs to conduct the study. If that is the case, then the analyst should state the legal basis for the study's authorization in this section.

Contrast this with research in the social and behavioral sciences—where, if the study involves human subjects, then approval to conduct research must be granted by an ethics committee. But as we are discussing secret intelligence research—not research that will be disseminated via public avenues (e.g., scholarly journals)—the issue of ethics takes on a different dimension.

Results

The *results* section can also be referred to as the study's *findings*. Some scholars even refer to this section as *analysis*. Any of these terms are fine, as all are in common usage.

The results section of a strategic intelligence report will be presented in three sections. The first is a description of how the data were prepared for analysis. In doing so, the analyst needs to be brief to focus on the more unique aspects of the analytic technique.

This is, then, followed by descriptive statistics of the most relevant or important information (if the study is quantitative). Again, these results need to be brief to avoid overwhelming the reader with volumes of results—doing so will run the risk of confusing them by inadvertently obscuring the assessment's central line of reasoning (i.e., the idiom "miss the forest for the trees" applies in this situation). These descriptive data need to be carefully considered and well organized by such techniques as summary tables and graphs, maps, or other diagrams.

The third section links any inferential analyses to the research question or hypothesis. If statistical analyses were not used, then this section would discuss the results of any of the qualitative analytic techniques that were employed to critically analyze the research question, such as a SWOT, PEST, or force field analysis, or other method for examining unstructured data.

The main consideration here is that only the results are presented. Analysts need to restrain their urge to add their interpretation to these findings—that is done in the Discussion section.

Discussion

This section presents a discussion about the implications or ramifications of the study's results—hence the name *discussion*. The analyst interprets the findings and discusses them in the context of the problem (i.e., background and rationale) and the theoretical base, but always in terms of what it means for the research question. In doing so, caution should be exercised regarding the language used and the conclusions drawn—journalist terms and phrases must be avoided; that is, language should be objective and conclusions based on the results of the study (i.e., *evidence-based*).

Conclusion and Recommendations

In intelligence writing, there is a need to present findings in tentative terms and to avoid the temptation of absolutism. Put the intelligence assessment's conclusions or judgments into a few paragraphs or a page or two, depending on the length of the report. This section is intended to reinforce why the research was important and what the ramifications might mean for policy or field operations.

References Cited

List the references that have been used in compiling the assessment using the Harvard style of referencing. The purpose of this section is to make transparent the information and intellectual authority the study relied on, so the reader can make a judgment as to their scholastic adequacy. Once complete, check the document for consistency in referencing and double-check the report for inadvertent errors, such as not citing other scholars' intellectual work. If the data are classified, then there is likely to be an agency recommendation for how confidential sources are noted; analysts need to adhere to this, as exposure of a covert source or clandestine means of information gathering could risk lives or jeopardize operations past, present, and future.

Appendices or Annexures (Optional)

Sometimes it is important to attach information that could prove helpful to the reader in understanding how a judgment was made or to show relationships that would be too voluminous to explain in narrative form in the body of the report. This type of information is better appended to a separate section and referred to in the body of the report.

[1] Former CIA director George Tenet's reply to the then president George W. Bush's question about the threat posed by Iraq, as cited in Bob Woodward, *Plan of Attack* (London: Simon & Schuster, 2004), 249.

Figures and Tables in the Assessment

Representing complex data in the strategic intelligence assessment will often take the form of a graph, chart, or table—or a picture, such as a photograph, diagram, or drawing. When doing so, the analyst needs to label this symbolic representation correctly, so the reader can identify it in the body of the report.

There are just two terms used to do this—figures and tables. Graphs, charts, diagrams, photographs, and any other illustrations are known as *figures*. A *table* is where data are arranged in rows and columns. Both are numbered sequentially as they appear in the text and independent of each other—that is, figures are numbered as a group, and tables are numbered as another group. If there are more than a few of either, it is worth considering a separate section in the front of the report, after the table of contents, entitled "List of Figures and Tables." If there are a great number of these, then there could be a separate list of figures and a separate list of tables.

Thoughts on Finalizing the Assessment

Analysts will frequently consider the question of what constitutes a good intelligence assessment at the culmination of their inquiries. Given that there are only two ways analysts communicate with decision makers—orally and in writing—deliberation will invariably center on clarity of expression.

Decision makers are people with busy agendas, tight budgets, and substantial pressures, so an analyst's assessment needs to be concise and precise. If a decision maker cannot find the important information in a report, then, to a large degree, the assessment has failed. Remember, the purpose of intelligence is to provide insight, so the best possible decision can be made. This is why the above examples and templates have been described in this section—they have been tested many times by many agencies and by busy managers. Some key points to remember are:

- Double-check that the report's conclusions and recommendations dovetail with the original aim of the inquiry;
- Comply with the agency's in-house style or template for reports;
- Do not selectively omit data items if they do not support a "preferred" position—this is not only unethical but can lead to civil and criminal charges against individuals or the agency if a court or commission of inquiry finds the intelligence investigation did not act in good faith;
- Use several analytic techniques to distil the data so that the clearest picture emerges;
- When formulating judgments, make it clear what the limitations are—do not give false or misleading indications;

- Follow the agency's policy on making and couching recommendations; provide options in objective terms; and avoid "rivers of blood" prognoses that manipulate decision makers (doing so is bordering on the unethical);
- Aim to write several drafts and have each version reviewed by a colleague who is senior in years of service. This is because he or she is likely to have experienced many of the pitfalls common in presenting reports and can steer a new analyst around the "holes in the road." It is better that someone close to you critically reviews your work than to have an executive in your agency do it with the potential consequence of getting a "black mark" against your reputation; and
- Always get someone else to proofread your work—it is more likely that he or she will note spelling and typographical errors than you as the author.

Key Words and Phrases

The key words and phrases associated with this chapter are listed below. Demonstrate your understanding of each by writing either a short definition or a one- or two-sentence explanation.

evidence-based conclusions
intelligence product
oral briefing

research question
statement of guiding purpose

Study Questions

1. Describe the "hourglass" approach to report writing and its advantages.

2. Explain the major parts of a strategic intelligence assessment.

3. Explain the main attributes of the Harvard style of referencing.

Learning Activity

Suppose you are requested to present the findings of your research into an issue facing your agency. To demonstrate the skills learned in this chapter, construct an electronic slideshow that will be the basis of your oral presentation. Use the hourglass approach to do this—that is, start from the general, work to the specific, and then end back at the general, like the shape of an hourglass. For the subject material, use the topic of report writing. Do this using no more than eight slides—short and concise.

Notes

1. Don McDowell, *Strategic Intelligence: A Handbook for Practitioners, Managers, and Users*, revised edition (Lanham, MD: Scarecrow Press, 2008), 5.

2. For a detailed tutorial on preparing accurately written intelligence reports, see James S. Major, *Communicating with Intelligence: Writing and Briefing in the Intelligence and National Security Communities* (Lanham, MD: Scarecrow Press, 2008), and Major, *Writing Classified and Unclassified Papers for National Security*.

3. Major, *Writing Classified and Unclassified Papers for National Security*, 8.

Appendix

Critical Values of Chi-Square Distribution

TABLE A.1 **Critical Values of Chi-Square Distribution**

Degrees of Freedom	$P = 0.05$	$P = 0.01$
1	3.84	6.64
2	5.99	9.21
3	7.82	11.35
4	9.49	13.28
5	11.07	15.09
6	12.59	16.81
7	14.07	18.48
8	15.51	20.09
9	16.92	21.67
10	18.31	23.21
11	19.68	24.73
12	21.03	26.22
13	22.36	27.69
14	23.69	29.14
15	25.00	30.58
16	26.30	32.00
17	27.59	33.41
18	28.87	34.81
19	30.14	36.19
20	31.41	37.57
21	32.67	38.93
22	33.92	40.29
23	35.17	41.64
24	36.42	42.98
25	37.65	44.31

Note: This is a facsimile of a table of critical values of chi-square. It has been reproduced here using data that is in the public domain.

Index

Page references for figures and tables are italicized.

Henry (**Hank**) **Prunckun**, BS, MSocSc, MPhil, PhD, is a research criminologist at the Australian Graduate School of Policing and Security, Charles Sturt University, Sydney. He is a methodologist who specializes in the study of transnational crime—espionage, terrorism, drugs and arms trafficking, and cyber-crime. He is the author of numerous reviews, articles, chapters, and books. Dr. Prunckun has served in several strategic research and tactical intelligence capacities within the criminal justice system during his previous twenty-eight-year operational career, including almost five years as a senior counterterrorism policy analyst. In addition, he has held operational postings in security and investigation.